브라운편입

편입영어,

이 종 현으로 통한다!

이것이 독해다

이종현 저

Part 1 기본유형 총정리

도서출판 상학당

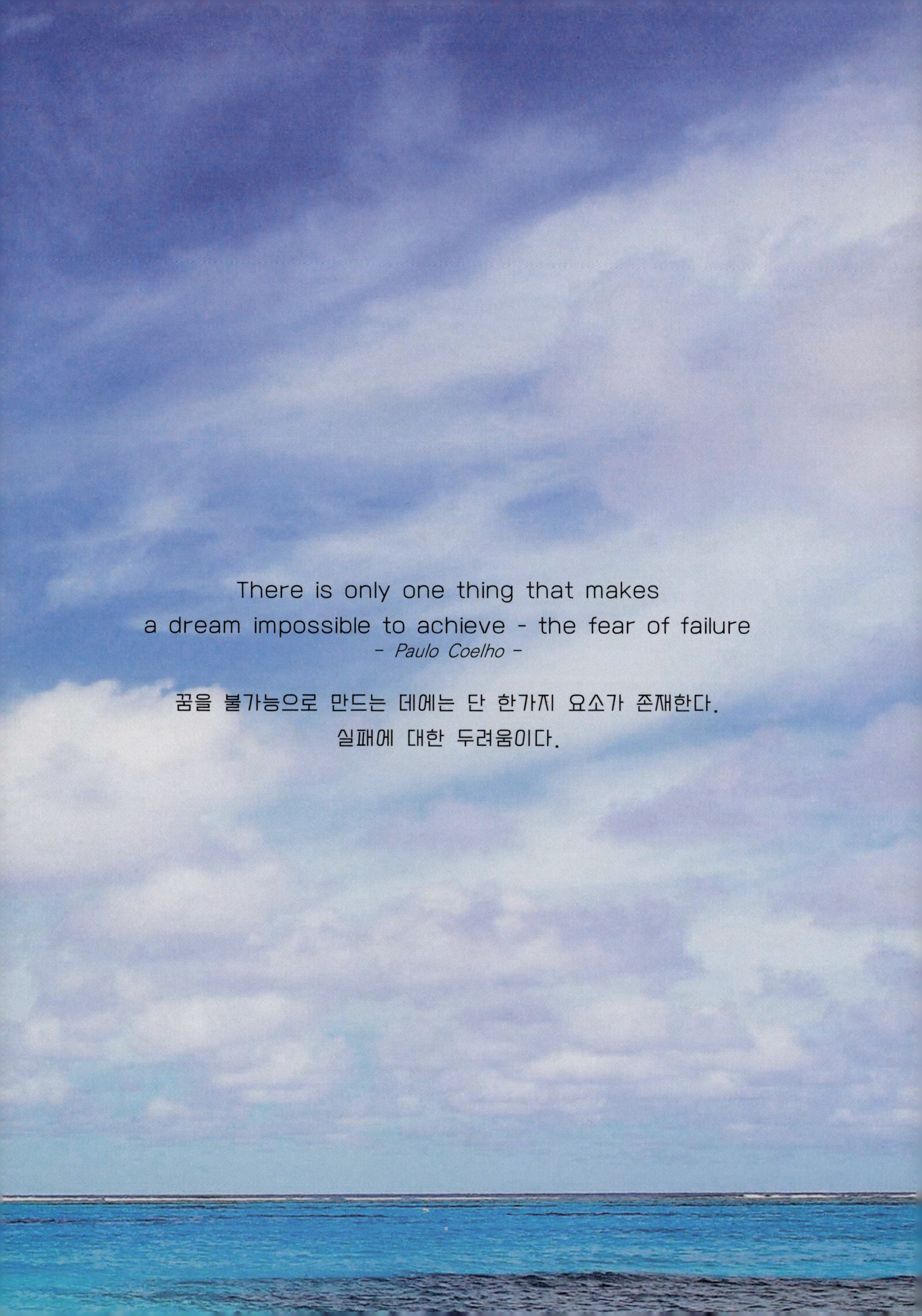

There is only one thing that makes
a dream impossible to achieve - the fear of failure

- Paulo Coelho -

꿈을 불가능으로 만드는 데에는 단 한가지 요소가 존재한다.
실패에 대한 두려움이다.

이 종 현

(전) 평촌 학원가 학원 고3 대표강사

(현) 브라운 편입 영어 대표강사

PREFACE 머리말

학생들이 편입영어를 공부하다 보면 독해 부분에서 막힌 기분이 들 때가 많습니다. 영어 구문을 공부해도 무슨 말인지 해석을 못하고 문제를 못 푸는 경우도 허다합니다. 이 이유를 살펴보면 대부분의 경우 문제는 영어 독해력입니다. 이 책은 그런 학생들을 위해 진짜 독해력을 키우기 위한 책입니다.

영어 문장들이 모여 영어 독해 지문을 형성하게 됩니다. 그럼 이 지문들은 일정한 구조를 가지게 됩니다. 이를 글의 구조라고 합니다. 학생들이 가장 먼저 익혀야 하는 것은 바로 이러한 글의 구조입니다. 글의 구조를 알아야 다음에 어떤 내용이 나올지를 정확하게 추론하면서 독해를 할 수 있고 필요한 부분과 필요하지 않은 부분을 나누어서 글을 바라볼 수 있게 됩니다.

그리고 그 이후 학생들에게 필요한 것은 유형별 독해 풀이법입니다. 실제로 편입시험엔 여러 유형의 문제들이 출제가 됩니다. 각각의 유형들을 정확하게 풀이하기 위한 연습이 필요합니다. 모든 유형엔 접근법이라는 것이 있고 이 접근법대로 풀 수 있다면 답을 못 찍는 독해 문제는 없어질 것입니다.

모든 독해 문제의 정답은 지문 속에 있습니다. 이 책을 통해 여러분들이 문제 풀이법을 정확하게 익혀서 어떤 독해 문제를 만나도 정확하게 답을 찍고 편입에 성공하기를 소망합니다.

차례

Unit 5 장문 유형 … 105

정답 및 해설 … 131

글의 논리를 잡아가는 방법

글을 이해한다는 것은 결국 결과가 바뀌어가는 포인트를 잡아내는 것이다. 즉 우리는 첫 번째 문장을 볼 때 원인과 결과의 관계를 잡아낼 수 있어야 한다. 원인이 없고 결과만 있는 문장도 있는데, 이런 문장은 행동/상태를 나타내주는 문장이다. 우린 이렇게 잡은 첫 문장의 논리, 그 중에서도 결과를 가지고 결과가 어떻게 바뀌어가는지를 판단하는 것이다.

1 기본은 첫 문장의 결과가 발생하는 이유/방법을 보여준다.

➔ 대부분의 문장은 첫 문장의 결과의 원인을 보여준다. 그래서 이를 중간 논리라고 부르는 것이다. 글의 주제는 바뀌는 것 없이 그냥 글은 계속 첫 문장의 결과가 발생한/변한 이유/방법으로 진행이 된다.

2 그러다 결과가 원인 자리에 가서 그 원인 때문에 생기는 결과가 나오면, 첫 문장의 결과 때문에 생기는 또 다른 결과가 추가된 것이므로 여기부터 글의 주제는 바뀐다. 이제 새롭게 바뀐 결과가 생기는 이유/방법에 대한 글이 되는 것이다.

3 첫 문장의 원인이 결과 자리로 와 있는 지문도 있는데, 이건 다시 결과의 결과로 흘러간다면 그냥 중간논리인 것이고, 그 문장부터 이 문장의 인과관계를 중심으로 간다면 이것은 글의 주제가 바뀌는 포인트가 된다.

ex) 비 때문에 홍수가 났다. 비가 많이 왔던 이유는 이상 기후 현상 때문이었다.

➔ 이렇게 글이 전개된다면, 이 다음에 다시 비가 많이 와서 홍수가 났다는 방향으로 글이 전개가 되면 여전히 첫 문장의 결과가 핵심 결과가 되는 것이고, 만약 여기서부터 계속 이상 기후 현상에 대한 중간 논리로 이어진다면 비가 많이 온 이유/이상 기후 현상의 영향 등이 주제가 된다.

4 불특정 결과, 불특정 원인으로 가는 글이 있다. 불특정 결과로 가는 글은 결과가 확실하게 정해지지 않고 뒤에 논리 추가의 형태가 나온다. 불특정 원인으로 가는 글은 결과는 고정인데 원인이 정해지지 않은 논리 추가의 글이 된다. 불특정 원인이 나올 땐 그냥 결과 고정이라고 생각하면 되고, 불특정 결과일 땐 원인 중심으로 봐서 A 때문에 생기는 여러 결과 등이 주제가 된다고 생각하면 된다.

5 반박의 논리가 되는 형태가 나오면, 인과관계 반박인지, 문제점 반박인지가 중요하다. 구별할 수 있는 가장 중요한 포인트는 However 같은 표현이 들어간 문장에서 결과가 바뀌었는지 아닌지이다. 결과가 안바뀌었다면 그것은 인과관계 반박의 논리이고 결과가 그대로이므로 주제도 크게 바뀌지 않는다. 그런데 문제점 반박이 된다면 결과가 바뀌게 되므로 주제가 바뀌게 된다. 그리고 문제점 반박이 나왔을 땐, 뒤에 결과의 결과 표현이 나온다면 거기부터 해결책이 될 수 있다.

6 첫 문장에 대한 판단이 어려울 땐, 어디에서 판단을 시작할지를 정해주는 것이 좋다. 그 때 요약해주는 표현들을 활용할 수 있고, 요약이 될 수 있는 표현들은 결과의 결과가 되기도 하는 부분이다. 그래서 그냥 의미없이 두 번째 문장을 보는 것이 아닌 판단을 멈추고 일단 어떤 문장부터 다시 판단을 시작할지 정해야 한다.

요약해주는 표현

- Therefore, Thus, As a result, As a consequence 등의 인과관계 부사 표현이 있는 문장
- Question, 명사절 that절, 명사절 how/why절 등
- 모든(every, all), 어떤 ~라도(any ~), 각각(each), 항상(always) 등이 들어간 문장

이런 문장부터 판단을 시작하겠다는 생각을 하면 아주 좋다.

7 중간 논리에서 우리가 기억할 수 있으면 좋은 부분은 비교 대상이 나오는 부분이다. 비교 대상을 볼 줄 아는 눈은 주제 문제를 풀 때 보다는 일치/불일치 문제를 풀 때 도움이 될 것이다.

8 실험/연구로 가는 글이라면 이 땐 비교 집단은 주제를 잡는데 중요할 수 있다. 비교될만한 두 집단이 반대될만한 결과를 낸다면 인과 관계를 증명하는 논리가 되고, 비교되는 두 집단이 같은 결과를 낸다면 인과관계를 부정하는 글이 된다.

9 지문에 Question, why/how 명사절 의 형태가 나왔다는 것은 거기부터 거의 대부분 결과가 고정된다는 것이다. 이제 해당 문장의 결과가 이 지문의 핵심 결과라고 생각하고 나머지를 보면 된다. 물론 Question, why/how절이 한 번 더 나온다면 얼마든지 결과는 바뀔 수 있다. 다만 이런 경우가 별로 없다.

10 차이점/공통점으로 시작하는 글도 있다. 이런 경우 그러한 차이/공통점 때문에 생기는 결과가 나오면 결과의 결과가 되는 것이고, 그렇지 않다면 그냥 둘의 차이/공통점 이 핵심 논리가 된다. 두 대상이 실제로 어떤 차이가 있고, 어떤 공통점이 있는지는 중간 논리의 비교 대상에 해당하게 된다.
물론, 차이점이 나오는 글의 반박은 공통점이고, 공통점을 반박하면 기본이 차이점이 된다.

11 만약 인물의 행동/상태 등으로 나오는 글이라면 반드시 '상황 → 인식 → 발생 → 발전 → 결과 but 내려감 → 사라짐'이 방향으로 판단하는 것을 기억한다. 그 중에서도 인식을 통해 발생하는 부분, 발전을 통해 결과가 만들어지는 부분, 내려가기 시작하는 부분이 핵심 논리라고 할 수 있다.

Unit 1

주제/제목/요지/주장/목적 유형

주제 문제를 풀 땐 말 그대로 핵심 논리 하나를 명확하게 잡으면 된다. 그 중에 가장 중요한 것은 결과다. 특히 첫 문장의 논리를 잡았을 때 결과 중심으로 주제를 이해하는 연습이다.

가령, 첫 문장이 "AI 때문에 인간은 발전해왔다."로 시작하는 글이면, 이걸 본 순간 우리가 해야 하는 생각은 "아 '이 글 주제는 인간이 발전할 수 있었던 이유'가 될 수 있겠구나." 생각을 하고 다음을 가는 것이다. 지금부터 인간이 발전하면서 생긴 결과가 뒤에 또 나오거나, 문제점 반박이 나오지 않는 이상 이 글의 결과는 바뀌지 않는다. 그러니 마지막까지 그런 포인트를 잡지 못했다면 그냥 첫 문장이 주제가 되는 것이고, 그럴 땐 선지로 가기 전에 일단 내가 잡은 결과가 선지에 써 있는 것부터 답을 찍겠다고 생각하면 된다. 그리고 답을 못 찍겠으면 원인을 중심으로 있는 선지를 찍으면 된다.

여기서 주의할 점은 인과관계 반박은 기본적으로 결과가 바뀌지 않는 글이다. 이 점을 꼭 기억하자.

예시문제

1. Its unmistakable smell permeates Seoul subway carriages during the rush hour, and admirers claim it is the healthiest food on the planet. Once valued as a source of vitamin C before the arrival of refrigerators, kimchi now crops up on menus far from its birthplace on the Korean peninsula. The spicy, garlicky cabbage dish is to be found as a pizza topping and taco filling in the UK, Australia and the US. Kimjang, the traditionally communal act of making kimchi, was recently awarded world cultural heritage status by UNESCO. But despite its growing popularity in restaurants from Los Angeles to London, Korea's national dish is in crisis in its country of origin. To kimchi's basic ingredients of napa cabbage, garlic, seasoning and copious amounts of chilli power, we can now add a trade war with China and fears of lasting damage to Korean cultural identity.

① Kimchi : Soaring in Popularity
② How does Kimchi Impact Health?
③ Korea Wins a Trade War Against China
④ Kimjang : Put Forward for UNESCO Award
⑤ Popularity and Crisis of Korea's National Dish

2. Innovative solutions—to prevent, monitor and clean (PMC) marine litter—are necessary to restore healthy oceans and maintain their well-being over time. And again, little is known about how many of these solutions have been developed and implemented, and to what extent they have been effective as information is scattered across platforms and not easily accessible. In a global analysis by Bellou and colleagues, also in Nature Sustainability, the researchers identify 177 PMC solutions and find that 106 of them address monitoring; 33 address prevention (mostly via wastewater treatment); only 30 address cleaning. They also find an inconsistent use of litter size terms across the various developers, which required a harmonization effort to assess the type of litter addressed—results show that 137 of the solutions targeted macrolitter. Overall, only few solutions reached technical readiness and no solution was validated for efficiency and environmental impacts.

① Saving Marine Animals : Target the Microlitter
② A Passive Journey to the Marine Discovery
③ Oceanic Threats to Human Race
④ Want to Heal the Ocean? More Work Needed
⑤ Questioning the Utility of Sea Wastes Recycling

3. After observing the "care" given to the aged in the United States, I can only conclude that personalization in that culture involves not only the acquisition of certain symbols and statuses, but also the achievement of a series of successes. By that token, an individual who fails or who has lost the capacity to succeed is considered less a person, because he or she has withdrawn from the success mechanism. Old people in the United States, because they have withdrawn or have been displaced from the occupational system, are deprived of the ability to succeed or fail; they are seen as scarcely persons at all — unless they can still symbolize their past success by continued consumption capability. In this way an individual's retention of consumption capability, even after he or she has withdrawn from the success machinery, is taken as an adequate substitute for success, because, through this consumption, an indispensable service is rendered to the economy.

① various strategies of personalization
② a typical misconception about old people
③ problems of aged care in the United States
④ one aspect of personalization in the United States
⑤ contribution of consumption to the United States economy

4. It is simply unclear just how technologies can be inevitable, at least from an ethical perspective, and how they can be autonomous. Some individuals elect to use a given technology; others do not. For any technology, it could be the case that all individuals elect not to use it. A competitor could arise, or moral argument may appear and convince a critical number of people no longer to use a technology. That technology then ceases to be implemented because of individuals' decisions. The technology, or at least its implementation, is thus not inevitable. Insofar as it depends upon individuals' electing to maintain it, it is not autonomous. An effort to fashion an ethics of technology based upon technologies' inevitability and autonomy would not reflect the way that people make choices, much less ethical decisions, nor reflect the entire relationship between individuals and technologies.

① technical critiques against autonomy
② the impact of ethics on the innovative technology
③ how to understand and utilize an ethical technology
④ reasons why people have to publicize their favorite technology
⑤ the destiny of a technology determined by individual choices

5. The flood of people-foreign-born and native-born, white and black—fit no single profile. A minority were professionals: businessmen and teachers, doctors and lawyers, priests, ministers, and rabbis. Most were working people who filled the factories, built the homes, scrubbed the floors, and nursed the babies of the well-to-do. These new residents brought more than brawn to the cities, though. They brought their religions, their politics, their institutions, and their art. They jammed the streets on the feast days of their village saints and they emptied them on the Day of Atonement. They opened tiny storefront churches and substantial fraternal lodges. They rushed to vaudeville theaters, where Jewish entertainers honed their craft, and to the ghetto dancehalls, where ragtime bands pushed the boundaries of American music. And they elbowed their way into the cities' public life.

① American frontiers overcame unexpected troubles.
② The perilous damage was begot by the new people.
③ Diverse immigrants engendered the political renaissance.
④ Minor cultures are transformed so as to fit into American public life.
⑤ The immigrants released their own cultures into the American mainstream.

6. The power of apologies as a display of caring lies at the heart of the veritable avalanche of them that we are now seeing in the public sphere. Government, for instance, can demonstrate that they care about a group that was wronged, such as when the United States apologized in 1997 to African-American men who were denied treatment for syphilis as part of a medical experiment. Offering an apology to another country is an effective way to lay the ground work for future cooperation. In the late 1990s, the Czech Republic remained the only European nation with which Germany had not reached a settlement providing restitution for Nazi persecution during World War II. Germany refused to pay Czech victims until the Czechs formally apologized for their postwar expulsion of ethnic Germans from the Sudetenland. In the interest of receiving both reparations and Germany's support for inclusion in NATO, the Czech government offered the apology in 1997. Germany responded by setting up a philanthropic fund for the benefit of the Czechs, and both NATO and the European Union have invited the Czech republic to join their ranks.

① Germany did not pay Czech victims until the Czechs expressed apologies for their postwar behavior.
② Apologies help people repair schisms between the rich and the poor countries.
③ Apologies restore equilibrium in domestic and international relations.
④ Apologies are often manipulated to suggest that people let bygones be bygones.
⑤ The United States apologized to African-American men who were denied treatment for syphilis.

7. Nothing is more jarring to the nervous system than repeated interruptions when you're in the midst of concentrating on an important problem. One of the worst mistakes is to get into the habit of taking every phone call no matter what you're doing. A good way to handle the telephone is to concentrate your calls in one time segment, say between nine and ten in the morning or four and five in the afternoon. During that time you take all calls, and call people back who called you. You aren't being rude to refuse a call because you are busy. You are being wise. If you are a victim of the telephone, telephone screening can change your work life.

① Consciously project ease and enjoyment.
② Beware of any lingering fears of success.
③ Become aware of your natural optimum work cycles.
④ Think of success as a process, not a final destination.
⑤ Insulate yourself as much as possible from interruption.

8. The inherent fragility of the economic system does not mean that it cannot be made safer. A lot can be done, has been done, and can still be done. But in designing reforms, it's important to choose the objective carefully. The goal should not be to eliminate the risk of the failure of individual banks or large institutions. Failure has its merits. It's important for creating the right incentives, spurring innovation, and promoting efficiency. Rather, policymakers should strive to enhance the resilience of the broader financial system. Even when the system is under extreme stress, it needs to remain able to perform its basic functions of providing payment, clearing, and settlement services; offering credit; and transferring risk. In other words, policymakers should try to build a system in which an idiosyncratic event does not turn into a systemic crisis. This means seeking not only to reduce the probability of financial distress but also to increase the probability that the real economy remains insulated from it.

① drafting economic policies based on statistics
② building an economy based on idiosyncratic events
③ putting the needs of people ahead of corporations
④ predicting potential problems in the economic system
⑤ reforming an economic system to withstand distress

9. After language had evolved as the principal communication system of modern humans, people were left with the question of who to communicate with through music. Music is, after all, a derivative of 'Hmmmmm,' which itself evolved as a means of communication, so the communicative function could not easily be dropped; there remained a compulsion among modern humans to communicate with music, as there still is today. How could this be fulfilled? Communication with other humans was now far better achieved by language than by music, other than for prelinguistic infants. But in the minds of modern humans there was now another type of entity with whom they could and should communicate: supernatural beings. So the human propensity to communicate through music came to focus on the supernatural — whether by beating the shaman's drum or through the compositions of Bach.

① effects of music on our views on the supernatural
② functional diversity of music compared to language
③ music as a means to communicate with the supernatural
④ advantages of language as a medium of communication
⑤ influence of music on the development of language

10. The EU, with its 512 million citizens, has, until recently, led the charge into a zero-emission green economy. The People's Republic of China, with its nearly 1.4 billion people, has roared onto the field in recent years with its plan to transition into a postcarbon era. And now the United States, with its 325 million citizens, is poised to join the herd. Without all three elephants marching in sync, sharing best practices, establishing common codes, regulations, standards, and incentives, and reaching out together to bring the rest of humanity into the fold, the race to a zero-carbon civilization in less than twenty years will be lost.

① Population problems need to be addressed before racing to a postcarbon era.
② With all three elephants marching in sync, no competitor will win the race.
③ China's participation is an optimistic sign for the zero-emission economy.
④ Cooperation among the key members is essential for a zero-carbon world.
⑤ A zero-carbon civilization is destined to backfire within twenty years.

11. Traditionally, research has treated goal pursuit as a solitary endeavor. But everyday experiences show that our relationships can either foster or impede our progress. If you want to wake up earlier each morning, you're better off with a spouse who shuts off his bedside lamp at 10 p.m. If you want to become a vegetarian, your spouse's feelings on tofu versus steak will probably have an impact. Now researchers are examining that influence. A Washington University study found that being married to a spouse who is highly conscientious — that is, organized and reliable — predicts future job satisfaction and higher income. Research by Wilhelm Hofmann at the University of Cologne in Germany indicates that high relationship satisfaction positively affects feelings of control over goal pursuit. Hofmann posits that the stability of happy relationships makes it easier to focus. According to Hofmann, "When people's everyday life feels stable and predictable, they feel more in control of their ability to pursue their goals."

① The chances of achieving your goals hinge on your spouse.
② Psychological stability is the main indicator of your wellbeing.
③ Setting a realistic goal is heavily influenced by your partner.
④ Personal feelings are directly related to pursuing your goals.
⑤ The conscientiousness of your spouse leads to a successful marriage.

12. In the U.S., windmills have been estimated to kill at least 45,000 birds and bats each year. That sounds like a lot of birds and bats. To place that number in perspective, consider that pet cats that are allowed to wander in and out of their owners' houses have been measured to kill an average of more than 300 birds per year per cat. If the U.S. population of outdoor cats is estimated at about 100 million, then cats can be calculated to kill at least 30 billion birds per year in the U.S., compared to the mere 45,000 birds and bats killed per year by windmills. That windmill toll is equivalent to the work of just 150 cats.

① Policies on birds and bats should be based on statistics.
② Cat owners are advised not to let their cats roam free outdoors.
③ Windmills need to be regulated to meet environmental standards.
④ Windmills do not threaten avian wildlife as much as outdoor cats.
⑤ The outdoor cat population must be curbed for ecological balance.

13. Since 1967, median household income in the United States, adjusted for inflation, has stagnated for the bottom 60 percent of the population, even as wealth and income for the richest Americans have soared. Changes in Europe, although less stark, point in the same direction. Corporate profits are at their highest levels since the 1960s, yet corporations are increasingly choosing to save those profits rather than invest them, further hurting productivity and wages. And recently, these changes have been accompanied by a hollowing out of democracy and its replacement with technocratic rule by globalized elites.

① Inflation : A Huge Hurdle for the Economy
② Public Demand for Corporate Transparency
③ If a Technocrat Sneezes, Do Banks Catch a Cold?
④ The Butterfly Effect of a Faltering European Economy
⑤ Economic Outlook for the Average Joe : Cloudy with Rain

14. I am lying here in my private sick bay on the east side of town between Second and Third avenues, watching starlings from the vantage point of bed. Three Democrats are in bed with me: Harry Truman (in a stale copy of the Times), Adlai Stevenson (in Harper's), and Dean Acheson (in a book called A Democrat Looks at His Party). I take Democrats to bed with me for lack of a dachshund, although as a matter of fact on occasions like this I am almost certain to be visited by the ghost of Fred, my dash-hound everlasting, dead these many years. In life, Fred always attended the sick, climbing right into bed with the patient like some lecherous old physician, and making a bad situation worse. All this dark morning, I have reluctantly entertained him upon the rumpled blanket, felt his oppressive weight, and heard his fraudulent report. He was an uncomfortable bedmate when alive; death has worked little improvement — I still feel crowded, still wonder why I put up with his natural rudeness and his pretensions.

① Books Versus Pets : Who Makes a Better Companion?
② Reminiscing About a Bedfellow on a Dark Morning
③ A Message of Hope from My Beloved Dash-hound
④ Unexpected Arrival of a Dog : A New Beginning
⑤ The Truth Behind the Politics of Medical Care

15. 다음 글의 주제로 가장 적절한 것은?

Divorce statistics are often used as a measure of family disorganization, and the present high divorce rate is cited as proof that the U.S. family is in serious trouble. However, higher divorce rates today than in the past are not entirely the result of more family unhappiness. In earlier generations, many couples avoided divorce even though their married life was unhappy. They avoided it because it meant social ostracism or, in the case of women, poverty because there were few opportunities for them to earn a good living. As the possibilities for divorced people increased and it became easier to get divorces, more unhappy couples have chosen this route.

① uses of divorce statistics
② collection of divorce statistics
③ reasons why people get divorced
④ cautious interpretation of divorce statistics
⑤ coping with divorce and family breakdown

16. 다음 글의 요지로 가장 적절한 것은?

When infant mortality rates are high, as they are in much of the developing world, parents tend to have high numbers of children to ensure that some will survive to adulthood. There has never been a sustained drop in birth rates that was not first preceded by a sustained drop in infant mortality. One of the most important distinctions in our demographically divided world is the high infant mortality rates in the less-developed countries. Better nutrition, improved health care, simple oral rehydration therapy, and immunization against infectious diseases have brought about dramatic reductions in infant mortality rates, which have been accompanied in most regions by falling birth rates. It has been estimated that saving 5 million children each year from easily preventable communicable diseases would avoid 20 or 30 million extra births.

① Infant mortality rates affect birth rates.
② Infant mortality around the world is declining very rapidly.
③ Disparities of wealth are reflected in infant mortality rates.
④ A primary cause of infant mortality is poor quality of water.
⑤ Good prenatal care has been linked to reduced infant mortality.

17. 다음 글의 제목으로 가장 적절한 것은?

People can actually do two or more things at once, such as walk and talk, or chew gum and read a map; but, like computers, what we can't do is focus on two things at once. Our attention bounces back and forth. This is fine for computers, but it has serious repercussions in humans. Two airliners are cleared to land on the same runway. A patient is given the wrong medicine. A toddler is left unattended in the bathtub. What all these potential tragedies share is that people are trying to do too many things at once and forget to do something they should do. When you try to do two things at once, you either can't or won't do either well. If you think multitasking is an effective way to get more done, you've got it backward. It's an effective way to get less done.

① Fallacy of Multitasking
② The ABCs of Multitasking
③ Multitasking : Why and How
④ Coping Strategies for Multitasking Demands
⑤ Simple Truth behind Great Results : Multitasking

18. 다음 글의 목적으로 가장 적절한 것은?

Please let me take this opportunity to introduce myself and to welcome you to the neighborhood. My wife, Monica, and I live at #19, just up the road from your new home. We have lived on Meadow Street for the past twenty years. Most likely because I'm older than everyone else around here, I am often addressed as the unofficial "mayor" of the neighborhood.

I have been asked by several of our neighbors to communicate their wishes about a problem that has arisen since you moved in. We all love music, and most of us have had, or will have, teenagers. We would, though, appreciate it if you would ask your teens to turn down the volume.

We all look forward to meeting and greeting you properly after you have the chance to settle in.

① to solicit donations for needy neighbors
② to invite a neighbor to a block party
③ to offer best wishes to a leaving family
④ to request an exchange for a better stereo
⑤ to complain about a neighbor's loud music

19. 다음 글의 요지로 가장 적절한 것은?

Laughter is one clue to compatibility. It tells you how much you will enjoy each other's company over the long term. If your laughter together is good and healthy, and not at the expense of others, then you have a healthy relationship to the world. Laughter is the child of surprise. If you can make each other laugh, you can always surprise each other. If you can always surprise each other, you can always keep the world around you new. Beware of a relationship in which there is no laughter. Even the most intimate relationships based only on seriousness have a tendency to turn dour. Over time, sharing a common serious viewpoint on the world tends to turn you against those who do not share the same viewpoint, and your relationship can become based on being critical together.

① A key to a healthy relationship is laughing together.
② "No action, talk only" is the seed of relationship failures.
③ Serious talk leads to endless criticism of one another.
④ The element of surprise brings laughter into your relationship.
⑤ Laugh a lot, and you will end up with new relationships.

20. In the U.S. the proportion of infants who were nursed at all by their mothers, and the age at which those nursed infants were weaned, decreased through much of the 20th century. For example, by the 1970s only 5% of American children were being nursed at the age of six months. In contrast, among hunter-gatherers not in contact with farmers and without access to farmed foods, infants are nursed far beyond six months, because the only suitable infant food available to them is mother's milk: they have no access to cow's milk, baby formula, or soft food replacements. The age of weaning averaged over seven hunter-gatherer groups is about three years old, an age at which children finally become capable of fully nourishing themselves by chewing enough firm food.

① relationship between the age of weaning and available food
② necessity of early weaning in hunter-gatherer societies
③ controversy over the role of weaning in children's health
④ agricultural motivations for early weaning in children
⑤ demographic contrasts between farmers and hunter-gatherers

21. Never has China's bond market had such a stormy spring. It has already set a record for defaults in the second quarter. The cost of credit for firms has shot up. Even the state-owned companies that invest in infrastructure, previously sacrosanct, are seen as risks. What has gone wrong? The answer is nothing at all. Defaults are progress for China, which needs to clear a backlog of accumulated debt. This year's casualties amount to a mere 0.1% of the bond market. But that is still an improvement on the recent past, when investors assumed that the government would rescue any big firm in trouble.

① the hidden pitfalls of China's economy
② the risky investments on China's infrastructure
③ the critical need for governmental intervention in China
④ the unwarranted concern about China's bond market
⑤ the doomed future of China's accumulating debt

22. 다음 글의 제목으로 가장 적절한 것은?

Do we live on a rare earth? One so exceptional that it is pretty much alone in hosting a rich diversity of life, with almost all other planets being home to simple microbes at best? Or are we in a universe teeming with living things as complex as those here, meaning that we exist as part of a vast, cosmic zoo? Debate on this rages on, but we say it is time to accept that the latter is very likely. To date we know of at least 3,700 exoplanets and there are likely to be trillions of other potentially habitable exoplanets and exomoons in our galaxy and beyond. We do not know how commonly life arises on them, but many scientists think that it may well emerge from the chemical and physical properties of any suitable planet.

① Earth, the Extraordinary Home
② The Intergalactic Superhighway
③ Are Microbes Our True Ancestors?
④ The Cosmic Zoo : The Big Hoax
⑤ Is Anybody Out There?

23. Catholicism held that the only God-given vocation was priesthood, but Protestants thought that people could be called to any of the secular crafts and trades. The belief that they were serving God encouraged them to work with religious fervor, leading them to produce more goods and make more money. Weber believed that the Protestant faith led inevitably to a capitalist economic society because it gave believers the chance to view the pursuit of profit as evidence of devotion, rather than of morally suspect motives such as greed and ambition. The idea of predestination also meant that believers need not worry about social inequalities and poverty, because material wealth was a sign of spiritual wealth.

① role of religion in creating social equality
② reasons for the rise of the Protestant faith
③ influence of Protestantism on economic ideals
④ importance of morality in economic activities
⑤ differences between Protestants and Catholics

24. Whether out of curiosity, vanity, or a motive as yet unexplored, people throughout the ages have wanted to see their own reflection. As early as 2500 B.C. the Egyptians had mirrors of highly polished metal, usually of bronze, occasionally of silver or gold. The first commercial glass mirrors were made in Venice in 1564; these were made of blown glass that was flattened and coated with an amalgam of mercury and tin. The Venetians proceeded to supply Europe with mirrors for centuries. It wasn't until 1840 that a German chemist named Justus Liebig came up with the method of silvering that we use today. By this technique, silver-ammonia compounds are subjected to the chemical action of a reducing agent, such as invert sugar, Rochelle salt, or formaldehyde, and the resulting metallic silver is spread evenly over the back of a smooth pane of plate glass.

① economic motivations behind the invention of the mirror
② outstanding achievements of German chemists
③ development of commercial glass mirror technology
④ human desires hidden in commercial glass mirrors
⑤ commonalities of ancient mirror technology in Europe

25. 다음 글의 목적으로 가장 적절한 것은?

What could be more comforting than seeing your dog or cat curled up in blissful sleep? Both species spend almost half their day engaged in some form of sleep. But not all find it restful: older animals, those with muscular or joint issues, or very active dogs will often pace or relocate frequently. If your companion fits into one of these categories, he might benefit from a therapeutic bed. These specialized products offer support and comfort unlike regular beds or an impromptu sleeping spot. Regardless of age and health, a good bed promotes muscular-skeletal health and offers additional rejuvenating and healing benefits.

① to prevent domestic animal abuse
② to promote specialized pet furniture
③ to explain the benefits of good sleep
④ to inform pet owners of furniture hazards
⑤ to warn pet owners of poor pet sleep habits

26. 다음 글의 요지로 가장 적절한 것은?

You cannot buy happiness. You cannot go to the nearest grocery store and order a pound of happiness as you would a pound of butter. But, since happiness comes from within, you can secure a measure of happiness by your own acts. You can find that feeling of contentment by helping your less fortunate fellowmen. You can help those who, because of ill-fate, will not have a happy Christmas unless we share with them. During this season of peace and good will, let us not force those in need to look at happiness through our eyes. Rather, let us help them to see and find happiness through their own eyes. Let us not fail the less fortunate of the community.

① Measure your true happiness level by acts of good will.
② Catch the happiness virus in your local community.
③ Do not force your happy ways on your neighbors.
④ Exercise self-contentment to achieve mental well-being.
⑤ Find happiness by helping the needy around you.

27. The center of mining and armor technology was Augsburg, in Germany, and that was no coincidence. Augsburg was near one of Europe's major deposits of iron ore, and the demand for metal from feudal states building forces of armored knights soon created a booming mining industry and an equally flourishing armorer business. To the annoyance of their customers throughout feudal Europe, the Germans charged sky-high prices, aware that those customers had no alternative: German armor was the best in the world, and if a customer didn't like the prices, he could sally forth on his next war with sticks and stones. Underwritten by these lavish profits, the German armorers could afford an extensive research and development effort. It resulted in stronger armor, for example, steel helmets with movable visors that covered the entire head.

① Farewell to Arms and Armors
② Past and Future of Armor Business
③ Stones vs. Steel : The Obvious Choice
④ Germany, the Hub of Armor Technology
⑤ High Quality and Low Prices : A Double-Edged Sword

28. Hate to haggle? You're not alone. A national survey found that just 48 percent of shoppers tried bargaining for a better deal on everyday goods and services in the past three years, down from 61 percent in 2007. But if you're chicken, you lose. Eighty-nine percent of those who haggled were rewarded at least once. Successful furniture hagglers saved $300 on average, as did those who questioned a health-related charge. Those who challenged their cell-phone plans saved $80. Clearly, people who don't haggle are leaving money on the table.

① Can't Hurt to Ask
② ABCs of Haggling Better
③ Furniture Haggling Made Easy
④ Shopping Around : Reap the Rewards
⑤ Does Haggling Actually Inflate Prices?

29. The emotional reaction of disgust is often associated with the obdurate refusal of young children to consume certain vegetables. While such disgust may seem absurd to parents determined to supply their children with nutritious foods, scientists interested in hygienic behavior have a rational explanation. This theory contends that people have developed disgust as a protective mechanism against unfamiliar and possibly harmful objects. A recent study shows that disgust not only deters the ingestion of dangerous substances, but also dissuades people from entering potentially contagious situations. For instance, subjects of the study declared crowded railcars to be more disgusting than empty ones and lice more disgusting than wasps.

① the role of disgust in keeping people safe
② the advantages of getting proper nutrition
③ the difference between danger and contagion
④ the importance of avoiding harmful substances
⑤ the necessity of practicing good hygienic behavior

30. Success as a scientist is not simply a function of the quality of the ideas we hold in our heads, or of the data we hold in our hands, but also of the language we use to describe them. We all understand that "publish or perish" is real and dominates our professional lives. But "publish or perish" is about surviving, not succeeding. You don't succeed as a scientist by getting papers published. You succeed as a scientist by getting them cited. Having your work matter, matters. Success is defined not by the number of pages you have in print but by their influence. You succeed when your peers understand your work and use it to motivate their own.

① the enduring belief of 'the more writing, the better'
② the importance of influencing others in scientific writing
③ the necessity for pursuing research in unexplored areas
④ the favorable peer reviews needed for journal acceptance
⑤ the working ethics and strict quality control in publications

31. 다음 글의 요지로 가장 적절한 것은?

You don't have to go vegan, pledge allegiance to an exercise cult or become a full-time meditator to get the longevity benefits of healthy habits. The latest science is showing quite the opposite, in fact: that extending healthy life is attainable for many of us with just a few small changes that aren't especially hard to do—and won't make you miserable. Researchers have learned that logging hours at the gym cannot counteract the negative effects of sitting for long periods, for instance—but something as simple as fidgeting can. They've also discovered that cutting down on how much you eat doesn't have to be excruciating—and it can improve your chance for a longer life.

① Living a healthy lifestyle is easier said than done.
② Key changes in your diet can help you live longer.
③ Exercising is important for people with sedentary lifestyles.
④ Physical and mental well-being can be achieved with hard work.
⑤ Achieving longevity is not as difficult as one might imagine.

※ [32-33] 다음 글의 제목으로 가장 적절한 것을 고르시오.

32. When you're carrying extra pounds, the extra expenses add up, starting with health care. In a 2013 Duke study, researchers tracked health care spending by body mass index (BMI) levels. The average annual cost for a person with a low BMI of 19 was $2,541. With a BMI of 25—considered overweight—it was $2,893. At a BMI of 33, what's deemed obese, the costs topped $3,439. "The risk of illness starts increasing already from the lower end of 'normal weight,'" says lead researcher Truls Ostbye. The add-ons don't end at the doctor's office. A 2010 McKinsey study estimated that obese Americans spend an aggregate of $30 billion extra on clothes. It is also estimated that a 40-year-old obese man will pay twice as much for life insurance.

① Increasing Costs of Health Care
② Lose Weight, Lower Risk of Illness
③ The Price You Pay for Extra Pounds
④ Do Obese People Spend More on Clothes?
⑤ BMI : Not an Accurate Indicator of Weight

33. Climbing the automobile ladder was hard work, and staying on top was even harder. Each year, employing the practice of perceived obsolescence, Chevrolet would roll out an entirely redesigned, and usually larger, model. A car that had been the height of fashion yesterday would look small, embarrassing, and worn-out tomorrow. As you would imagine, all of this provoked a good deal of anxiety from the bottom to the top of American society. Then in 1959, seemingly out of nowhere, simple full-page newspaper ads began to appear with an unadorned image of the Volkswagen Beetle and the headline "Think Small." The ad didn't say much more, except that the car was modest and efficient—it even called the Beetle a "flivver," contemporary slang for a piece of junk. People found the ads shockingly honest and hilarious, allowing them to publicly express an unnamed anxiety that marketers had been instilling in them for years. Will I make it to the top of the ladder? Who Cares?

① Hard Economic Times : Think Small
② At the Top of the Automobile Ladder
③ New Ad : Step Down From Your Ladders
④ Does Your Car Represent Your Social Status?
⑤ International Automobile Warfare : Size Matters

[34-35] 다음 글의 주제로 가장 적절한 것을 고르시오.

34. Music that was exciting to the contemporaries of Bach and Beethoven is still exciting, although we do not share their culture. The early Beatles' songs are still exciting although the Beatles have unfortunately broken up. Similarly, some Venda songs that must have been composed hundreds of years ago still excite me. Many of us are thrilled by Koto music from Japan, sitar music from India, Chopi xylophone music, and so on. I do not say that we receive music in exactly the same way as the players, but our own experiences suggest that there are some possibilities of cross-cultural communication. I am convinced that the explanation for this is to be found in the fact that at the level of deep structures in music there are elements that are common to the human psyche, although they may not appear in the surface structures.

① the potential of music to enrich culture
② the gradual divergence of music from culture
③ the ability of music to nourish the human psyche
④ the advantages of cross-cultural transmission of music
⑤ the universality of music that transcends time and culture

35. We often see stories of inspiring people and wonderful successes. Some of us put their pictures on our walls or clip notable quotes from them. But what does that do for us if the inspiring person has done things we will never or could never do? For many of us, the choice of a role model invites comparison; and if our abilities and outcomes do not measure up, the role model serves not as an inspiration but as a source of frustration and defeat. Choose as your role model someone who has accomplished something you can accomplish and something you want to accomplish. There is tremendous value in using co-workers or family members who you admire rather than famous athletes, leaders, or historical figures, who have experienced great successes but whose experience has less in common with yours.

① the success stories of a realistic role model
② the source of frustration in emulating a role model
③ the importance of selecting a reachable role model
④ the necessity for having an inspiring person around
⑤ the positive effects of imitating a person of high status

36. 다음 글의 요지로 가장 적절한 것은?

Recently I was reading about the endangered grizzly bears on the coast of British Columbia. The authors emphasized how the cubs were keen observers of their mothers' skills in searching for and consuming food. What the cubs learned by the mothers' modeling was a matter of life and death; without that knowledge the cubs probably would not survive. The same principle applies to us. How can we believe that when we live life like a rat race, our children somehow will not? That as we mindlessly acquire and consume, our children will somehow know moderation and meaning in their relationship to things? If I regularly cheat on little things—like not returning the extra change I receive at the counter, or pocketing found money without trying to find its owner—I am teaching that behavior to children.

① Parents are spending more time reading books on wildlife.
② Mindful consumption lies at the center of being good parents.
③ Good parenting begins and ends with setting a good example.
④ Teaching good behavior to children outweighs earning money.
⑤ Children's behavior is subconsciously mirrored by their parents.

[37-38] 다음 글의 제목으로 가장 적절한 것을 고르시오.

37. The earliest Robin Hood ballad was printed in 1450, and it does not portray the dashing hero that we have come to know in popular culture. He was a yeoman, rough and cruel at times. The legend was more than likely based on a robber who kept the money he stole from the rich and occasionally helped the poor. He did not want to set up an ideal society in the forest. He and his men sought mainly to rectify social injustices and to live well. Robin Hood became so popular by the seventeenth century that people named places and ships after him. By the nineteenth century, many stories and songs had brought about major changes in the Robin Hood legend. His yeoman origins disappeared, and he increasingly became the heroic outlaw of Sherwood Forest who defended the rights of the poor.

① Robin Hood as a Robber
② Origins of Medieval Yeomen
③ Earlier Struggles of Robin Hood
④ Ideal Society in Sherwood Forest
⑤ Transformations in the Robin Hood Character

38. In one study a hundred men and women wore devices that took readings of their blood pressure whenever they interacted with someone. When they were with family or enjoyable friends, their blood pressure fell; these interactions were pleasant and soothing. When they were with someone who was troublesome, there was a rise. But the biggest jump came while they were with people they felt ambivalent about: an overbearing parent, a volatile romantic partner, or a competitive friend. A mercurial boss looms as the archetype, but this dynamic operates in all our relationships.

① High Blood Pressure : The Silent Assassin
② Uneasy Relationships : Your Body Doesn't Lie
③ Don't Be Bossed Around by Your Biorhythm
④ Can Health Monitoring Devices Save Your Life?
⑤ How Can You Deal with Uncomfortable Interactions?

[39-40] 다음 글의 주제로 가장 적절한 것을 고르시오.

39. Observational studies provide information as to some of the things mothers do around children, but little about their feelings, ideas and beliefs concerning children, child care and themselves. Mothers hold a range of views about children and parenting which are not necessarily in agreement with those of formal psychology and these may influence how they interact with their children. Some mothers find that being sensitive to their children does not come easily. This may be because they cannot relate easily to their children, because they are depressed or isolated, or because they do not believe that sensitivity is an important part of their relationship with the child. For some mothers there may be a mismatch between their behavior and feelings and those prescribed by psychological theories; and there may be conflict between their own needs and those of their children.

① reasons for mothers' negligence in child-rearing
② necessity to establish a philosophy of mothers' parenting
③ gaps between what mothers want and what their children want
④ psychological underpinnings of conflict between mothers and children
⑤ discrepancy in the concept of parenting between mothers and psychologists

40. Alexander the Great launched Egypt's Greco-Roman period in 332 B.C. After conquering parts of western Asia, the Macedonian general was welcomed in Egypt by a people politically weary after several hundred years of unrest and occupation by outsiders. The mixing of Greek (and later Roman) influences with a still rich Egyptian culture helped set social and religious change spinning around the Mediterranean. In this newest period of vibrancy the Egyptians' styles of dress and sculpture worked their way to Greece and Rome, while Egyptian gods and demigods mingled with their counterparts in Greek and Roman mythology. The mother goddess Isis would eventually have temples built to her in the land of the Caesars, while many Greco-Roman gods and heroes would be honored in temples throughout Egypt.

① Egypt's social reform efforts during the Greco-Roman period
② political unrest in Egypt caused by Alexander the Great
③ cultural interchanges between Egypt and Greece/Rome
④ penetration of Egyptian lifestyles into the Greco-Roman world
⑤ Greek and Roman influences on Egyptian peasants' daily lives

41. 다음 글의 주장으로 가장 적절한 것은?

A lapse is a single event during which you take up an old behavior you've been trying to change. The key to overcoming lapses is to expect them on occasion just as traffic tie-ups and road construction may delay you on the highway. Think about the last time you embarked on a long road trip. Chances are you encountered something along the way that slowed you down — but you did not give up, turn the car around, and head home. You still reached your intended destination, though it may have taken you a little longer than expected. It's the same with personal change. Let's say you've been balancing your plate, adding more fruits and vegetables, but suddenly give in to the urge to eat a fast-food hamburger. You've just had a lapse.

① You should remind yourself of the direction you'd like to be headed in.
② When you have an urge to resume an old habit, try to resist the urge.
③ Take a shortcut when your plan for change meets unforeseen delays.
④ Occasional deviations encountered on your way to change are not abnormal.
⑤ Seek support from those who are trying to change the same behavior as you are.

[42-43] 다음 글의 제목으로 가장 적절한 것을 고르시오.

42. You must follow Cross-Continent Enterprise's (CCE) processes and adhere to the system of internal controls around supplier selection. Supplier selection should never be based on receipt of a gift, hospitality or payment. When supplier selection is a formal, structured invitation for the supply of products or services (often called a 'tender'), it is most important we maintain documentation supporting our internal controls. In the public sector, such a tender process may be required and determined in detail by law to ensure that such competition for the use of public money is open, fair and free from corruption. A tender process includes an invitation for other parties to make a proposal, on the understanding that any competition for the relevant contract must be conducted in response to the tender, no parties having the unfair advantage of separate, prior, closed-door negotiations for the contract where a bidding process is open to all qualified bidders and where the sealed bids are in the open for scrutiny and are chosen on the basis of price and quality.

① CCE's Regulations of the Supplier Selection Process
② Why Is Supplier Selection Important at CCE?
③ How to Boost Employee Morale of the Company
④ Legal Issues Surrounding the Tender Competition Process
⑤ Documentation Requirements in the Bidder Selection Proces

43. As light hits the Earth's atmosphere, the different colors react in different ways. Some of them get absorbed by the gas molecules while others do not. Most of the longer-wavelength colors (such as red and orange) pass straight through the atmosphere and are unaffected, while many of the shorter-wavelength colors (such as violet and blue) get absorbed by the gas molecules, because the wavelengths (i.e., the distance between the peaks of each wave) of these colors are similar in size to the diameter of an atom of oxygen. The gas molecules then radiate these colors and scatter them across the sky, causing the sky to appear blue.

① The Fate of Colors Destined by Wavelengths
② Science Behind the Science of Gas Molecules
③ The Nature of Light : The Longer, the Brighter
④ Gas Molecules vs. Wavelengths : Who Wins?
⑤ How Do Our Naked Eyes Perceive Colors?

[44-45] 다음 글의 주제로 가장 적절한 것을 고르시오.

44. The belief that optimism can keep you alive — or at least stave off cancer — gained traction after the release of a study on recovering breast-cancer patients in the Lancet medical journal in 1979. Since then, it has become a household idea that patients with a "fighting spirit" fare better than those with feelings of hopelessness. However, a few recent large-scale meta-analyses have found a lack of convincing evidence that optimism really extends the lives of cancer patients. Despite the lack of definitive data, the belief in the power of positive thinking has become so widespread that it might actually be doing harm. Cancer patients may feel inclined to act upbeat even when they are distraught, hide their despair instead of seeking solace or treatment, or blame themselves if their disease progresses.

① the dangers of hopelessness for cancer recovery
② the necessity of optimism for recovering patients
③ the downfalls of positive thinking for cancer patients
④ the importance of a sound doctor-patient relationship
⑤ the discovery of new preventative measures for cancer

45. Aristarchus of the Aegean island of Samos first suggested that the earth and the other planets moved about the sun —an idea that was rejected by astronomers until Copernicus proposed it again 2,000 years later. After Copernicus, the Danish astronomer Tycho Brahe watched the motions of the planet Mars from his observatory on the Baltic island of Hveen; as a result Johannes Kepler was able to show that Mars and the earth and the other planets move in ellipses about the sun. Then Isaac Newton proposed his universal law of gravitation and laws of motion, and from these it was possible to derive an exact description of the entire solar system. This occupied the minds of some of the greatest scientists and mathematicians in the centuries that followed.

① human endeavors to understand the solar system
② distortions of the solar system by ancient scientists
③ superstitions about the solar system in ancient times
④ history of pre-Newtonian physical laws and principles
⑤ some newly discovered information about planet movements

46. 다음 글의 요지로 가장 적절한 것은?

In commercial society based upon exchange, every man "becomes in some measure a merchant." The pursuit of self-interest in the market, with its division of labor and his resulting dependence on others, leads him to adapt his behavior to the expectations of others. The market itself is therefore a disciplining institution. "The real and effectual discipline which is exercised over a workman, is not that of his corporation," Adam Smith wrote, "but that of his customers. It is the fear of losing their employment which restrains his frauds and corrects his negligence." In order to become successful in his economic exchanges with others, the individual is led to develop the moderate level of self-command which Smith calls "propriety." The character that the market promotes includes prudence and the ability to defer short-term gratification for long-term benefits.

① 시장에서의 개인의 경제 활동은 자기훈육을 가져오게 된다.
② 개인의 이득추구는 자기조절에 의해 절제되어야 한다.
③ 노동자는 동료 노동자보다 고객에게 더 관심을 가져야 한다.
④ 개인은 지속적인 이득을 위해 즉각적인 만족을 희생해야 한다.
⑤ 시장에서의 개인 활동은 분업과 타인에의 의존을 바탕으로 한다.

47. 다음 글의 주장으로 가장 적절한 것은?

Purported to treat a variety of ailments, from fevers to measles to epilepsy, rhinoceros horns have been prized ingredients in Chinese medicines for thousands of years. Sought after for their horns, white rhinos saw their population fall to 100 animals in South Africa by 1910. Today, despite a 1977 ban on the selling of rhino parts, Africa's rhinos once again are facing extinction. Since the ban has not been able to protect the rhinos from illegal poaching, ironically, legalizing a highly regulated trade in rhino horns can end up saving the animals. Rhino horns can be cut or shaved without injuring the animals, and they grow back. If tightly controlled by a single centralized organization, the current demand can be satisfied through legal horn cuttings, along with stockpiles of confiscated black-market horns and those collected from rhinos that die naturally.

① Rhino horns should be considered as an alternative to conventional medicine.
② Legalizing and regulating the trade of rhino horns can save the rhinos.
③ The government must strictly enforce the penalties of illegal poaching.
④ Confiscated black-market rhino horns need to be put to better use.
⑤ Cutting the horns of rhinos is inhumane and should be abolished.

[48-49] 다음 글의 제목으로 가장 적절한 것을 고르시오.

48. When billionaires turn to philanthropy after making their fortune, they often fund scholarships for poor students, work to improve health care, or contribute to the arts. Chang Yung-Fa's mission is nothing less than to "reorganize" social values. Five years ago he started a cartoon-illustrated magazine, Morals, that each month seeks to uplift people's sense of morality in Taiwan and around the world. Whether he's making money or giving away money, morality underpins much of what the 85-year-old Chang does. He believes that his Evergreen Group — which includes the world's fourth-largest container shipping company, hotels, EVA Airways and long-distance buses to the island's main airport — prospers largely because of congenial staff relations backed by the company culture of morality.

① Bothered Philanthropist in Taiwan
② Higher Morality, Greater Happiness
③ Instilling Morality in Taiwanese Companies
④ Entrepreneur Turned to Morality Missionary
⑤ Business and Morality : Like Oil and Wate

49. Perhaps the scientists most excited about reigniting the lunar program are not lunar specialists, but astronomers studying a wide range of subjects. Such scientists would like new missions to install a huge telescope with a diameter of 30 meters on the far side of the moon. Two things that a telescope needs for optimum operation are extreme cold and very little vibration. Temperatures on the moon can be as frigid as 200 degrees Celsius below zero in craters on the dark side. Because there is no seismic activity, the moon is a steady base. Permanent darkness means the telescope can be in constant use. Proponents claim that under these conditions a lunar-based telescope could accomplish as much in seventeen days as the replacement for the Hubble telescope will in ten years.

① Lunar Program : Once in a Blue Moon
② The Case for a Lunar Space Observatory
③ Moon Exploration : One Small Step for Mankind
④ The New Hubble Telescope : Is It Worth It
⑤ Lunar Specialists vs. General Astronomers

[50-51] 다음 글의 주제로 가장 적절한 것을 고르시오.

50. There is consideration to which some advocates of freedom attach too little importance. In a community of children which is left without adult interference there is a tyranny of the stronger, which is likely to be far more brutal than most adult tyrannies. If two children, two or three years old, are left to play together, they will, after a few fights, discover which is bound to be the victor, and the other will then become a slave. Where the number of children is larger, one or two acquire complete mastery, and the others have far less liberty than they would have if the adults interfered to protect the weaker and less pugnacious. Consideration for others does not, with most children, arise spontaneously, but has to be taught, and can hardly be taught except by the exercise of authority. This is perhaps the most important argument against the abdication of the adults.

① the importance of freedom in child care
② understanding children's behaviors in various learning contexts
③ the relation of victors to slaves in a community of children
④ the necessity for adult interference in child care
⑤ various factors affecting children's leadership

51. The place of secondhand smoke in causing disease has been under study for years. A mid-sized city in a western state unexpectedly added to the data. Smoking in public and in workplaces was banned and six months later the ban was lifted. During the time that smoking was prohibited in public places, the rate of hospital admissions for heart attacks was 24. During the typical six-month period, the rate is 40 admissions. The researchers believed that the drop was evidence of the negative effects of secondhand smoke. Secondhand smoke contributes to heart attacks by elevating heart rate and decreasing the ability of blood vessels to dilate.

① effects of smoking in the workplace
② causes of heart attacks in mid-sized cities
③ the importance of a stress-free working environment
④ the relationship of secondhand smoke and heart attacks
⑤ the necessity of banning smoking in public and workplaces

52. 다음 글의 주장으로 가장 적절한 것은?

If there is a garbage crisis, it is that we are treating garbage as an environmental threat and not as what it is: a manageable—though admittedly complex—civic issue. Although many old urban landfills are reaching their capacity, the reality is that there is—and always will be—plenty of room in this country for safe landfill. We've chosen to look at garbage not as a management issue, however, but as a moral crisis. The result is that recycling is now seen as an irreproachable virtue, beyond the scrutiny of cost-benefit analysis. But in the real world, the money municipalities spend on recycling is money that can't be spent on schools, libraries, health clinics, and police. In the real world, the sort of gigantic recycling programs that many cities and towns have embarked upon may not be the best use of scarce government funds.

① 쓰레기 매립지의 확대는 바람직하지 않다.
② 쓰레기 재활용은 도덕적 관점에서 접근해야 한다.
③ 쓰레기 재활용에는 충분한 사전 홍보가 선행되어야 한다.
④ 쓰레기 재활용에 쓰이는 과다한 정부 기금은 재고되어야 한다.
⑤ 쓰레기 재활용 프로그램은 공공기관부터 참여해야 한다.

[53-55] 다음 글의 제목으로 가장 적절한 것을 고르시오.

53. The amount of sunshine that reaches the Earth dropped by 10 percent between the early 1950s and the early 1990s. Scientists have found that the problem is not the sun. No instruments have recorded any dimming of the sun's rays. The problem appears to be between the Earth and the Sun. Pollution has gotten in the way. Particulates in pollution reflect sun back into outer space. Pollution also causes increased condensation in the air. This condensation forms thicker, darker clouds. To verify their theory, scientists point to areas with little or no pollution. Instruments in those places have shown sunshine as bright as ever.

① Let's Give the Sun a Vacation
② Sunshine : The More the Better
③ Pollution : An Unnatural Sunshade
④ How Can We Stop the Sun's Dimming?
⑤ Look for a Silver Lining in Every Cloud

54. Walter Benjamin identifies traditional storytelling not only with the traveller, who returns from his wanderings with something to tell, but also with the preserver of local traditions, rooted in his native place. In the Middle Ages, these two types of storytelling interpenetrated because of the craft structure, whereby the resident master craftsman and the travelling journeyman came together in the workplace. But through the workings of "the secular productive forces of history," narrative has been taken from the realm of living speech. What stands in opposition to storytelling, what is in the process of replacing it entirely, is of course the novel, inseparably linked to the invention of printing and the notion of the book. The novelist is necessarily isolated, invisible, a hidden god who does not have the capacity to enter into colloquy with his fellow man, and thus cannot communicate that wisdom that is good counsel.

① Two Times, One Narrative
② Storytelling : Living Speech vs Dead Letters
③ A Solitary Hero in the Modern Narrative
④ The Decline of Storytelling, the Rise of the Novel
⑤ Craftsman and Journeyman : Two Sides of the Coin

55. Modern psychology has been called "the science of the behavior of the college sophomore." During the 1960s and 1970s, several psychologists analyzed four journals in the field and found that 58 percent to 96 percent of the articles were based on studies with college students. More recently, I analyzed the articles in two of those journals in 1991 and found that 77 percent reported on research done with college students. Melvin Manis, a University of Michigan psychologist, who is also an editor of one of the journals studied, explains that convenience dictates the choice of subjects in other fields as well. "There's very little genetic research going on with elephants," he says. "Most of it is done with fruit flies, not only because they have short life spans but because they're much cheaper." That's fine if elephants and fruit flies have comparable genetic mechanisms. But do college students think, behave, and feel as their non-college peers do? Or, for that matter, as older adults do? The answer to both questions is "no."

① College Students : Now and Then
② Genetic Research : Smaller is Better?
③ Sampling Error in the Study of Psychology
④ College Students in Psychology : Too Many?
⑤ Thought Patterns of College Students and Older Adults

56. 다음 글의 제목으로 가장 적절한 것은?

Hunters, spending their lives in the fields and woods, in a peculiar sense a part of Nature themselves, are often in a more favorable mood for observing her, in the intervals of their pursuits, than philosophers or poets even, who approach her with expectation. She is not afraid to exhibit herself to them. The traveller on the prairie is naturally a hunter. He who is only a traveller learns things at second-hand and by the halves, and is poor authority. We are most interested when science reports what those men already know practically or instinctively, for that alone is a true humanity, or account of human experience.

① Conditions for Productive Research in Natural Science
② Hunter, the Master of Understanding Nature
③ Benefits of Second-hand Learning
④ Why Hunting Should Be Banned in the Wilderness
⑤ Which Approach Is Preferred, Philosophical or Scientific?

57. 다음 글의 주제로 가장 적절한 것은?

The greatest asset of the next President, perhaps, will be that the world wants the U.S. to be great, or at least inspiring. Similarly, Americans want their President to be great, or at least admirable. For all the dissent and despair, Americans are not yet cynics, and have not yet lost their capacity for enthusiasm. Voters are looking for a presidential hero, a figure who will not only accept the U.S. assumption that one man is equal to the task, but who will also be responsive to the people as well as responsible for them. Will they find them? If the present field does not look brilliant, history proves that Presidents, like monarchs, show their true qualities only once they are in power. At any rate, in seeking the ideal man for the White House, or at least an approximation of the ideal, the electorate can ultimately rely only on a little reason, and muchinstinct, and a great deal of luck — which is sometimes knownas destiny.

① dilemmas that a U.S. President faces
② international expectations of a U.S. President
③ attributes that voters envision in a U.S. President
④ logical approaches to the U.S. President election
⑤ the ideal schooling for a U.S. President

[58-59] 다음 글의 요지로 가장 적절한 것을 고르시오.

58. As a conceptual framework, semiotics teaches students to formulate cogent, well-supported interpretations. It emphasizes the examination of assumptions and of the way language shapes our apprehension of the world. And, because semiotics focuseson how beliefs are formulated within a social and political context (rather than just judging or evaluating those beliefs), it's ideal for discussing sensitive or politically charged issues.

As an approach used in literature, media and communications studies, anthropology, art and design coursework, sociology, law, and market research (to name only some of its more prominent field applications), semiotics has a cross-disciplinary appeal that makes it ideal for a writing class of students from a variety of majors and disciplines. We recognize that semiotics has a reputation for being highly technical or theoretical; rest assured that this book does not require students or instructors to have a technical knowledge of semiotics.

① Semiotics can be used to interpret culturally sensitive issues.
② Our apprehension of the world relies on correct semiotic interpretations.
③ Politicians should utilize a semiotic framework appropriate for their beliefs.
④ Using this book for a course does not entail any technical knowledge of semiotics.
⑤ The cross-disciplinary nature of semiotics allows for efficient market research.

59. Nicholas Goldberg asks where all the English majors have gone. The answer is simple: They've gone where they've always gone. They'll probably become teachers or lawyers. The question many liberal arts majors may be asking themselves is this: Why did I get myself into debt by attending a "highly ranked" college if I'm going to end up being a teacher? After all, California State University schools are the best teacher prep colleges in the state. And liberal arts majors who decide to become lawyers may be asking themselves a similar question: Would it have been better to attend a state school instead of going into debt at a "highly ranked" college and actually have some money to attend law school? Getting into a "highly ranked" undergraduate school is good for bragging rights, but a good teacher is still a good teacher, and a good lawyer is still a good lawyer, no matter what colleges they attended. So to answer Goldberg's question, the English majors are doing just fine.

① Teachers should be more highly valued than lawyers.
② Making money is just as important as attending college.
③ Liberal arts majors are better off not going to law school.
④ Highly ranked colleges do not always provide better education.
⑤ Majoring in English is fine as long as one does not go into debt.

Unit 2

일치/불일치/추론 유형

일치/불일치/추론 유형도 마찬가지로 절대 하나씩 찾는 유형이 아니다. 우린 지문의 논리를 잡아가면서 정답의 우선순위를 잡아갈 수 있는 연습이 필요하다. 즉 일치/불일치 문제를 잘 풀게 되는 단계는 아이러니하게도 모든 선지를 완벽하게 판단할 수 있는 실력을 갖추게 되었을 때가 아니고, 다른 선지는 모르겠지만 이건 정답이겠다 라는 판단을 할 수 있을 때이다.

꼭 기억하자! 여기서 글을 원래부터 잘 읽고 그렇지 못한 학생 간의 차이도 심해진다. '잘할수록 답은 이거겠다'라는 판단을 잘하고, '잘하지 않을수록 하나하나 모든 것을 따지겠다'는 생각으로 망치게 될 확률이 높다.

특히 불일치하는 선지를 판단해야 하는 경우엔, 지문의 논리가 맞지 않아서 불일치, 지문에 안 써 있어서 불일치 등의 판단도 필요한 경우가 있다. 이런 판단을 완벽하게 해낼 수 있으려면 답을 찍는 기준을 먼저 알아야 한다. 기준의 핵심은 큰 판단부터 작은 판단으로 좁혀가는 것이다.

답을 찍는 기준

1) 글의 구조로 판단이 되는 선지

- 반박의 논리가 있는 글 ➡ 항상/모두/무조건 ~하다(불일치)
- 시간에 따라 변한다는 논리가 있는 글 ➡ 시간이 흘러도 변하지 않는다(불일치)
- Mystery 논리로 가는 글 ➡ 확정적인 인과관계(불일치), 방법/이유를 확실하게 알았다(불일치)
- 불특정 결과(결과 자리에 several 복수명사, some/many/most 복수, all ~) ➡ 결과가 하나밖에 없다(불일치)
- A와 B의 공통점으로 가는 글 ➡ A와 B는 차이가 있다(불일치)
- A와 B의 차이점으로 가는 글 ➡ A와 B는 같다(불일치)

2) 핵심 논리로 판단이 가능한 선지

두 번째는 핵심 논리로 판단이 되는 선지들이다. 지문에서 잡아 놓은 핵심 논리를 그대로 쓰면 일치, 반대로 쓰면 불일치라고 판단하는 것이다.

3) 중간 논리에선 비교 대상

비교 대상이 중간 논리로 등장하면 그 비교 대상의 특징을 반대로 쓴 선지도 불일치가 될 수 있다. 이건 가장 마지막에 하는 판단이다.

이것 말고 일치/불일치에서 따져야 하는 것은 없다. 그러니 지엽적으로 어떻게든 단어 찾기를 하지 말고 이런 판단을 연습해야 한다.

예시문제

1 글의 구조로 판단이 가능한 지문

1) A 때문에 여러 결과가 있다(불특정 결과)로 시작하는 글

일치/불일치 문제 선지에서 A 때문에 생기는 결과는 하나밖에 없다 = 불일치

Climate change has led to a multitude of consequences that affect ecosystems, economies, and human lives in profound and unpredictable ways. Rising sea levels are forcing the displacement of entire coastal communities, creating a growing population of climate refugees. Changing weather patterns have disrupted agricultural systems, leading to food shortages and increased vulnerability in regions already struggling with poverty. Additionally, higher global temperatures have accelerated the loss of biodiversity, as many species face extinction due to habitat loss or an inability to adapt to rapidly shifting environments. Coral reefs, for instance, are experiencing mass bleaching events, which threaten marine ecosystems and the livelihoods of millions dependent on them.

Beyond ecological impacts, climate change has intensified the frequency and severity of extreme weather events such as hurricanes, droughts, and wildfires, causing widespread destruction of natural landscapes and human infrastructure. Economic costs are mounting as governments and communities allocate increasing resources to disaster response, recovery, and mitigation efforts. These interconnected effects underscore the complexity of climate change, which manifests in a wide array of ways and leaves no sector untouched. The repercussions extend beyond immediate damage, as cascading effects ripple through global systems, challenging the capacity of nations and individuals to respond effectively.

Question 1 : Which of the following is the best title of the passage?

A. "The Narrow Scope of Climate Change Impacts"
B. "The Broad and Interconnected Consequences of Climate Change"
C. "Rising Sea Levels and the Sole Threat of Climate Change"
D. "How Climate Change Primarily Affects Agriculture"

Question 2 : Which of the following cannot be inferred from the passage?

A. Climate change has led to a wide range of ecological, economic, and social consequences.
B. Rising temperatures and changing weather patterns are contributing to biodiversity loss and food shortages.
C. Extreme weather events caused by climate change place increasing financial strain on governments and communities.
D. Climate change leads to only one significant outcome, primarily the displacement of coastal communities.

2) 반박의 논리로 흘러가는 글

항상/무조건 ~하다 = 불일치

Some proponents of the "digital detox" argue that extended breaks from technology are essential for mental health, fostering greater creativity, focus, and emotional well-being. They claim that by disconnecting from constant notifications and online distractions, individuals can reclaim their time and reengage with the world more meaningfully. However, this perspective oversimplifies the relationship between technology and mental health, failing to account for its nuanced role in contemporary life.

For instance, while it is true that excessive screen time can lead to burnout or diminished attention spans, technology also provides critical tools for stress relief and productivity. Many people use apps for guided meditation, time management, or virtual therapy sessions, which have been shown to improve mental health outcomes. Furthermore, digital platforms can foster meaningful connections and offer support systems for those who might otherwise feel isolated. A complete "detox" ignores the reality that for some, technology is an indispensable resource for coping and thriving in the modern world.

The argument for digital detoxes also overlooks the importance of individual variability. Not everyone experiences the same degree of harm from technology use, nor do all benefit equally from disconnection. For some, moderate use of digital tools is far more effective than abstinence. While intentional breaks can indeed be beneficial, framing them as universally necessary fails to consider the diversity of experiences and the positive contributions technology can make to well-being.

Question 3 : Which of the following is the best title of the passage?

A. "The Universal Benefits of Disconnecting from Technology"
B. "Reconsidering the Digital Detox : A Balanced Perspective"
C. "Why Technology Is Always Harmful to Mental Health"
D. "The Dangers of Ignoring Screen Time Limits"

Question 4 : Which of the following cannot be inferred from the passage?

A. Digital detoxes may oversimplify the complex role of technology in mental health.
B. Technology can serve as a beneficial tool for stress management and social support.
C. Not everyone is equally affected by technology use, nor benefits equally from disconnection.
D. Disconnecting from technology is always the best solution for improving mental health.

3) 시간에 따른 변화

시간이 지나도 변하지 않았다 = 불일치

The role of libraries has undergone profound transformations over the centuries, evolving in response to societal needs and technological advancements. In ancient times, libraries served as exclusive repositories of knowledge, accessible only to elites such as scholars, priests, and royalty. The Library of Alexandria, for example, symbolized intellectual power, its collections guarded and curated for the few deemed worthy. With the invention of the printing press in the 15th century, libraries began to democratize, transitioning from elite institutions to public resources as books became more affordable and widely available. By the 19th century, the establishment of public libraries reflected a growing societal emphasis on education and equality, enabling people from all walks of life to access knowledge.

In the digital age, libraries have once again transformed, embracing technology to maintain relevance. They now provide access to digital databases, e-books, and online learning platforms, often serving as hubs for technological literacy. However, these changes have sparked debates about the future of physical books and traditional library spaces. While libraries continue to adapt, their core mission remains rooted in the democratization of knowledge, even as the methods and mediums evolve. This trajectory underscores the fluid nature of libraries, which have continually reshaped themselves to meet the demands of their times.

Question 5 : Which of the following is the best title of the passage?

A. "The Timeless Role of Libraries as Static Knowledge Repositories"
B. "From Elite Archives to Digital Hubs : The Evolution of Libraries"
C. "Why Libraries Have Lost Their Purpose in the Digital Age"
D. "The Invention of the Printing Press : A Historical Footnote"

Question 6 : Which of the following cannot be inferred from the passage?

A. Libraries were initially exclusive spaces accessible only to societal elites.
B. The advent of the printing press played a key role in making libraries more accessible to the public.
C. In the digital age, libraries have adapted to include modern technologies like e-books and online platforms.
D. Libraries have remained unchanged in their structure and purpose throughout history.

4) Mystery 논리로 진행하는 글

확정적인 원인을 알았다 = 불일치

The phenomenon of bird migration, an awe-inspiring natural spectacle, is well-documented, yet the precise mechanisms driving this behavior remain elusive. Every year, millions of birds travel thousands of miles, navigating across continents with astonishing accuracy. While it is clear that this remarkable ability ensures access to food and favorable breeding conditions, the question of how birds accomplish such feats is far from resolved. Researchers have identified several factors that may play a role, including magnetic fields, celestial cues, and inherited genetic programming. Some studies suggest that birds possess magnetoreceptors allowing them to sense the Earth's magnetic field, while others highlight the role of memory and learned routes. However, none of these explanations fully accounts for the reliability and precision with which even first-time migratory birds find their way.

Adding to the mystery, migration patterns are not uniform across all species. Some birds follow strict, linear routes, while others wander erratically before reaching their destinations. Environmental changes and disruptions such as climate change have also introduced additional variables, making it even harder to determine the primary factors governing this behavior. Despite decades of research, the exact combination of instincts, learned behaviors, and environmental influences that enable migration remains one of biology's enduring puzzles.

Question 7 : Which of the following is the best title of the passage?

A. "The Solved Mystery of Bird Migration : A Journey Fully Understood"
B. "Bird Migration : Nature's Enigma in Motion"
C. "Magnetic Fields and Genetics : The Singular Explanation for Migration"
D. "The Decline of Bird Migration in the Age of Climate Change"

Question 8 : Which of the following cannot be inferred from the passage?

A. Bird migration ensures access to better feeding and breeding conditions.
B. Magnetic fields and celestial cues are among the potential factors influencing migration.
C. Environmental changes have complicated efforts to fully explain migratory behavior.
D. Scientists have definitively identified the primary cause of bird migration.

9 다음 글의 내용과 일치하는 것은?

If we suppose our extraneous observer to be a being of pure reason, devoid of instincts himself and unaware of the way in which all instincts in general and aggression in particular can miscarry, he would be at a complete loss how to explain history at all. It is a mere commonplace to say that the ever-recurrent phenomena of history are caused by what common parlance so aptly terms "human nature." Unreasoning and unreasonable human nature causes two nations to compete, though no economic necessity compels them to do so; it induces two political parties or religions with amazingly similar programs of salvation to fight each other bitterly, and it impels an Alexander or Napoleon to sacrifice millions of lives in his attempt to unite the world under his scepter. We have been taught to regard some of the persons who have committed these and similar absurdities with respect, even as "great" men, we are wont to yield to the political wisdom of those in charge, and we are all so accustomed to these phenomena that most of us fail to realize how abjectly stupid and undesirable the historical mass behavior of humanity actually is.

① Historical events, however commonplace they may be, have reasonable causes.
② It is economic rivalry that forces nations to fight against one another.
③ The unreasoning quality in human nature led great conquerors to seek world power.
④ Great men in history wanted to be respected, having minimized absurdities to gain political wisdom.
⑤ We generally recognize the time in which human beings act irrationally.

10 다음 글의 내용과 일치하지 않는 것은?

Most of us rely on expiration dates to know whether our groceries are still fresh. But as British-based industrial designer Solveiga Pakštaite learned when she interviewed blind people for a project on public transportation, if you can't see, you can't read those dates. The revelation inspired the 23-year-old to design the Bump Mark, a series of raised bumps coated with a layer of gelatin on food packaging. As the gelatin protein decays, the bumps become tangible. That's when you know the food is past its prime. This works because gelatin—made from animal hooves—rots at roughly the same rate as a steak, fish fillet, or bag of salad. The potential for this technology is even greater than what you might think. Printed dates are just guidelines, not true indicators of food spoilage, so we waste a lot of perfectly good food. (In the U.K., grocery stores and consumers throw away a total of 12 million tons of food every year.) Because the Bump Mark measures real rates of decay, the invention could help fix that. Pakštaite is now doing market research, studying manufacturing, and running lab tests to increase the accuracy of the gelatin-to-food decay rate. From a fresh idea, fresh food.

① For a project on public transit, Pakštaite spoke with blind persons.
② Food packaging bearing the Bump Mark features a number of raised bumps covered in gelatin.
③ The bumps become noticeable when the food has lost its freshness.
④ The rate of deterioration of gelatin is faster than that of a steak.
⑤ Printed dates are only recommendations rather than accurate indicators of food degradation.

11 다음 글의 내용과 일치하지 않는 것은?

Born into a wealthy Roman family, Marcus Terentius Varro led a long and adventurous life. After studying under the pre-eminent scholar Lucius Aelius Stilo, he travelled to Athens to study philosophy. Varro returned to fight on the losing side in one of the power struggles in which Caesar eventually triumphed. He was forgiven and rose to a position of prominence under Caesar's protection, then fell precipitously out of grace under Antony in 43 BCE. Varro escaped death, but suffered the destruction of his private library. He retired to spend the latter half of his life reading and writing, dying at age 89. Estimates vary, but on some accounts he produced 620 books — granted that most Roman books are the length of modern chapters. Varro wrote on virtually every topic: astronomy, geography, agriculture, mathematics, law, history, philosophy, and language. He also left behind poetry, speeches and letters.

① Varro studied philosophy in Athens.
② Varro fought on the losing side in a power struggle.
③ Varro was forgiven by Antony and rose to prominence.
④ Varro is thought to have produced over 600 books.
⑤ Varro wrote on astronomy, mathematics, and language, among other things.

12 다음 글의 내용과 일치하지 않는 것은?

Where a matter directly involves criminal issues, much of the practical investigation is carried out by the police on behalf of the criminal justice system, a system in which a coroner plays little part in most jurisdictions. In these circumstances, there is a practical basis for concluding that the pathologist in fact is carrying out a service for the police investigators. In reality, a criminal investigation involves many phases. Traditionally, the forensic pathologist was involved in that phase of an investigation that was centered on a death or injury, and in particular the examination of an injured or deceased person to ascertain the nature and cause of their injuries. In practice, however, forensic pathologists play a wider role in the criminal investigation. For example, they may become involved in the examination of scenes of death, or in the examination of suspects who may have inflicted injuries on the victim. They may evaluate medical records for medico-legal purposes, and examine the statements of other witnesses with regard to medical matters. In practice, therefore, forensic pathologists have a wider role than just dealing with suspicious deaths. The vast majority of autopsies conducted by forensic pathologists involve unconfirmed natural deaths which society requires to be scrutinized and confirmed. The investigation of non-suspicious natural deaths, fatal accidents, deaths from suicide and deaths from other forms of intentional and non-intentional injury forms the vast majority of their casework.

① The police carry out much of the investigation involving criminal issues.
② Forensic pathologists traditionally focused on the investigation of deaths or injuries.
③ Forensic pathologists are often involved in the examination of suspects and scenes of death.
④ The majority of autopsies performed by forensic pathologists involve unconfirmed natural deaths.
⑤ The investigation of suspicious deaths constitutes the vast majority of the casework handled by forensic pathologists.

13 다음 글의 내용과 가장 거리가 먼 것을 고르시오.

By the late eighteenth century, the discipline of natural history was dominated by so-called parson-naturalists — vicars, parsons, abbots, deacons, and monks who cultivated their gardens and collected plant and animal specimens to service the wonders of divine Creation, but generally veered away from questioning its fundamental assumptions. The result was a peculiar distortion of the field. Even as taxonomy — the classification of plant and animal species — flourished, inquiries into the origin of living beings were relegated to the forbidden sidelines. Natural history devolved into the study of nature without history. It was this static view of nature that Darwin found troubling. A natural historian should be able to describe the state of the natural world in terms of causes and effects, Darwin reasoned, just as a physicist might describe the motion of a ball in the air. The essence of Darwin's disruptive genius was his ability to think about nature not as fact but as process, as progression, as history.

① Parson-naturalists identified and classified plants and animals.
② Parson-naturalists had a static view of nature in describing nature.
③ Parson-naturalists fiercely investigated the origin of living beings.
④ Parson-naturalists celebrated the immense diversity of living beings created by an omnipotent God.
⑤ Darwin believed that a natural historian should ask how nature has progressed in terms of causes and effects.

14 다음 글의 내용과 가장 거리가 먼 것을 고르시오.

The French philosopher Gaston Bachelard once wrote an analysis of what he called the poetics of space. The inside of a house, he said, acquires a sense of intimacy, secrecy, security, real or imagined, because of the experiences that come to seem appropriate for it. The objective space of a house its corners, corridors, cellar, rooms is far less important than what poetically it is endowed with, which is usually a quality with an imaginative or figurative value we can name and feel; thus a house may be haunted, or homelike, or prisonlike, or magical. So space acquires emotional and even rational sense through a kind of poetic process, whereby the vacant or anonymous reaches of distance are converted into meaning for us here.

① Bachelard described locations in the house as places of intimacy and memory.
② Bachelard placed emphasis on the inside of the house with a sense of intimacy.
③ Bachelard examined the home as the manifestation of the soul through the poetic image.
④ Bachelard suggested that one should transcend mere description in order to grasp the essential qualities of space.
⑤ Bachelard suggested that poetic spaces of the house are dependant on our ability to observe and examine them objectively.

15 다음 글의 내용과 가장 거리가 먼 것을 고르시오.

The Swiss pastor Johann Casper Lavater wrote confidently that the chin signifies strength in a man. He claimed that an angular or receding chin is seldom found in "discreet, well disposed, firm men." He also asserted that horizontal eyebrows that are "rich and clear always convey understanding, coldness of heart, and the capacity to frame plans." Perhaps not surprisingly, he thought that European facial physiognomy was superior to others. In a curious connection, Fitz Roy, the commander of the Beagle, was a Lavater fan. The Beagle is the ship that took Darwin around the world to gather evidence from which he later developed his theory of evolution. Darwin wrote in his biography that the captain doubted that anyone with Darwin's nose had "sufficient energy and determination for the voyage." Of course, this was the nose that led Darwin through 5 years of arduous travel that inspired his theory of evolution.

① Lavater linked an individual's appearance to racial stereotyping.
② Lavater suggested that men with horizontal eyebrows are likely to be rational rather than emotional.
③ Lavater suggested that discreet, well disposed, and firm men are likely to have an angular chin.
④ Lavater confidently wrote about the relationship between an individual's outward appearance and inner character.
⑤ The captain of the Beagle doubted that Darwin had enough determination for the arduous voyage.

16 위 글의 내용과 가장 거리가 먼 것을 고르시오.

In strong opposition to methodological naturalism in the field of sociology, historicism claims that some of the characteristic methods of physics cannot be applied to the social sciences, owing to the profound differences between sociology and physics. Physical laws, or the 'laws of nature', it tells us, are valid anywhere and always; for the physical world is ruled by a system of physical uniformities invariable throughout space and time. Sociological laws, however, or the laws of social life, differ in different places and periods.

Although historicism admits that there are plenty of typical social conditions whose regular recurrence can be observed, it denies that regularities detectable in social life have the character of the immutable regularities of the physical world. For they depend upon history, and upon differences in culture. They depend on a particular historical situation. Thus one should not, for example, speak without further qualification of the laws of economics, but only of the economic laws of the feudal period, or the early industrial period, and so on; always mentioning the historical period in which the laws in question are assumed to have prevailed.

Historicism asserts that the historical relativity of social laws makes most of the methods of physics inapplicable to sociology. Typical historicist arguments on which this view is based concern generalization, experiment, the complexity of social phenomena, the difficulties of exact prediction, and the significance of methodological essentialism.

① Historicism claims that most of the methods of physics are not applicable to sociology because of the historical relativity of social laws.

② Historical relativity makes it possible to discover scientific laws or trends that underlie the evolution of history.

③ According to historicism, the regularities detectable in social life depend on a particular historical situation.

④ Historicism assumes that history and culture have no such uniformity that physics has in its studies.

17 다음 글을 바탕으로 유추할 때 적절하지 않은 것을 고르시오.

Any velocity once imparted to a moving body will be rigidly maintained as long as the external causes of acceleration or retardation are removed, a condition which is found only on horizontal planes; for in the case of planes which slope downwards there is already a cause of acceleration; while on planes sloping upwards there is retardation; from this it follows that motion along a horizontal plane is perpetual; for, if the velocity be uniform, it cannot be diminished or slackened, much less destroyed.

① The velocity shows whether or not external forces are acting on a body.
② A pull in the direction of motion increases the speed of the moving body.
③ If no external forces act on a body, every body perseveres in its state of uniform motion.
④ A push in the direction opposite to that of motion decreases the speed of the moving body.

18 다음 글의 내용과 일치하지 않는 것을 고르시오.

Linguists repeatedly run up against the myth that working-class people and the less educated members of the middle class speak a simpler or coarser language. This is a pernicious illusion arising from the effortlessness of conversation. Ordinary speech, like color vision or walking, is a paradigm of engineering excellence — a technology that works so well that the user takes its outcome for granted, unaware of the complicated machinery hidden behind the panels. Behind such "simple" sentences as Where did he go? and The guy I met killed himself, used automatically by any English speaker, are dozens of subroutines that arrange the words to express the meaning. Despite decades of effort, no artificially engineered language system comes close to duplicating the person in the street.

① It is an illusion that working-class people speak a ruder and plainer language.
② We are often aware of the complicated machinery hidden behind ordinary speech that works so well.
③ An engineer has not yet developed an artificially constructed language system close to ordinary speech.
④ Dozens of subroutines are arranged to express the meaning in such a "simple" sentence as Where did he go?

19 다음 글의 내용과 일치하지 않는 것을 고르시오.

The starling flies from its net to a feeding site, searches for a beak-full of leatherjackets by probing in the grass, and then takes them home to the nestlings. The starling's problem is when to give up. If it gives up too early it spends a lot of time travelling for a small load; if it struggles on too long it spends time in ineffective search which could be better spent by going home to dump its load and starting again. A similar problem is faced by a worker honeybee as it flies from flower to flower filling its honey crop with nectar to take back to the hive. Bees also often return to the hive with less than the maximum load they could carry and their behaviour can be explained by a model similar to that used for the starling. There is, however, an important difference: the bee experiences a curve of diminishing returns neither because the nectar in its crop makes it less able to suck more flowers nor because of resource depression but because the weight of nectar in the crop adds an appreciable energetic cost to flight. The more the bee loads up its crop the more of its load it will burn up as fuel before it gets home.

① The bee flies home with less than the maximum load it can carry.
② The bee knows when to go home and empty its crop to maximize efficiency.
③ The starling's best option is that it stays long enough for the maximum load on each trip.
④ There is the difference between bees and starlings in maximizing the currency of carrying a load.

20 다음 글의 내용과 일치하지 않는 것을 고르시오.

Why are you reading Spinoza's Ethics? Perhaps it is assigned reading on a university course. Maybe you are a philosopher who wants to brush up on a neglected area. Or perhaps you are led by curiosity about the nature of reality, the mind and human behaviour. If you fall into any of these categories, this book—and indeed, Spinoza's Ethics itself—was written for you.

It may surprise you to hear that Spinoza's Ethics was written just as much for a non-expert audience in the twenty-first century as for the philosophical world of the seventeenth. Spinoza anticipated that his book would be read largely by those steeped in the philosophical traditions of the time. (If you do have some philosophical background, you may hear echoes of Plato, Aristotle, the Stoics, Descartes and Hobbes in his work, as well as anticipations of Nietzsche, Sartre, Foucault and Deleuze.) But Spinoza would be delighted to learn of non-experts reading his work more than 300 years later, for his aim is to help as many people as possible understand the truth. The Ethics is a workbook designed to enable the reader to develop his or her own understanding. Spinoza thinks that if more people read the Ethics, then reason and virtue amongst human beings will increase, leading to more peaceful and tolerant societies.

That is not to say that the Ethics is a kind of early self-help manual. Spinoza's Ethics is a rich and complex work of metaphysics, epistemology and ethics. Undoubtedly, it is one of the most difficult philosophical books you will ever read. You will grapple with language and concepts that are unfamiliar and encounter ideas with which you may disagree profoundly. But it is also one of the most exciting philosophy books ever written. Spinoza gives us a programme for being human beings in the best way possible—a programme based on a deep understanding of the nature of reality that anyone can attain. He leads us on a journey that reveals to us the truth about what we are and our place in the universe. Understanding the truth about ourselves is the basis for positive human relationships, true scientific knowledge and good political organisation. Spinoza can lead you to think differently about yourself and your life, about nature, about God, about freedom and about ethics. So perhaps the best reason for reading Spinoza's Ethics is this: it is a book that may change your life.

① Understanding the truth about ourselves is prerequisite for true scientific knowledge.
② As a whole, Spinoza's Ethics is committed to influencing its readers' lives.
③ The author of the Ethics aimed to help as many people as possible understand the truth.
④ Those who were stuck with the philosophical tradition of the time did not like the Ethics.

21 다음 글의 내용과 가장 일치하는 것을 고르시오.

Let us assume that crises are a necessary precondition for the emergence of novel theories and ask next how scientists respond to their existence. Part of the answer, as obvious as it is important, can be discovered by noting first what scientists never do when confronted by even severe and prolonged anomalies. Though they may begin to lose faith and then to consider alternatives, they do not renounce the paradigm that has led them into crisis. They do not, that is, treat anomalies as counter-instances, though in the vocabulary of philosophy of science that is what they are. In part this generalization is simply a statement from historic fact, based upon the examples which hint what our later examination of paradigm rejection will disclose more fully: once it has achieved the status of paradigm, a scientific theory is declared invalid only if an alternate candidate is available to take the place. No process yet disclosed by the historical study of scientific development at all resembles the methodological stereotype of falsification by direct comparison with nature. That remark does not mean that scientists do not reject scientific theories, or that experience and experiment are not essential to the process in which they do so. But it does mean—what will ultimately be a central point—that the act of judgment that leads scientists to reject a previously accepted theory is always based upon more than a comparison of that theory with the world. The decision to reject one paradigm is always simultaneously the decision to accept another, and the judgment leading to that decision involves the comparison of both paradigms with nature and with each other.

① Scientists give up the existing theories when they begin to consider alternatives.
② Scientists think that a new scientific theory should usually be tested with the falsification stereotype through direct comparison with nature.
③ The final decision to accept one scientific paradigm used to be made after the comparison of both paradigms with nature as well as with each other.
④ The advantages and disadvantages of a scientific theory are well revealed by a study of anomalous scientific phenomenon in which the theory becomes invalid.

22 다음 글의 내용과 가장 거리가 먼 것을 고르시오.

Isaac Newton believed, in part because shadows had sharp edges without spreading out, that light behaved as if it were a stream of tiny particles. He thought that red light was composed of the largest particles and violet the smallest. Huygens argued that instead light behaved as if it were a wave propagating in a vacuum, as an ocean wave does in the sea—which is why we talk about the wavelength and frequency of light. Many properties of light, including diffraction, are naturally explained by the wave theory, and in subsequent years Huygens's view carried the day. But in 1905, Einstein showed that the particle theory of light could explain the photoelectric effect, the ejection of electrons from a metal upon exposure to a beam of light. Modern quantum mechanics combines both ideas, and it is customary today to think of light as behaving in some circumstances as a beam of particles and in others as a wave. This wave-particle dualism may not correspond readily to our common-sense notions, but it is in excellent accord with what experiments have shown light really does.

① Electrons are emitted from a metal that is exposed to a beam of light.
② Wave-particle duality is one of the great puzzles of Newtonian physics.
③ Quantum mechanics demonstrates that light behaves both like particles and waves.
④ Light as a wave traverses through space in a manner similar to a wave spreading across the surface of the sea.
⑤ If light as particles encounters the edge of a barrier, then it casts a shadow because the particles do not spread out behind the edge.

23 다음 글의 내용과 가장 거리가 먼 것을 고르시오.

A theory of heredity, Darwin realized, was not peripheral to a theory of evolution; it was of pivotal importance. For a variant of gross-beaked finch to appear on a Galápagos island by natural selection, two seemingly contradictory facts had to be simultaneously true. First, a short-beaked "normal" finch must be able to occasionally produce a gross-beaked variant—a monster or freak. And second, once born, that gross-beaked finch must be able to transmit the same trait to its offspring, thereby fixing the variation for generations to come. If either factor failed, nature would be mired in a ditch, the cogwheels of evolution jammed.

① The organism must be able to occasionally produce variants.
② Variations could lie dormant for several generations before reappearing.
③ For Darwin's theory to work, heredity has to possess stability and mutation.
④ Inheritance of acquired characters is the driving force of Darwin's theory of evolution.
⑤ Variations experienced by the organism must be able to occasionally be transmitted to its offspring.

24 다음 글의 내용과 가장 거리가 먼 것을 고르시오.

Any physical theory is always provisional, in the sense that it is only a hypothesis: you can never prove it. No matter how many times the results of experiments agree with some theory, you can never be sure that the next time the result will not contradict the theory. On the other hand, you can disprove a theory by finding even a single observation that disagrees with the predictions of the theory. As philosopher of science Karl Popper has emphasized, a good theory is characterized by the fact that it makes a number of predictions that could in principle be disproved or falsified by observation. Each time new experiments are observed to agree with the predictions the theory survives, and our confidence in it is increased; but if ever a new observation is found to disagree, we have to abandon or modify the theory.

① A scientific theory must take measures to make the observed reality fit its predictions.
② When a scientific theory is falsified by observations, scientists have to respond by modifying it.
③ A scientific theory is characterized by entailing predictions that future observations might reveal to be false.
④ The process of revising scientific theories must aim at the production of predictions that could be disproved.
⑤ Scientific practice is characterized by its continual effort to make revisions based on the outcomes of observations.

25 According to the passage, which of the following is NOT true?

BRK Brands, Inc. ("BRK") the maker of First Alert brand product, warrants that for a period of five years from the date of purchase, this product will be free from defects in material and workmanship. BRK will repair or replace this product or any component of the product found to be defective during the warranty period. Replacement will be made with a new or remanufactured product or component. If the product is no longer available, replacement may be made with a similar product of equal or greater value. This is your exclusive warranty.

This warranty is valid for the original retail purchase from the date of initial retail purchase and is not transferable. Keep the original sales receipt. This warranty does not cover normal wear of parts or damage resulting from any of the following: negligent use of the product, use on improper voltage or current, or use contrary to the operating instructions by anyone other than BRK. Further, the warranty does not cover acts of God, such as fire, flood, hurricanes and tornadoes.

① The warranty does not cover the damage of the product resulting from careless use.
② The product may be replaced by a new one if natural disaster such as flood has damaged it.
③ You may receive a product better than the one you purchased if the same model is not available.
④ Only for the original retail purchase will this warranty be valid.

26 다음 글의 내용과 가장 거리가 먼 것은?

Machiavelli's unpardonable sin was to reveal that, if they are genuinely practiced and not just hypocritically professed, Christian humility, loving kindness and trust bring ruin to any state that honors them. In contrast, what Machiavelli called virtú — a pagan resolve to do whatever may be necessary for the attainment of civic glory and greatness — enables the state to achieve republican self-government, which he considered the supreme political good. No ruler can govern for long without a constant readiness to dispose of his enemies. Yet the sword is a blunt instrument if it is wielded without the mask. A ruler must not be one person, the righteous sovereign as described in medieval "mirrors for princes" that were written to guide nobles who had succeeded to power. Instead, they must have many personae, changing the face they present to the world as circumstances require. Personal authenticity is a luxury they cannot afford, and truth a weapon that must be used sparingly. As much as the readiness to eliminate their enemies, rulers need constant exercise in dissimulation. Success in any political project depends on traits that Christianity condemns as vices. Machiavelli reports these facts without sadness or regret. There is no trace in his writings of the narcissistic anguish of the disillusioned humanist.

① Republican self-government was the best form of state for Machiavelli.
② Machiavelli's writing is characterized by dispassionate and reasoned lines of argumentation.
③ For Machiavelli, civic glory and greatness were among the most highly regarded Christian virtues.
④ Machiavelli insisted that the political leader should have a multifaceted personality to handle volatile political situations.
⑤ According to Machiavelli, Christian humility and personal authenticity were negative qualities for political leadership.

27 다음 글을 통해 추론할 수 있는 것으로 가장 적합한 것을 고르시오.

The Fourth Industrial Revolution, a moniker initially coined by the World Economic Forum to refer to the newest innovations in labor and productivity, which can include near-feature robotic and AI innovation, refers to an age when digital technology ceases to be trapped within the confines of a desktop computer. The Internet of Things promises the insertion of computational technology in virtually all physical products. The quantified self suggests the digital capture of every human sense and action, from heart rate and blush response to emotional fluency and activity tracking. Digital and physical surveillance unite to provide a complete picture of each person's physical and online activities in a unified holistic picture. Massive networking promises that information is richly fused, creating secondary knowledge that was otherwise impossible to capture, such as demographic data, purchasing habits, and the chances of loan defaults. Robotic innovations threaten prevailing concepts of aging and injury, suggesting exoskeletons and other robotic orthotics that change how human and machines can couple in the physical world.

① The revolution redefines our human relationship to the Internet of Things.
② The revolution reduces our holistic relationship with computation and digital intelligence.
③ The revolution gives digital technology the chance to break out of the computer and pervade the entire world.
④ The revolution envisions the production of a computer and all its associated products and systems.

28 다음 글을 통해 추론할 수 있는 것으로 가장 적합한 것을 고르시오.

In our brains, a neuron has a body, dendrites, and an axon. The signal from one neuron travels down the axon and transfers to the dendrites of the next neuron. That connection where the signal passes is called a synapse. Neurons by themselves are kind of useless. But when you have lots of them, they work together to create some serious magic. That's the idea behind a deep learning algorithm! You get input from observation and you put your input into one layer. That layer creates an output which in turn becomes the input for the next layer, and so on. This happens over and over until your final output signals. Think of the input layer as your senses: the things you see, smell, and feel, for example. These are independent variables for one single observation. This information is broken down into numbers and the bits of binary data that a computer can use. You'll need to either standardize or normalize these variables so that they're within the same range. They use many layers of nonlinear processing units for feature extraction and transformation. Each successive layer uses the output of the previous layer for its input. What they learn forms a hierarchy of concepts. In this hierarchy, each level learns to transform its input data into a more and more abstract and composite representation.

① Deep learning process is an abstract collection of neurons.
② Many layers of nonlinear processing units work independently for the next step.
③ The information collected from one single observation is converted into bits of binary data.
④ One layer deletes an input data by a repeated process of independent variables.

29 Which of the following is true about Keith Haring according to the passage?

The particular fascination of Keith Haring's art lies in his ability to combine his strongly graphic style with a great deal of imagination. His figures and forms are subject to continuous transformations and new creations, providing ongoing proof of his qualities as a draftsman, painter and sculptor. Within his oeuvre, we witness a steady stylistic evolution. His constant search for new challenges is accompanied by experimentation with changing surfaces on which to paint. No matter whether he chooses to paint on walls, items of clothing, automobiles or airships and most of all on paper, canvas, untreated cotton or vinyl, Haring's hallmark is perfection of execution. Neither for his formally planned projects nor for his spontaneous mural designs are his lines based on sketches or studies. We can discern no errors or corrections, no asymmetries of proportion. Spontaneity and assurance are the outstanding attributes of his work.

① He does his works without the benefit of prior planning.
② Figures and forms remain constant throughout his works.
③ His paintings on cars reveal flaws in his execution style.
④ One of his shortcomings was lack of variety in art form.

30 Choose the one that is not true according to the passage.

Rome owed its success to its traditions, which combined to create a distinctly Roman identity. Among these was the determination never to be ruled by kings. Even during the empire, the forms of old Roman government were preserved. The standards carried by Roman legions did not carry the emperor's name, but the letters SPQR, which stood for "for the senate and people of Rome." Family was considered to lie at the very heart of Roman life, and the names of eminent families recur over the centuries in Roman history. It was very important for a man to gain success in war or civil life in order to add to the prestige of his family. Another Roman characteristic was the way the city was unyielding toward its foes. Many enemies of Rome beat the Romans in a battle, but few were able to defeat them in a war. Finally, the Roman system of government allowed ambitious men to succeed. The consular system, in which two consuls served in partnership for a year, encouraged each consul to do what he could to make a success of his year in office. This arrangement often led to foolhardy mistakes, but it also contributed to great successes. In spite of attempts by senators to protect their position, the Roman system eventually allowed wider groups of people to participate in government.

① Romans were tenacious in fending off aggression from abroad.
② Rome favored monarchy over any other from of governance.
③ Familial fidelity marked an important facet of the Roman psyche.
④ The consular arrangement did not always yield positive outcomes.

Unit 3

지칭 추론 유형

Unit 3 지칭 추론 유형

지칭 추론 유형은 함축 의미 추론 유형이라고도 한다. 밑줄 친 부분이 뜻하는 의미를 고르는 문제가 가장 흔하게 출제가 된다.

1) 우리는 밑줄을 보면서 이 밑줄의 근거를 어떻게 찾을지에 대해 먼저 생각을 해야 한다. 밑줄의 근거를 찾기 위해 밑줄 문장의 앞으로 갈지, 뒤로 갈지, 아니면 밑줄 문장만 가지고 끝낼지 등을 정하는 것이 필요하다.

2) 그 다음 밑줄 부분이 문장의 원인 자리에 있는지 결과 자리에 있는지를 판단을 해야 한다. 그리고 찾기로 한 부분을 찾으러 가서 답의 근거를 발견하면 된다.

3) 만약 내 생각에 답의 근거를 발견했다면 그걸 그대로 선지에서 찾으면 된다. 없다고 느껴진다면, 근거를 못 찾은 것일수도 있지만, 일단 이건 밑줄 자체의 의미를 묻는 문제겠다 라고 생각하고 그 부분이 무슨 의미인지를 알 땐 풀고 모를 땐 안 풀면 된다.

예시문제

1. 밑줄 친 <u>hunting the shadow, not the substance</u>가 다음 글에서 의미하는 바로 가장 적절한 것은?

The position of the architect rose during the Roman Empire, as architecture symbolically became a particularly important political statement. Cicero classed the architect with the physician and the teacher and Vitruvius spoke of "so great a profession as this." Marcus Vitruvius Pollio, a practicing architect during the rule of Augustus Caesar, recognized that architecture requires both practical and theoretical knowledge, and he listed the disciplines he felt the aspiring architect should master: literature and writing, draftsmanship, mathematics, history, philosophy, music, medicine, law, and astronomy — a curriculum that still has much to recommend it. All of this study was necessary, he argued, because architects who have aimed at acquiring manual skill without scholarship have never been able to reach a position of authority to correspond to their plans, while those who have relied only upon theories and scholarship were obviously "<u>hunting the shadow, not the substance</u>."

① seeking abstract knowledge emphasized by architectural tradition
② discounting the subjects necessary to achieve architectural goals
③ pursuing the ideals of architecture without the practical skills
④ prioritizing architecture's material aspects over its artistic ones
⑤ following historical precedents without regard to current standards

2. 밑줄 친 <u>Now I zip along the surface like a guy on a Jet Ski</u>가 다음 글에서 의미하는 바로 가장 적절한 것은?

In 1890, William James described attention as "the taking possession by the mind, in clear and vivid form, of one out of what seem several simultaneously possible objects or trains of thought." Attention is a choice we make to stay on one task, one line of thinking, one mental road, even as attractive off-ramps signal. When we fail to make that choice and allow ourselves to be frequently sidetracked, we end up in "the confused, dazed, scatterbrained state" that James said is the opposite of attention. Staying on one road got much harder when the internet arrived and moved much of our reading online. Every hyperlink is an off-ramp, calling us to abandon the choice we made moments earlier. Nicholas Carr, in his 2010 book, grieved his lost ability to stay on one path. Life on the internet changed how his brain sought out information, even when he was off-line trying to read a book. It reduced his ability to focus and reflect because he now craved a constant stream of stimulation: "Once I was a scuba diver in the sea of words. <u>Now I zip along the surface like a guy on a Jet Ski</u>."

① Ironically, the convenience of downloading digital creations restrains people's creativity.
② By uncritically accepting information, we get trapped in a cycle of misunderstanding.
③ People's attention is naturally drawn to carefully analyzed and well-presented data.
④ We now deal with the information in a skin-deep manner, constantly being distracted.
⑤ With the help of the internet, we comprehend the information quickly and thoroughly.

3. 밑줄 친 <u>from their verandas</u>가 다음 글에서 의미하는 바로 가장 적절한 것은?

Around the turn of the twentieth century, anthropologists trained in the natural sciences began to reimagine what a science of humanity should look like and how social scientists ought to go about studying cultural groups. Some of those anthropologists insisted that one should at least spend significant time actually observing and talking to the people studied. Early ethnographers such as Franz Boas and Alfred Cort Haddon typically traveled to the remote locations where the people in question lived and spent a few weeks to a few months there. They sought out a local Western host who was familiar with the people and the area (such as a colonial official, missionary, or businessman) and found accommodations through them. Although they did at times venture into the community without a guide, they generally did not spend significant time with the local people. Thus, their observations were primarily conducted <u>from their verandas</u>.

① seeking to build long-lasting relationships with the natives
② participating in collaborative research with natural scientists
③ engaging in little direct contact with the people being studied
④ cooperating actively with Western hosts in the local community
⑤ struggling to take a wider view of the native culture examined

4. 밑줄 친 <u>the breadcrumbs of the conversation</u>이 다음 글에서 의미하는 바로 가장 적절한 것은?

In improv, the actors have no control of the conversation or the direction it takes. They can only react to the other actors' words or nonverbal communication. Because of this, the actors become experts at reading body language and reading between the lines of what is said. If they are unable to do this, they are left in the dark and the performance crumbles. This applies to our daily conversations, but we're usually too self-centered to notice. Just like the improv actors become adept at picking up on <u>the breadcrumbs of the conversation</u>, we need to do the same. When people want to talk about something specific, rarely will they come out and just say it. 99 percent of people won't say, "Hey, let's talk about my dog now. So...." Instead, they will hint at it. When they bring up a topic unprompted, or ask questions about it, they want to talk about it. Sometimes, when the other person seems to not pick up on these signals, they will keep redirecting the conversation to that specific topic. If they seem excited whenever the topic comes up, they want to talk about it.

① roundabout hints revealing the speaker's intention
② opening words to make the topic more interesting
③ part of the conversation that distracts the listeners
④ characteristics that are unique to the actors themselves
⑤ unexpected reactions of the audience to the performance

5. 밑줄 친 Burnout hasn't had the last word가 다음 글에서 의미하는 바로 가장 적절한 것은?

To balance the need for breadth (everyone feels a bit burned out) and depth (some are so burned out, they can no longer do their jobs), we ought to think of burnout not as a state but as a spectrum. In most public discussion of burnout, we talk about workers who "are burned out," as if that status were black and white. A black-and-white view cannot account for the variety of burnout experience, though. If there is a clear line between burned out and not, as there is with a lightbulb, then we have no good way to categorize people who say they are burned out but still manage to do their work competently. Thinking about burnout as a spectrum solves this problem; those who claim burnout but are not debilitated by it are simply dealing with a partial or less-severe form of it. They are experiencing burnout without being burned out. Burnout hasn't had the last word.

① Public discussion of burnout has not reached an end.
② There still exists room for a greater degree of exhaustion.
③ All-or-nothing criteria are applicable to burnout symptoms.
④ Exhaustion is overcome in different ways based on its severity.
⑤ Degrees of exhaustion are shaped by individuals' perceptions.

6. 밑줄 친 Approximate perfection is better than perfect perfection이 다음 글에서 의미하는 바로 가장 적절한 것은?

Turn the lights out and point the beam of a small flashlight up into one of your eyes. Shake the beam around while moving your gaze up and down. You should catch glimpses of what look like delicate branches. These branches are shadows of the blood vessels that lie on top of your retina. The vessels constantly cast shadows as light streams into the eye, but because these shadows never move, the brain ceases responding to them. Moving the flashlight beam around shifts the shadows just enough to make them momentarily visible. Now you might wonder if you could cause an image to fade just by staring at something unmoving. But that is not possible because the visual system constantly jiggles the eye muscles, which prevents the perfect stabilization of images of the world. These muscle movements are unbelievably small, but their effect is huge. Without them, we would go blind by tuning out what we see shortly after fixating our gaze! It's an interesting notion: Approximate perfection is better than perfect perfection.

① What makes your vision blurry actually protects your eyes.
② The more quickly an object moves, the more sensitively eyes react.
③ Eyes exposed to intense light are subject to distortion of images.
④ Constant adjustment of focusing makes your eye muscles tired.
⑤ Shaky eye - muscle movements let us see what the brain might ignore.

7. 다음 밑줄 친 <u>you taste its price</u>가 의미하는 바로 가장 적절한 것은?

That perception is a construction is not true just of one's perception of sensory input, such as visual and auditory information. It is true of your social perceptions as well — your perceptions of the people you meet, the food you eat, and even of the products you buy. For example, in a study of wine, when wines were tasted blind, there was little or no correlation between the ratings of a wine's taste and its cost, but there was a significant correlation when the wines were labeled by price. That wasn't because the subjects consciously believed that the higher-priced wines should be the better ones and thus revised whatever opinion they had accordingly. Or rather, it wasn't true just at the conscious level. We know because as the subjects were tasting the wine, the researchers were imaging their brain activity, and the imaging showed that drinking what they believed was an expensive glass of wine really did activate their centers of taste for pleasure more than drinking a glass of the same wine that had been labeled as cheaper. That's related to the placebo effect. Like pain, taste is not just the product of sensory signals; it depends also on psychological factors: you don't just taste the wine; <u>you taste its price</u>.

① Customer ratings determine the price of a product.
② We fool ourselves into thinking our unplanned buying was reasonable.
③ We immediately dismiss opposing opinions without any consideration.
④ The brain shows consistent response regardless of personal preference.
⑤ The perceived value of a product influences one's subjective experience of it

Unit 4

빈칸 유형

Unit 4 빈칸 유형

빈칸에 알맞은 것을 고르는 유형은 지칭 추론을 풀 때와 비슷한 방식으로 접근하면 된다. 우선 우리가 해야 할 일은 빈칸 문장에서 내가 빈칸의 근거를 어디에서 찾을지에 대해 판단하는 것이다. 빈칸이 있는 문장의 앞 부분에서 찾을지, 빈칸이 있는 문장의 뒷 부분에서 찾을지, 아니면 빈칸이 있는 문장으로 판단을 끝낼 것인지를 정하는 것이 가장 중요하다.

1) 이것을 정할 때 가장 많이 활용할 수 있는 것이 바로 글의 구조가 바뀔 수 있는 포인트다.
   빈칸이 있는 문장에 반박의 부사, 인과관계의 부사 상황이 바뀌는 표현, 인물의 표현이 있을 때 : 빈칸의 근거는 기본적으로 뒤에 가서 찾는다. 물론 앞으로 가서 찾는 것도 있겠지만 일단 뒤에 가서 찾는 것을 기본으로 하고 어떤 경우에 앞에 가서 찾는지를 정하는 연습을 하면 된다.
   - 빈칸이 있는 문장 다음 문장에 반박의 부사, 인과관계의 부사 상황이 바뀌는 표현, 인물의 표현이 있을 때 : 이 땐 빈칸의 근거는 기본적으로 빈칸이 있는 문장 앞에서 찾는다. 이것 또한 뒤에 가서 찾을 때도 있겠지만 기본은 앞이라는 것을 기억하고 접근하면 된다.
   - 빈칸이 있는 문장에 반박의 부사, 인과관계의 부사 상황이 바뀌는 표현, 인물의 표현이 있을 때가 있고 빈칸이 있는 문장 다음에도 반박의 부사, 인과관계의 부사 상황이 바뀌는 표현, 인물의 표현이 있을 때 : 이 땐 빈칸 문장만으로 판단을 끝내고 빈칸을 채우겠다고 생각하면 된다.

2) 그 다음 빈칸이 원인 자리인지 결과 자리인지에 대해 판단해본다. 빈칸이 원인에 있다면 지문 속에서 결과에 해당하는 것을 찾고, 그 결과가 있는 문장에 원인에 있는 내용이 빈칸의 근거라고 생각하면 되고, 빈칸이 결과 자리에 있다면 지문에서 원인 자리에 있는 표현을 찾고 그 문장의 결과 자리에 있는 내용이 빈칸의 근거라고 생각하면 된다.
3) 이렇게 빈칸의 근거를 찾은 후 빈칸을 주관식으로 만들어준다. 내가 만들어 둔 주관식을 바탕으로 선지를 판단하면 된다.
4) 선지 판단의 기본은 내가 잡은 주관식과 반대를 말하는 선지, 내가 잡은 주관식과 아무 관련이 없는 내용의 선지가 있다.

예시문제

1. Are we alone in the Universe? It's probably the most profound question science has yet to answer. But so far the search for extraterrestrial life has only found ________. However, over the next few years the search for alien life is about to seriously ramp up. All being well, the most powerful telescope ever built, the James Webb Space Telescope, will start sending back images to Earth by the end of March. Its sensors and tech will let scientists take a closer look at Earth-like exoplanets than ever before. In 2023, the Vera Rubin Observatory in Chile will open its shutters to survey the stars. This telescope will have the largest camera of any ever built and will enable astronomers to map and catalogue the Universe in unprecedented detail. But it's not all about new tech. A handful of scientists have also hatched a plan to look for alien life in a completely new way. Instead of searching for signals, for traces of the ingredients for life, or the by-products of living creatures, these astronomers think we ought to be searching for something altogether bigger and therefore easier to find: alien technology. It sounds like the stuff of science fiction, but there's some serious science behind it.

① shadows
② miracles
③ blueprints
④ shelters
⑤ pinnacles

2. Animal liberationists generally draw the line of moral consideration at the boundary of sentience or feeling. For Singer, this is somewhere between crustaceans and molluscs, leaving mussels on the menu but taking crab and lobster off. Environmental ethics, on the other hand, places far less emphasis on the individual organism, but demands moral consideration for inanimate things such as rivers and mountains, assuming pain and suffering to be a necessary part of nature. These ethical conflicts have practical consequences, in that liberationists are generally ________________, whereas ecophilosophers argue that in some cases exploding populations of a certain species must be culled if they threaten a local environment as whole. Such conflicts have become especially pressing in cases where non-native predators or destructive herbivores threaten fragile ecologies.

① opposed to hunting
② insensitive to animal pain
③ interested in the bio-community
④ inclined to focus on inanimate objects
⑤ favorable to the control of foreign predators

3. I suppose now that my mother was locked in some dark world of sadness, but at the time, all I knew was that I had lost not only a father, but a mother as well. At eleven years old, with my sister just seven, I took over as head of the family. There was no choice. I bought our food at the market and cooked it as best as I could and tried to keep my sister and myself looking presentable. Because if it had become known that my mother could no longer care for us, the district would have taken us away from her and ________________________. I'd grown up seeing those home kids at school. The sadness, the marks of angry hands on their faces, the hopelessness thatcurled their shoulders forward. I could never let that happentomy sweet sister, who cried when I cried before she even knewthe reason, who brushed and plaited my mother's hair beforewe left for school, who still polished my father's shavingmirror each night because he'd hated the layer of coal dustthat settled on everything in the Seam. The community homewould crush her like a bug. So I kept our predicament asecret.

① asked us to work for ourselves
② placed us in the community home
③ kept me from seeking my father's inheritance
④ provided us with a new comfortable home
⑤ sent my sister to school in the village

4. A team from the University of California, Davis, has developed a genetically modified strain of lettuce that could help prevent astronauts from ____________________. Regular lettuce has already been grown successfully aboard the International Space Station (ISS), so the team decided to see if they could create a strain of the plant that produces a bone-stimulating chemical called human parathyroid hormone(PTH), which would help counter the bone-depleting effects of spending extended periods in the microgravity of space. Recent NASA studies carried out on Scott Kelly and Christina Koch(the first two astronauts to spend a year on the ISS) found that they lost more than 1 per cent of their bone density during each month of their stay. With a mission to Mars likely to last around three years, scientists are searching for ways to counter these effects. Medicine is one possibility and food is another, which may be more practical.

① losing bone density during long space journeys
② controlling the spaceship more effectively
③ examining the solidity of the bone for the counter effects
④ having hallucinations while piloting the ship
⑤ acquiring an unknown mutation in bone marrow

5. As everyone knew at the time, the release of the mega-hit movie Avengers: Endgame in 2019 did not in the least signal the conclusion of the most profitable cinematic franchise in history. For like the real-world universe it inhabits, the Marvel Cinematic Universe promises to expand indefinitely, with no end in sight. But as Maya Phillips notes in her aesthetic approach to the M.C.U., such an expansive and interconnected story line presents __________ to its creators, requiring the development of a nontraditional narrative format attuned to the complex interplay of old comics and new movies that underlies the whole enterprise. Will the whole thing collapse under its own weight eventually? Stay tuned.

① artistic outlets
② special challenges
③ unexpected benefits
④ manageable burdens
⑤ golden opportunities

6. Can we really be sure that science can always trace effects back to their causes? It certainly tries to do that. Descartes wanted to explain the attraction among heavenly bodies in terms of the central dogma of his physics, that in the last analysis all phenomena were due to a chain of mechanical contacts, a domino effect on a cosmic scale. What keeps the Moon in its orbit around the Earth? In order to ______________, Descartes could only hypothesize that there were particles of some invisible substance — the ether — between the Moon and the Earth, and that a huge vortex whose fulcrum is the Earth imprisoned the Moon.

① recalibrate his belief system
② be consistent with his dogma
③ repudiate the accepted theories
④ be distinguished from his peers
⑤ instantiate the less popular ideas

7. Pain and pleasure are simple ideas, incapable of definition. People are not liable to be mistaken in their feelings, but they are very frequently wrong in the names they give them, and in their reasonings about them. Many are of opinion that pain arises necessarily from the removal of some pleasure as they think pleasure does from the ceasing or diminution of some pain. For my part, I am rather inclined to imagine, that pain and pleasure, in their most simple and natural manner of affecting, are each of a positive nature, and by no means necessarily ______________________.

① influenced by sadness and despair
② defined by essential emotions of animate beings
③ impertinent to their own designations and meanings
④ irrelevant to changes caused by mutual interactions
⑤ dependent on each other for their existence

8. Though Glinda the Good Witch from The Wizard of Oz and the Sanderson sisters in Hocus Pocus had colorful wardrobes, the base of the standard witch costume is typically a black dress, cloak or robe. "Historically, healing women and others who would later be called witches would wear what everyone else in their village community did—homemade clothes that were made to be functional," says Katherine Walker, an assistant professor of English at the University of Nevada, Las Vegas. "In the medieval period and beyond, these clothes would feature cloaks or hoods. So it's very likely that, in terms of dress, witches at first were not ______________." It didn't take long, however, for these garments to be affiliated with witches. "The connection with a black dress in particular is probably the result of the association of the color black with the devil and 'black magic' throughout the Renaissance," Walker explains.

① visually distinct from their neighbors
② susceptible to their neighbors' criticism
③ meant to be harmful to their neighbors
④ considered as frugal as their neighbors
⑤ identical with their neighbors in costumes

9. Only in the twentieth century did non-European cultures adopt a truly global vision. This was one of the crucial factors that led to the collapse of European hegemony. Thus in the Algerian War of Independence (1954-62), Algerian guerrillas defeated a French army with an overwhelming numerical, technological and economic advantage. The Algerians prevailed because they were supported by a global anti-colonial network, and because they worked out how to harness the world's media to their cause—as well as public opinion in France itself. The defeat that little North Vietnam inflicted on the American colossus was based on a similar strategy. These guerilla forces showed that even superpowers could be defeated if __________________.

① their strategy was exposed to the enemy
② no lessons were learned from previous invasions
③ they didn't have a well-trained, elite unit
④ they engaged the adversary in fierce combat
⑤ a local struggle became a global cause

10. When you're inside the walls of high tech, whether for an interview or for a temporary work assignment, there's one thing you should keep in mind. You'll be judged largely on your attitude. High-tech people like others who are enthusiastic and show it. If that sounds corny, sorry, but it's true. A positive attitude, a smile, a sense of humor—these can do wonders for you when you come in. When you're interviewing for a position, you'll not only see the hiring manager, you'll be interviewed by three to six others, usually people who would be your future associates if you get the job. Each of these people is going to judge you mainly by something called "fit." Yes, you have to be smart, demonstrate that you understand the job and can perform it. But you can do all that and still strike out on the question of "fit." Your attitude and demeanor during the interviews will, it's hoped, settle the question of ____________________.

① how well you'll perform in your future job
② how politely you'll respond to your supervisors
③ how humorous you are in the workplace
④ how enthusiastic you are towards demanding tasks
⑤ how well you'll fit into the group

11. We have a tendency to imagine that life can not exist under conditions other than terrestrial, and that the other worlds can only be inhabited on the condition of being similar to our own. But terrestrial nature itself demonstrates to us the error of this way of thinking. We die in the water: fishes die out of the water. Again, short-sighted naturalists affirm categorically that life is impossible at the bottom of the sea: first, because it is in complete darkness; second, because the terrible pressure would burst any organism; third, because all motion would be impossible there, and so on. There is no light in these depths: they make it with their own phosphorescence. Other inquirers visit subterranean caverns, and discover animals and plants whose organs have been transformed by ________________.

① enormous pressure of water
② adaptation to their gloomy environment
③ interbreeding tendencies across different species
④ natural inclination of marine lives
⑤ sudden environmental changes

12. What Ptolemy saw in the movements of the stars led him to the conclusion that they were bright points attached to the inside of a tremendous globe. The movements of this globe were only compatible with the supposition that the earth occupied its center. The obvious fact that the sun, the moon, and the stars rose day by day, moved across the sky in a glorious never-ending procession, and duly set when their appointed courses had been run, demanded some explanation. The circumstance that the fixed stars preserved their mutual distances from year to year, and from age to age, appeared to Ptolemy to prove that the sphere which contained those stars, and on whose surface they were believed by him to be fixed, revolved completely around the earth once every day. He would thus account for all the phenomena of rising and setting consistently with the supposition that ______________________.

① the constellation of stars affects our globe
② our globe was stationary
③ the sun is the center of the universe
④ our globe revolves around the sun
⑤ our globe was dynamic

13. Perhaps the most serious obstacle impeding the evolution of a land ethic is the fact that our educational and economic system is headed away from, rather than toward, an intense consciousness of land. People today are separated from the land by many middlemen, and by innumerable physical gadgets. They have no vital relation to it; to them it is the space between cities on which crops grow. Turn them loose for a day on the land, and if the spot does not happen to be a golf links or a 'scenic' area, they are bored stiff. If crops could be raised by hydroponics (water culture) instead of farming, it would suit them very well. Synthetic substitutes for wood, leather, wool, and other natural land products suit them better than the originals. In short, land is ______________________.

① the model they aspire to copy
② something they have outgrown
③ the spot for their organic products
④ something profitable to them in any case
⑤ what they cultivate with the assistance of mediators

14. According to Heidegger, the whole of Being and Time is concerned with a single question — the question of the meaning of Being. But what does he mean by the term 'Being'? What, if anything, does it signify? It is no accident that Heidegger provides no clear and simple answer to this question —neither at the opening of his book nor at any later point within it; for, in his view, it will take at least the whole of his book to bring us to the point where we can even ask the question in a coherent and potentially fruitful way. Nevertheless, he also takes a certain, preliminary understanding of Being to ________________________; so it should be possible, even at this early stage, to indicate at least an initial orientation for our thinking.

① be absent in the way most of us behave
② lack completely in any meaningful manner
③ be irrelevant in pursuing his line of thinking
④ offer no clear answers to his ultimate questions
⑤ be implicit in everything human beings say and do

15. What is art really and why does it appear to be so tightly linked with what it means to be a human? We are the only mammal species that produces art, and while it is important to us, it is in no way necessary for our physical survival. Still, the examples are numerous on how humans have risked, even sacrificed, their lives for the right to express themselves artistically. Art comes in many forms, from literature with its prose and poetry to sculptures and paintings, movie making, the composition of music, but also bodily expressions such as dance. But what is it that we seem so eager to express through art? By studying the various artworks over the millennia, a few themes keep appearing, namely that of expressing the human condition and our sometimes anxious deliberations over life and death, including the existence of a soul and similar ethereal phenomena. These are typically depicted in a contemporary setting, sometimes through metaphors that in particular will resonate with its intended audience, which will come in variations, and the many manifests of art do take different shapes and forms over time, culture, and geography, and in the past at least, they also came with ____________________________.

① mandates of theatrical art compliance
② guidelines for cultural narrative expectations
③ standards of athletic performance evaluations
④ requirements of aesthetic minimum standards
⑤ conditions for environmental sustainability plan

16. The creed which accepts as the foundation of morals, Utility, or the Greatest Happiness Principle, holds that actions are right in proportion as they tend to promote happiness, wrong as they tend to produce the reverse of happiness. By happiness is intended pleasure, and the absence of pain; by unhappiness, pain, and the privation of pleasure. To give a clear view of the moral standard set up by the theory, much more requires to be said; in particular, what things it includes in the ideas of pain and pleasure; and to what extent this is left an open question. But these supplementary explanations do not affect the theory of life on which this theory of morality is grounded — namely, that pleasure, and freedom from pain, are the only things desirable as ends; and that all desirable things (which are as numerous in the utilitarian as in any other scheme) are desirable either for the pleasure inherent in themselves, or as means to ________________.

① the promotion of pleasure and the prevention of pain
② the acquisition of wealth and the escape from poverty
③ the pursuit of knowledge and the avoidance of ignorance
④ the attainment of power and the liberation from oppression
⑤ the cultivation of virtues and the achievement of moral excellence

17. During the years of the July Monarchy (1830-48) and influenced by Louis-Philippe's more informal lifestyle and the devotion of the royal parents for their children, the ideal of family life had taken a strong hold on the public imagination and become the keystone of bourgeois society. The care and education of children and the development of the infant personality became a matter of great interest. This preoccupation with the family and the child's role initcontinued in the Second Empire under Napoleon III (1852-70), who with his wife, the Empress Eugénie, cultivated an image of ________________. The same phenomenon occurred in Britain, where prints of Queen Victoria and Pince Albert playing with their offspring adorned the walls of many homes. It is this period from 1850 onwards, a period noted for itseconomic prosperity, civic improvement, and bourgeois self-assurance, that can be regarded as the most fruitful in the development of children's literature in the nineteenth century. The novel of domestic realism, or the family novel, developed from the moral tale of the first half of the century and mirrored the development of the realist novel for adults.

① family intimacy
② a happy mother
③ a dominant family
④ a flourishing group
⑤ middle classes' desire

18. The Columbus myths enabled white Americans to find a beginning, to declare a courageous opening to their 'story'. It was part of the influential dream myth of origin so prevalent in America. F. Scott Fitzgerlad's The Great Gatsby is aware both of the power of American dreams and the problems of seeking them out in lived experience. The ideals of endless progress, self-creation, achievement and success — __________ incorporated in the spirit of Columbus — are played out in the figure of Jay Gatsby as seen through the eyes of Nick Carraway. The novel concerns itself with issues of identity and in particular with the temptation to believe in a 'dream' which is manifested in Gatsby's yearning for Daisy Buchanan, a woman he almost married in the past, who encompasses 'the endless desire to return to "lost origin", to go back to the beginning'.

① the frustrated plan
② the fulfilled scheme
③ the unattainable aim
④ the fruitless longing
⑤ the mythicised dream

19. Literature can be helpful in the language learning process because of the __________ it fosters in readers. Core language teaching materials must concentrate on how a language operates both as a rule-based system and as a sociosemantic system. Very often, the process of learning is essentially analytic, piecemeal, and, at the level of the personality, fairly superficial. Engaging imaginatively with literature enables learners to shift the focus of their attention beyond the more mechanical aspects of the foreign language system. When a novel, play or short story is explored over a period of time, the result is that the reader begins to 'inhabit' the text. He or she is drawn into the book. Pinpointing what individual words or phrases may mean becomes less important than pursuing the development of the story. The reader is eager to find out what happens as events unfold; he or she feels close to certain characters and shares their emotional responses. The language becomes 'transparent' — the fiction draws the whole person into its own world.

① linguistic insight
② artistic imagination
③ literary sensibility
④ alternative perspective
⑤ personal involvement

20. Education, at its best, teaches more than just knowledge. It teaches critical thinking: the ability to stop and think before acting, to avoid succumbing to emotional pressures. This is not thought control. It is the very reverse: mental liberation. Even the most advanced intellectual will be imperfect at this skill. But even imperfect possession of it ______________ of being 'stimulus-driven', constantly reacting to the immediate environment, the brightest colours or loudest sounds. Being driven by heuristic responses, living by instinct and emotion all the time, is a very easy way to live, in many ways: thought is effortful, especially for the inexperienced. But emotions are also exhausting, and short-term reactions may not, in the long term, be the most beneficial for health and survival. Just as we reach for burgers for the sake of convenience, storing up the arterial fat which may one day kill us, so our reliance on feelings can do us great harm.

① intensifies people's danger
② enhances our understanding
③ frees a person from the burden
④ allows us to accept the inevitability
⑤ requires one to have the experience

21. We are famously living in the era of the attention economy, where the largest and most profitable businesses in the world are those that consume my attention. The advertising industry is literally dedicated to capturing the conscious hours of my life and selling them to someone else. It might seem magical that so many exciting and useful software systems are available to use for free, but it is now conventional wisdom that if you can't see who is paying for something that appears to be free, then ____________________. Our creative engagement with other people is mediated by AI-based recommendation systems that are designed to trap our attention through the process that Nick Seaver calls captology, keeping us attending to work sold by one company rather than another, replacing the freedom of personal exploration with algorithm-generated playlists or even algorithm-generated art.

① all of your attention has already been spent
② the real product being sold is you
③ your privacy is being violated
④ the public may be sponsoring you
⑤ you owe the benefits to your friend AI

22. Centralized, formal rules can ____________________. The rules of baseball don't just regulate the behavior of the players; they determine the behavior that constitutes playing the game. Rules do not prevent people from playing baseball; they create the very practice that allows people to play baseball. A score of music imposes rules, but it also creates a pattern of conduct that enables people to produce music. Legal rules that enable the formation of corporations, that enable the use of wills and trusts, that create negotiable instruments, and that establish the practice of contracting all make practices that create new opportunities for individuals. And we have legal rules that establish roles individuals play within the legal system, such as judges, trustees, partners, and guardians. True, the legal rules that establish these roles constrain the behavior of individuals who occupy them, but rules also create the roles themselves. Without them an individual would not have the opportunity to occupy the role.

① categorize one's patterns of conduct in legal and productive ways
② lead people to reevaluate their roles and practices in a society
③ encourage new ways of thinking which promote creative ideas
④ reinforce one's behavior within legal and established contexts
⑤ facilitate productive activity by establishing roles and practices

23. After we make some amount of scientific and technological progress, does further progress get easier or harder? Intuitively, it seems like it could go either way because there are two competing effects. On the one hand, we "stand on the shoulders of giants": previous discoveries can make future progress easier. On the other hand, we "pick the low-hanging fruit": we make the easy discoveries first, so those that remain are more difficult. You can only invent the wheel once, and once you have, it's harder to find a similarly important invention. Though both of these effects are important, when we look at the data it's the latter effect that ____________________. Overall, past progress makes future progress harder. It's easy to see this qualitatively by looking at the history of innovation. Consider physics. In 1905, his "miracle year," Albert Einstein revolutionized physics, describing the photoelectric effect, Brownian motion, the theory of special relativity, and his famous equation, $E=mc^2$. He was twenty-six at the time and did all this while working as a patent clerk. Compared to Einstein's day, progress in physics is now much harder to achieve.

① predominates ② scatters ③ varies
④ vanishes ⑤ fades

24. Behavior is, for the most part, a product of genes and brain neuropathways. Consider the elegant chemistry at work when living organisms move, think, behave, and act. Certainly, the environment is a factor here because it can influence how we act. An analogy would illustrate this adequately. Think of the environment as gasoline, and our body as the engine. Truly, the engine does not run without the gasoline, but all the intricate parts of the engine are the product of physical architecture, designed and assembled for a reactive purpose long before the gasoline is injected. Inject more gas and the engine accelerates, less, and it slows. The same is true for an organism. Behavior is a response to the environment. We have 'free will,' but the ultimate characteristic of that response can only act with respect to the architecture of our genes and our brain. In other words, the environment can, effectively, accelerate or slow down a potential behavior, but the engine for that behavior ____________________; therefore, the environment is but a catalyst.

① malfunctions even with correct input
② is already built and functional
③ tends to shut down periodically
④ runs in an unpredictable manner
⑤ is subject to change without notice

25. The social-cognitive revolution at 1 year of age sets the stage for infants' second year of life, in which they begin to imitatively learn the use of all kinds of tools, artifacts, and symbols. For example, in a study by Meltzoff (1988), 14-month-old children observed an adult bend at the waist and touch its head to a panel, thus turning on a light. They followed suit. Infants engaged in this somewhat unusual and awkward behavior, even though it would have been easier and more natural for them simply to push the panel with their hand. One interpretation of this behavior is that infants understood that the adult had the goal of illuminating the light and then chose one means for doing so, from among other possible means, and if they had the same goal, they could choose the same means. Similarly, Carpenter et al. (1998) found that 16-month-old infants will imitatively learn from a complex behavioral sequence only those behaviors that appear intentional, ignoring those that appear accidental. Young children do not just imitate the limb movements of other persons, they attempt to ____________________.

① avoid looking awkward in the eyes of family members
② reproduce other persons' intended actions in the world
③ accept the value of chance incidents that turn out helpful
④ behave in an unprecedented way that others have missed
⑤ undermine any goal that does not coincide with their own

26. As an ideal of intellectual inquiry and a strategy for the advancement of knowledge, the scientific method is essentially a monument to the utility of error. Most of us gravitate toward trying to prove our beliefs, to the extent that we bother investigating their validity at all. But scientists gravitate toward falsification; as a community if not as individuals, they seek to disprove their beliefs. Thus, the defining feature of a hypothesis is that it has the potential to be proven wrong (which is why it must be both testable and tested), and the defining feature of a theory is that it hasn't been proven wrong yet. But the important part is that it can be — no matter how much evidence appears to confirm it, no matter how many experts endorse it, no matter how much popular support it enjoys. In fact, not only can any given theory be proven wrong; sooner or later, it probably will be. And when it is, the occasion will mark the success of science, not its failure. This was the crucial insight of the Scientific Revolution: that the advancement of knowledge depends on current theories ______________________.

① holding true regardless of temporal and spatial constraints
② collapsing in the face of new insights and discoveries
③ shifting according to scientists' pursuit of reputation
④ being exposed to the public and enjoying popularity
⑤ leaving no chance of error and failure

27. There has been a lot of discussion on why moths are attracted to light. The consensus seems to hold that moths are not so much attracted to lights as they are ______________ by them. The light becomes a sensory overload that disorients the insects and sends them into a holding pattern. A hypothesis called the Mach band theory suggests that moths see a dark area around a light source and head for it to escape the light. Another theory suggests that moths perceive the light coming from a source as a diffuse halo with a dark spot in the center. The moths, attempting to escape the light, fly toward that imagined "portal," bringing them closer to the source. As they approach the light, their reference point changes and they circle the light hopelessly trying to reach the portal. Everyone is familiar with moths circling their porch lights. Their flight appears to have no purpose, but they are, it is believed, trying to escape the pull of the light.

① warmed
② trapped
③ targeted
④ protected
⑤ rejected

28. One of the factors determining the use of technologies of communication will be the kinds of investments made in equipment and personnel; who makes them, and what they expect in return. There is no guarantee that the investment will necessarily be in forms of communication that ________________. Because the ownership of investment funds tends to be in the hands of commercial organisations, the modernisation of communications infrastructure only takes place on the basis of potential profitability. Take, for example, the installation of fibre-optic communications cable across the African continent. A number of African nations are involved in the development but its operational structures will be oriented to those who can pay for access. Many states that might wish to use it for education and information may not only find it too expensive but also simply unavailable to them. There can be no doubt that the development has been led by investment opportunity rather than community demand.

① require minimal cost and effort to maintain
② are most appropriate for the majority of people
③ are in line with current standards and global norms
④ employ some of the most advanced technologies
⑤ promote the commercial interests of companies

29. City quality is so crucial for optional activities that the extent of staying activities can often be used as a measuring- stick for the quality of the city as well as of its space. Many pedestrians in a city are not necessarily an indication of good city quality — many people walking around can often be a sign of insufficient transit options or long distances between the various functions in the city. Conversely, it can be claimed that a city in which many people are not walking often indicates good city quality. In a city like Rome, it is the large number of people standing or sitting in squares rather than walking that is conspicuous. And it's not due to necessity but rather that ________________. It is hard to keep moving in city space with so many temptations to stay. In contrast are many new quarters and complexes that many people walk through but rarely stop or stay in.

① the city quality is so inviting
② public spaces are already occupied
③ public transportation is not available
④ major tourist spots are within walking distance
⑤ the city's administrative buildings are concentrated

30. That people need other people is hardly news, but for Rousseau this dependence extended far beyond companionship or even love, into the very process of becoming human. Rousseau believed that people are not born but made, every individual a bundle of potentials whose realization requires the active involvement of other people. Self-development is a social process. Self-sufficiency is an impossible fantasy. Much of the time Rousseau wished passionately that it were not: Robinson Crusoe was a favorite book, and he yearned to be free from the pains and uncertainties of social life. But his writings document with extraordinary clarity __________________. Our sweetest existence is relative and collective, and our true self is not entirely within us." And it is kindness — which Rousseau analyzed under the rubric of pitié, which translates as "pity" but is much closer to "sympathy" as Hume and Smith defined it — that is the key to this collective existence.

① the necessity of philosophical study to understand human nature
② the development of self-sufficiency through literary works
③ the shaping of the individual by his emotional attachments
④ the making of the self-reliant man through his struggles
⑤ the difficulty of trusting other people wholeheartedly

MEMO

Unit 5

장문 유형

예시문제

1~3. 'Form follows profit' is the aesthetic principle of our times. Thus, design skill is measured today by the architect's ability to build the largest possible enclosure for the smallest investment in the quickest time. The factors that now determine the design of a building are maximum economic efficiency in terms of rentable space to gross space, wall to floor ratios and minimum story height. The result is invariably a single-activity building in the form of a thin-skinned box - a shopping center, an office building or a block of flats - with no unprofitable public space, no expressive or innovative structural features and certainly no room celebrate the art of Architecture. Arcades, gardens and balconies, even recessed windows, impinge on rentable space and are deemed incompatible with the profit principle. And because developers and their shareholders want a quick return on their investment - the horizons of stockbrokers and accountants do not extend to posterity - the cheapest materials must be used. Some clients refuse to plant even trees; no acorn will increase the rentable value of a property, and no investor, we are told, will wait for an oak. Most contemporary architecture is therefore the product of ________ rather than the work of a designer; it represents the logical product of a society which sees the environment in terms of profit.

1. Choose the one that best fills in the blank.

① stark economic forces
② environmental considerations
③ user-friendly interfaces
④ one-size-fits-all tendencies

2. According to the passage, which aspect is associated with the contemporary design of buildings?

① multi-functionality
② cube-like shape
③ greenery
④ unique style

3. What is the purpose of the passage?

① to accuse architects of being avant-garde
② to suggest architectural freedom should be restored
③ to criticize external influences on architecture
④ to extol the contributions of architecture to society

4~7. In the aftermath of terrorist attacks in Paris and San Bernardino, California, American support for accepting more Syrian refugees has withered. The Republican presidential hopeful Donald J. Trump has called for blocking all Muslims from entering the United States, saying we are at war with radical Islam. The focus on whether or not to admit these desperate people to the United States obscures the bigger question of the refugee crisis. A vast majority of the more than four million refugees want to return to Syria once the war there ends. For that reason, most have stayed in the region, often languishing for years in camps in Lebanon and Jordan, rather than migrating to Europe or attempting to enter the United States. These people are the responsibility of the international community, according to the 1951 Refugee Convention. The United States and all other signatories to the convention have a legal obligation to protect refugees and their well-being, which can mean resettlement when necessary. But the refugees face increasing burdens. Neither Jordan nor Lebanon allows them to work. Lebanon requires [A] re-registration fees every six months. The funds for refugee support, which the international community is supposed to provide, have fallen woefully short. As a consequence, the United Nations' World Food Program has had to cut food rations for Syrian refugees in Lebanon in half, down to $13.50 per person per month. How can anyone survive on less than 50 cents a day for food? That is a reason so many have left the camps for the often dangerous trip to Europe. Quite simply, the world has helped foster the migrant crisis by not supporting refugees in the Middle East. The United States prides itself on how much we have given to the refugee crisis, but we lag behind the European Union. On a per-capita basis, we are far outranked by many much smaller countries, among them Britain, Norway, Sweden and Denmark. Full funding of the United Nations Appeal would go some way toward <u>stemming</u> the flow of refugees. The United States alone could give at least $500 million more to the United Nations Appeal annually. At this time, when heightened anxiety about terrorism has become intertwined with the plight of millions of refugees, there must be those among us — leaders and ordinary citizens — who are clearheaded enough to act. Indeed, the cost of not doing so is far too high.

4. Select the word suitable for the blank [A].

① short-lived
② wakeful
③ exultant
④ blissful
⑤ onerous

5. Which can best replace the underlined stemming?

① destroying
② receiving
③ cherishing
④ halting
⑤ stepping

6. Which of the following is TRUE for the above passage?

① America has supported the international Refugee Convention wholeheartedly.
② The major cause of the Syrian Refugees' problem is the curtailing of the funds to support them.
③ In order to prevent terrorism, increasing of the funds to support the refugees is fundamental.
④ The immediate action must be initiated to stop the terrorist activities.
⑤ Jordan and Lebanon have increased the capacity to admit the Syrian Refugees.

7. Select the best title of the above passage.

① "Terror of Syrian Refugees"
② "The Best Way to Solve International Terrorism"
③ "Agony and Starvation in Syrian Refugees"
④ "Appeal to the Americans"
⑤ "Justice of the Syrian War"

8~11. Stephen Hawking, the pre-eminent physicist, recently warned that artificial intelligence (AI), once it surpasses human intelligence, could pose a threat to the existence of human civilization. If AI becomes an existential threat, it won't be the first one. Humanity was introduced to existential risk when I was a child sitting under my desk during the civil-defense drills of the 1950s. Since then we have encountered comparable specters, like the possibility of a bio-terrorist creating a new virus for which humankind has no defense. Technology has always been a double-edged sword, since fire kept us warm but also burned down our villages. The typical dystopian futurist movie has one or two individuals or groups fighting for control of "the AI." Or we see the AI battling the humans for world domination. But this is not how AI is being integrated into the world today. AI is not in one or two hands; it's in 1 billion or 2 billion hands. A kid in Africa with a smartphone has more intelligent access to knowledge than the President of the United States had 20 years ago. As AI continues to get smarter, its use will only grow. Virtually everyone's mental capabilities will be enhanced by it within a decade. AI today is advancing the diagnosis of disease, finding cures, developing renewable clean energy, helping to clean up the environment, providing high-quality education to people all over the world, helping the disabled (including providing Hawking's voice) and contributing in a myriad of other ways. We have the opportunity in the decades ahead to make major strides in addressing the grand challenges of humanity. AI will be the pivotal technology in achieving this progress. We have a moral imperative to realize this promise while controlling the peril. It won't be the first time we've succeeded in doing this.

8. Which of the following is NOT true for the above passage?

① Artificial Intelligence has advanced the skills detecting disease.
② Stephen Hawking had a negative view on AI.
③ In the future, AI will not become a threat to the grand challenges of humanity.
④ Technology has always been a one-way street to the human progress.
⑤ The movies dealing with AI do not reflect the true reality of AI.

9. Which can best replace the underlined access?

① investigation
② admittance
③ solution
④ reasoning
⑤ education

10. Select the best title of the above passage.

① "Finding Dangers in AI"
② "Future of AI"
③ "How to Make AI Positive"
④ "Grand Dream of Humanity"
⑤ "Misconception of Technology"

11. The author's tone on AI in the above passage can best be described as ________.

① objective
② affirmative
③ subjective
④ jaundiced
⑤ strict

12~14. History is necessary because it helps to explain current events. How do cultures rise and how do they fall? History will not give us the answers, but it will certainly help to focus our questions and our understanding of the forces at work in the world today.

Of course history is easily manipulated, though that makes it even more important for us to know what actually happened. We need a knowledge of history to spot the delusions of leaders and the media. As voters and citizens, we have to be able to see through these dangerous distortions. Besides, history is – or should be – interesting. The chain of cause and effect is fascinating as are the details. ________, many teachers who lack historical training themselves are naturally defensive, fearing to understand the mentality of their pupils.

I would never argue that historians or history teachers have a moral role. Their main obligation is to understand the mentality of the time and to pass on that understanding. Nor should they simplify for moral effects. History offers the richest imaginable source of moral examples and which are themselves the essence of great fiction, great drama, and life itself. Without an understanding of history, we are politically, culturally and socially impoverished.

12. Choose the one that best fills in the blank.

① Repulsed by this
② Shying away from this
③ In concordance with this
④ Motivated by this

13. Which of the following cannot be inferred from the passage?

① Morals of past events should be diluted through history education.
② Some teachers today do not seem confident about the appeal of history.
③ Understanding history helps us resist untruths propagated by power.
④ History enables us to form a perspective required for understanding the present.

14. What is the best title for the passage?

① Pitfalls of History
② Historical Insights for the Future
③ What History Tells
④ Competing Interpretations of History

15~17. In the late nineteenth century, a young man named Frederick Winslow Taylor carried a stopwatch into the Midvale Steel plant in Philadelphia and began a historic series of experiments aimed at improving the efficiency of the plant's machinists. He set a group of factory hands to work on various metalworking machines, and recorded and timed their every movement as well as the operations of the machines. By breaking down every job into a sequence of small, discrete steps and then testing different ways of performing each one, Taylor created a set of precise instructions - an "algorithm," we might say today - for how each worker should work. Midvale's employees grumbled about the strict new regime, claiming that it turned them into little more than automatons, but the factory's productivity soared. Taylor's ________ was embraced by manufacturers throughout the country and, in time, around the world. Seeking maximum speed, maximum efficiency, and maximum output, factory owners used time-and-motion studies to organize their work and configure the jobs of their workers. The goal was to identify and adopt, for every job, the one best method of work and thereby <u>to effect the gradual substitution of science for rule of thumb</u> throughout the mechanic arts. Once his system was applied to all acts of manual labor, Taylor assured his followers, it would bring about a restructuring not only of industry but of society, creating a utopia of perfect efficiency. Taylor's system is still very much with us; it remains the ethic of industrial manufacturing.

15. Choose the one that best fills in the blank.

① tight industrial choreography
② stringent job evaluation
③ impromptu machine orchestration
④ incessant laborer surveillance

16. Choose the one closest in meaning to the underlined part.

① to replace outdated factory facilities with cutting-edge business equipment
② to substitute automated machinery for manual labor
③ to substitute high-tech procedures for labor intensive jobs
④ to replace conventional ways of working with the systematic management of labor

17. Which of the following cannot be inferred about "Frederick Winslow Taylor"?

① His new methods of increasing productivity became widespread among manufacturing industries in and out of the country.
② His pioneering experiments benefited factory workers, for they boosted productivity by turning them into versatile machinists.
③ A methodical segmentation of the manufacturing process was what he believed enabled maximum efficiency.
④ His ambition to transform society through efficiency has been integrated in modern-day manufacturing.

18~20. When we create narratives, they are usually traditional ones, with protagonists and antagonists and a prescribed relationship between narrators, characters, and listeners. They have ______ plots with a fixed past, a present built coherently on it, and a horizon of possibilities projected coherently into the future. Digital technologies, on the other hand, are producing narratives that stray from this classic structure. New communicative interfaces allow for novel narrative interactions and constructions. Multi-user domains, massively multiplayer online role-playing games, hypertext and cybertext all loosen traditional narrative structure. Digital narratives, in their extremes, are co-creations of the authors, users and media. Multiple entry points into continuously developing narratives are available, often for multiple co-constructors. These recent developments seem to make possible limitless narratives lacking the defining features of the traditional structures.

18. Choose the one that best fills in the blank.

① multidimensional
② parallel
③ convoluted
④ linear

19. What is the best title for the passage?

① Interacting through Narratives on the Internet
② Impact of Technology on Literary Genres
③ Transformation of Narratives in the Digital Age
④ Traces of Classic Structure in Digital Narratives

20. Which of the following cannot inferred about "narratives"?

① Conventionally, their plots are premeditated and planned.
② They have traditionally shown interrelationships among the characters.
③ Nowadays, they are sometimes constructed by more than one author.
④ They have developed to become more flexible and open in cyberspace.

21~24. Energy drinks contain whopping doses of sugar, caffeine and other stimulatory ingredients. Although often marketed to and by athletes, they are not sports drinks. Sports drinks contain far less sugar or other sweeteners than energy drinks and rarely if ever contain caffeine. That fact has not slowed the growing popularity of energy drinks among athletes in college and younger. But the evidence that they can make you a better athlete is sketchy at best. It can, in the right circumstances, improve athletic performance. But the amounts of caffeine required to improve performance vary wildly from person to person, and the effects typically are lessened once an athlete is used to caffeine. And the large amounts of sugar in energy drinks have been known to cause diarrhea and other gastrointestinal upset.

The effects of energy drinks on young athletes are particularly mysterious. Very little research has been conducted, although two recently released studies are telling. In one, collegians were given energy drinks that contained different levels of caffeine (including none) and asked to complete a test. The students who drank the caffeinated energy drinks had quicker reaction times than those who did not, but the better times and more accurate reactions were in the group that had the least caffeine. In the second study, healthy children between the ages of 12 and 17 drank sweet, flat soft drinks spiked with varying amounts of caffeine. Then the children were set loose in the lab stocked with a variety of snack foods. The ones who had downed the most caffeine steered unerringly for the snacks containing the most sugar. That result indicates that there may be a link between caffeine use and intake of higher energy-density foods in children.

21. Which of the following is not a possible result of consuming energy drinks?

① stomach problems
② increased accuracy
③ fast reaction
④ sugar craving

22. Choose the one closest in meaning to the underlined "telling."

① significant
② succinct
③ superlative
④ suspect

23. Which of the following can be inferred from the passage?

① Sport drinks have been found to have no substantial effect on athletic activities.
② Researchers have been highly interested in the long-term effects of energy drinks.
③ Energy drinks are virtually identical with sports drinks.
④ Energy drinks may not enhance performance in sports.

24. What is the tone of the passage?

① acclamatory
② ambivalent
③ skeptical
④ exuberant

25~26. The dispute between rationalism and empiricism takes laces within epistemology, the branch of philosophy devoted to studying the nature, sources and limits of knowledge. We can form true beliefs just by making some lucky guesses. How we can gain warranted beliefs is unclear. Moreover, to know the world, we must think about it, and it is not clear how we gain the concepts we use in thought or what assurance, if any, we have that the ways in which we divide up the world using our concepts correspond to divisions that actually exist.

Rationalists claim that there are significant ways in which our concepts and knowledge are gained independently of sense experience. Empiricists claim that sense experience is the ultimate source of all our concepts and knowledge. Rationalists argue that there are cases where <u>the content of our knowledge outstrips the information that sense experience can provide</u>. Empiricists present complementary lines of thought. They develop accounts of how experience provides the information that rationalists cite, insofar as we have it in the first place.

25. According to the passage, which of the following is not a question asked in epistemology?

① where our conceptual tools come from
② how we can ascertain the truth of a belief
③ how valid our categorization of the world is
④ what kinds of knowledge are valuable

26. Choose the one closest in meaning to the underlined part.

① it becomes impossible to acquire knowledge from raw experience
② we may attain knowledge that surpasses the data garnered from experience
③ experience alone is sufficient to yield knowledge
④ experience is bound to produce information that distorts knowledge

27~29. The job of managing, like so many other things, is learned primarily by doing. It is therefore vital that people moving toward senior positions have the opportunity to acquire the necessary experience at the right time. Rather than such experience being left to chance, opportunities can be built into the organization's manpower planning system. The first of these is to carve out positions that enable people to have challenging jobs and overall accountability for running part of the business. This means that the organization must not be too ________. If the organization can devide up its work into profit and loss units, executives can gain the experience of running an operation which, while interdependent with the rest of the organization, stands on its own as a measurable business center.

Some business lend themselves more to this form of organization than others. Consider, for example, that in the retail industry managers often have an opportunity to take over management of a retail outlet while relatively young. It may be far more difficult to find similar profit center units in other, more technologically sophisticated, industries. Wherever possible, however, profit centers should be established so that young manage can have the experience of leading a team – whether it be five, a hundred, or five hundred people. They learn that 'the buck stops' with them for overall performance.

27. Choose the one that best fills in the blank.

① centrally constructed
② leniently managed
③ profit oriented
④ extrinsically motivated

28. What is the main idea of the passage?

① Managers need to be given the chance to run a part of the business independently.
② Playing an integral role in the organization is the target for a manger.
③ The success of an organization depends on how skilled managers are.
④ Specialized managers are more effective in raking in profits.

29. Which of the following can be inferred from the passage?

① The number of team members a manager oversees is indicative of how much power the manager has.
② Depending on the industry, age can make a difference in terms of the nature of a manager's job.
③ The more audacious managers are the more likely it is that they will be promoted to higher positions.
④ Managers are immune to accountability for the wrongdoings of their team members which result in losses for the business.

30~33. The cosmos is one of a genus of tropical herbs, numbering about twenty species. It is a tall, graceful, late-flowering animal or perennial, of many different varieties and feathery foliage. The word "cosmos" is derived from the Greek term, kosmos, and signifies "an ornament or beautiful thing." And after seeing the lovely graceful cosmos in bloom, one feels that this flower has indeed been rightly named. It is native to tropical and semitropical America. its American ancestors are said to have come from the warmer uplands of Mexico. The early kinds grown in the U.S. could not stand cold, for the cosmos glories in the sun. Often frost killed the plants before their seeds had ripened. However, new ones have been developed that now make the cosmos a fall as a summer flower.

The face that the cosmos flowers late, when many other plants have completed their work, makes it of more value to gardeners and flower lovers. For it truly comes into its own at the first frosts. This late, aster-like blossom, with its filmy leaves, not only is most attractive in garden beds or against walls but the cut flowers make beautiful bouquets for indoor decorations.

The most commonly cultivated type in the U.S. may grow to heights of from 7 to 10 feet, though some are not so tall. It has smooth stems, and its brightly rayed, showy flowers have yellow disks. The rays are in a variety of colors including white, pink, red, purple, shell, yellow, orange - in fact, almost any hue except blue. The early primitive kinds had flowers only about an inch across. But various breeders have worked with this desirable plant, and have in some cases shortened the steams and increased the size of the blooms, some of which grow singly, others in clusters.

30. Choose the one closest in meaning to the underlined part.

① the cosmos grows better at the time of the first frost
② the first frosts are not conducive in making the cosmos grow
③ when the first frosts come, the cosmos blooms to its fullest
④ the cosmos has developed skills to cope with frosts on its own

31. Which of the following cannot be inferred about the "cosmos"?

① It was originally a fall flower but now has developed into a summer one.
② Some types live for a few growing seasons.
③ The meanings of its name seems to suit the flowers well.
④ The origins of the ones found in the U.S. can be traced to Mexico.

32. According to the passage, which aspect is associated with why the cosmos is valued?

① It lasts a longer time than other kinds of cut flowers.
② It is a rare flower that cannot be found in warmer climates.
③ It is easy to cultivate since it does not need much water to grow.
④ It is pleasing to look at when planted in garden beds.

33. According to the passage, which of the following is not true about the appearance of the cosmos?

① Not all blooms are found in clusters.
② The color of the rays varied widely but does not include blue.
③ The average height is 7-10 feet with some types growing taller.
④ The stems are smooth and all flowers have yellow disks.

34~36. Atheism and Anarchy are not really ideologies, in that they are not complex ideological organisms. Each of these words represents opposition to a particular type of complex collective idea-organism. They both claim that the Idea-organism they are fighting is not necessary in order for people to lead good lives. There should be one word for both of them, but there is not, mostly because Church and State are not generally recognized as being the same sort of "multi-celled" ideological organism.

"Individualist" is perhaps the closest word we have to describing the autonomous human, standing apart from any collective mindset. A strong sense of individualism leads us to conclude that no Higher Power has any right to control our minds. Because both atheism and anarchy stand opposed to a number of large, popular, complex ideas there is a tendency to try to cast these (much simpler) ideas into the same mold; to make them into larger ideological constructs than they are, and to attach other ideas to them; in short, to turn them from simple ideas into complex idea-organisms.

Because of this, those who believe in the ideas of atheism and/or anarchy are often actually convinced to end up ________ like having strong faith in their Atheism of forming Anarchist groups to fight the powers that be.

34. What is the best title for the passage?

A. Simplifying Ideological Constructs
B. Anarchy as an Alternative to Atheism
C. The End of Collectivism
D. Rethinking Atheism and Anarchy

35. Choose the one that best fills in the blank.

A. compromising with each other
B. making use of different applications
C. doing strangely contradictory things
D. weakening their ideological stances

36. Which of the following cannot be inferred from the passage about "atheism" and "anarchy"?

A. The two are perceived to be a similar ideological construct.
B. Both cannot be considered full-fledged ideologies.
C. Both can be somewhat described with the word "individualist"
D. The two are accepted widely at the State and Church level.

37~39. While watching any sunset can be a moment of great beauty and reflection, connoisseurs of the phenomenon claim the few things are as rewarding to aficionados as the rate 'green flash,' a ball or semi-circle of vivid green light that appears for a few seconds after the sun has sunk below the horizon. This elusive evening event was long considered a myth, but it has recently been confirmed by atmospheric scientists as more than just a side effect of an extended happy hour.

When sunlight strikes the Earth's atmosphere, the colors in the light are diffused to different degrees depending on their wavelengths. The shorter wavelengths, such as blue and green, are more prone to scattering than the longer wavelengths of the warmer colors. When the sun is overhead, the widely scattered blue light causes the sky to appear blue. When the sun is at the horizons, we see it through so much more atmosphere that the cooler colors are blocked. The red, orange, and yellow light that reaches us gives the sky its classic sunset hues.

Under perfect conditions, however, the light from the sun is split into bands of color as it passes below the horizon. These bands run horizontally through all the colors of the rainbow, with red on the bottom and blue on top. Light from the sun follows a curved path in the atmosphere, so light curves over the horizon even though the sun has actually set. When everything is just right, the warm colors are blocked by the edge of the Earth, the blue is scattered by the atmosphere, but the green band briefly becomes visible as a 'green flash.'

37. Which of the following cannot be inferred from the passage?

A. Cooler colors in light tent to scatter more than warmer colors.
B. Green flashes begin to form immediately before the sun sets.
C. Red and blue are the colors at the bottom and top of a rainbow.
D. The sky appears to be blue because of scattered blue light.

38. What is the best title for the passage?

A. The Mystery of the Green Flash Explained
B. The Best Way to Enjoy a Sunset
C. The Sun: Source of Life and Energy
D. The Various Color Bands of Sunlight

39. According to the passage, what is true about a green flash?

A. It is an optical illusion much loved by sunset watchers.
B. It comes from a color in sunlight that is normally diffused by the atmosphere.
C. It is something that happens after a heavy rain shower.
D. It is a change in the wavelengths of the warm colors in sunlight.

40~41. In 1966, Eddie Arnold earned induction into the Country Music Hall of Fame. Ranked among the most popular country singers in U.S. history, Arnold used his smooth voice to escape from poverty. When his father died, the family farm was lost to creditors, and the Arnolds were forced to become sharecroppers. Even when achieving his lifelong dream of becoming a top-selling artist, <u>this country boy never lost touch with his roots</u>. Even while gaining a rather sophisticated fan base with his succession of hits, he always referred to himself as the "Tennessee Plowboy." In his mind, his background as a hard-working farm hand prepared him for the demanding role of a successful singer. From the beginning, he __________ from most of his contemporaries in the world of country singers. Unlike most of them who appeared either in jeans and plaid shirts or glittering sequins and spangles, Arnold always dressed in debonair attire. When he died in May 2008, the music world lost an immensely popular crooner of romantic ballads.

40. 윗글의 빈칸에 들어갈 가장 알맞은 것은?

① kept his figure
② cut a different figure
③ emerged a big figure
④ created a whole figure

41. 밑줄 친 "this country boy never lost touch with his roots"가 의미하는 것으로 가장 알맞은 것은?

① Arnold remained connected to the family farm and continued to pursue agriculture.
② Arnold eschewed his humble beginnings and indulged in a more sophisticated lifestyle.
③ Arnold liked to be known as a farm hand and favored jeans and cowboy boots when he performed.
④ Arnold continued to identify himself with the attitudes and values of hardworking rural Americans.

42~43. The relevance of formal economic models to real-world policy has been a topic of some dispute. The economists R. D. Norton and S. Y. Rhee achieved some success in applying such a model ___Ⓐ___ to the Korean economy over a fourteen-year period; the model's figures for output, prices, and other variables closely matched real statistics. The model's value in policy terms, however, proved less clear-cut. Norton and Rhee performed simulations in which, keeping long-term factors constant, they tried to pinpoint the effect of short-term policy changes. Their model indicated that rising prices for imported oil would increase inflation; reducing exports by five percent would lower Gross Domestic Product (GDP) and increase inflation; and slowing the growth of the money supply would result in slightly higher inflation. These findings are somewhat ___Ⓑ___. Many economists have argued that reducing exports will lessen, not increase, inflation. And while most view escalating oil costs as inflationary, few would think the same of slower monetary growth. The Norton-Rhee model can perhaps be viewed as indicating the pitfalls of a formalist approach that stresses statistical "goodness of fit" at the expense of genuine policy relevance.

42. 윗글의 목적으로 가장 알맞은 것은?

① to propose a new type of economic analysis
② to suggest an explanation for Korean inflation
③ to determine the accuracy of Norton and Rhee's analysis
④ to describe the limitations of a formal economic model

43. 빈칸 Ⓐ와 Ⓑ에 들어갈 가장 알맞은 것은?

① retrospectively - startling
② reflectively - promising
③ prospectively - anticipating
④ intensively - disappointing

44~45. Experts say that if you feel drowsy during the day, you haven't had enough sleep. If you routinely fall asleep within five minutes of lying down, you probably have severe sleep deprivation, possibly even a sleep disorder. Microsleeps, or very brief episodes of sleep in an otherwise awake person, are another mark of sleep deprivation. In many cases, people are not aware that they are experiencing microsleeps. The widespread practice of "burning the candle at both ends" in Western industrialized societies has created so much sleep deprivation that what is really abnormal sleepiness is now almost the norm.

Sleep-deprived people who are tested by using a driving simulator or by performing a hand-eye coordination task perform as badly as or worse than those who are intoxicated. Sleep deprivation also magnifies alcohol's effects on the body, so a fatigued person who drinks will become much more impaired than someone who is well rested. Since drowsiness is the brain's last step before falling asleep, driving while drowsy can and often does lead to disaster. Caffeine and other stimulants cannot overcome the effects of severe sleep deprivation. The National Sleep Foundation says that if you have trouble keeping your eyes focused, if you can't stop yawning, or if you can't remember driving the last few miles, you are probably too drowsy to drive safely.

44. 밑줄 친 "burning the candle at both ends"가 의미하는 것으로 가장 알맞은 것은?

① an ardent desire to sleep
② a state of extreme agitation
③ an unrelenting schedule that affords little rest
④ the unavoidable conflagration that occurs when two forces oppose each other

45 윗글의 목적으로 가장 알맞은 것은?

① to offer preventive measures for sleep deprivation
② to alert readers to the signs and risks of not getting enough sleep
③ to recommend the amount of sleep individuals need at different ages
④ to explain why sleepssness has become a common state in Western societies

46~48. If you read through the arguments and Op-Eds over the past few years about the impact of ______, you'll find that the debate keeps cycling back to two refrains: the impact of blogging on traditional journalism and the impact of Wikipedia on traditional scholarship. In both cases, a trained, institutionally accredited elite has been challenged by what the blogger Glenn Reynolds called an "army of Davids," with much triumphalism, derision, and defensiveness on both sides. This is a perfectly legitimate debate to have, since bloggers and Wikipedians are likely to do some things better than their professional equivalents and some things much worse, and we may as well figure out which is which. The problem with spending so much time hashing out these issues is that it overstates the importance of amateur journalism and encyclopedia authoring in the vast marketplace of ideas that the Web has opened up. The fact is that most user-created content on the Web is not challenging the authority of a traditional expert. It's working in a zone where there are no experts or where the users themselves are the experts.

46. Choose the one closest in meaning to the underlined "army of Davids."

A. people who have authority
B. people who have military inclinations
C. people who are ordinary
D. people who are adventurous

47. Choose the one that best fills in the blank.

A. Internet addiction
B. Web surfing
C. Internet access
D. Web amateurism

48. What is the purpose of the passage?

A. to contrast different types of writing venues on the Web
B. to suggest that the Web is an uninhibited sphere of activity
C. to argue that expertise on the Web should be fostered more
D. to persuade people to refrain from posting false information on the Web

49~51. At a distance a fish school resembles a large organism. Its members, numbering anywhere from two or three into the millions, swim in tight formations, wheeling and reversing in near unison. Either dominance systems do not exist or they are so weak as to have little or no influence on the dynamics of the school as a whole. There is, moreover, ______. When the school turns to the right or left, individuals formerly on the flank assume the lead. The average school size varies according to species, as does the spacing of its members, its average velocity, and its three-dimensional shape. Although the fish are usually aligned with military precision while the group is on the move, they assume a more nearly random orientation while resting or feeding. Their alignments also shift in particular ways when the fish are attacked by predators. Spacing within the moving school is evidently determined to a large extent by hydrodynamic force. Individual fish tend to seek positions in which they can be as close as possible to their neighbors without suffering serious loss of efficiency due to turbulence created by the other fish.

49. According to the passage, what does <u>not</u> influence school size?

A. the direction of the fish
B. the proximity of the fish
C. the type of the fish
D. the speed of the fish

50. Choose the one that best fills in the blank.

A. an opportunity to swim solo
B. no consistent leadership
C. little room for autonomy
D. a strong sense to diverge

51. Which of the following <u>cannot</u> be inferred about a "fish school"?

A. Its main role is to provide safety to its members.
B. Predators affect the alignment of the fish.
C. It refers to a group of more than two fish.
D. Feeding is an exception to uniform formation.

52~55. Taste develops with the definite preponderance of commodity production over any other kind of production. As a consequence of the manufacture of products as commodities for the market, people become less and less aware of the conditions of their production — not only of the social conditions in the form of exploitation, but of the technical conditions as well. The consumer, who is more or less expert when he gives an order to an artisan, is not usually knowledgeable when he appears as a buyer. Added to this is the fact that mass production, which aims at turning out inexpensive commodities, must be bent upon disguising bad quality. In most cases it is actually in its interest that the buyer has little expertise. The more industry progresses, the more perfect are the imitations which it throws on the market. The commodity is bathed in a profane glow; this glow has nothing in common with the glow that produces its 'theological capers', yet it is of some importance to society. In the same measure as the expertness of a customer declines, the importance of his taste increases — both for him and for the manufacturer. For the consumer it has the value of a more or less elaborate ______ of his lack of expertness. Its value to the manufacturer is a fresh stimulus to consumption which in some cases is satisfied at the expense of other requirements of consumption the manufacturer would find more costly to meet.

52. Choose the one that best fills in the blank.

A. awareness
B. expose
C. masking
D. deconstruction

53. What is the best title for the passage?

A. Commodities Galore: Products for the Masses
B. Basking in the Limelight of Commodities
C. The Hidden Agenda of Production and Consumption
D. Developing a Taste for the Good Life

54. According to the passage, what is true about "customer's expertise"?

A. It stays constant throughout different consumption contexts.
B. It is an illusion that is discredited by manufacturers.
C. It is used to discern good quality from bad quality.
D. It declines in reverse proportion to the importance of taste.

55. Which of the following can be inferred about "taste"?

A. It is acquired through the consumption of high-end commodities.
B. It becomes refined over a long period of time.
C. It is weakened through mass production.
D. It is perceived differently by the buyer and the manufacturer.

정답 및 해설

Unit 1. 주제/제목/요지/주장/목적 유형

UNIT 2. 일치/불일치/추론 유형

UNIT 3. 지칭 추론 유형

UNIT 4. 빈칸 유형

UNIT 5. 장문 유형

정답 및 해설

Unit 1. 주제/제목/요지/주장/목적 유형

1.⑤ 이 냄새는 출퇴근 시간대에 서울 지하철 객차에 스며들며, 찬미자들은 이 냄새가 지구상에서 가장 건강에 좋은 음식이라고 주장한다. 냉장고가 들어오기 전에 비타민C의 원천으로 평가받던 김치는 이제 한반도에서 멀리 떨어진 메뉴에서 떠오르고 있다. 맵고 마늘 냄새가 나는 양배추 요리는 영국, 호주, 미국에서 피자 토핑과 소를 채운 타코 음식으로 발견된다. 김치를 담그는 전통적인 공동 행위인 김장은 최근 유네스코로부터 세계문화유산으로 인정받았다. 그러나 로스앤젤레스부터 런던까지 한국 국적의 레스토랑에서 인기가 높아졌음에도 불구하고 요리는 원산지에서 위기에 처해있다. 배추, 마늘, 양념, 고춧가루 등 김치의 기본 재료에 중국과의 무역 전쟁이 한국문화의 정체성에 지속적인 손상을 우려하는 목소리가 더해진다.

이종현T의 독해 Point!

밑에서 4번째 줄의 But부터 한국 음식의 문제점에 대한 얘기가 시작되는 부분이고 문제점으로 끝나는 글이다. 따라서 한국 음식의 문제점이 들어간 선지를 찍으면 정답은 ⑤번이 된다.

2.④ 해양 쓰레기를 예방, 감시, 청소하기 위한 혁신적인 솔루션은 건강한 해양을 복원하고 시간이 지남에 따라 그것의 안녕을 유지하기 위해 필요하다. 또한 이러한 솔루션 중 몇 개가 개발 및 구현되었는지, 플랫폼 전체에 정보가 분산되어 쉽게 접근할 수 없는 상황에서 어느 정도까지 효과적인지 거의 알려지지 않았다. 세계적인 분석 또한 Nature Sustainability에서도 177개의 PMC 솔루션을 식별한 연구진은 그 중 106개가 모니터링, 33개는 (대부분 폐수 처리를 통해) 33개는 예방, 30개만 청소하는 것으로 나타났다. 그들은 또한 다양한 개발자에 걸쳐 쓰레기 크기 용어의 일관되지 않은 사용을 발견한다. 이는 처리 대상 쓰레기의 유형을 평가하기 위한 조화와 노력이 필요했으며, 이는 해결책 중 137개가 Microlitter를 대상으로 한다는 것을 보여준다. 전체적으로 기술 준비 상태에 도달한 솔루션은 거의 없었고 효율성 및 환경 영향에 대해 검증된 솔루션은 없었다.

이종현T의 독해 Point!

중간에 In a global analysis ~부터 연구가 나오기 시작하고, 그 연구의 결과를 찾겠다고 생각하면 마지막 문장이 연구의 결과이다. 해양 문제에 대해 아직 제대로 검증된 솔루션은 없었다 라는 얘기가 이 글의 주제가 될 것이고, 이게 들어간 선지를 찍으면 정답은 ④번이 된다.

3.④ 미국에서 노인들을 대상으로 한 '케어'를 관찰한 결과, 그 문화에서의 개인화는 특정한 상징과 지위의 획득뿐만 아니라 일련의 성공의 성취도 포함한다고 결론지을 수 있을 뿐이다. 그 징표에 따르면 성공할 능력이 상실되거나 실패한 개인은 성공 메커니즘에서 물러났기 때문에 덜한 사람으로 간주된다. 미국의 노인들은, 그들이 직업 체계에서 물러났거나 쫓겨났기 때문에, 성공하거나 실패할 수 있는 능력을 빼앗긴다. 그들은 여전히 지속적인 소비 능력으로 그들의 과거의 성공을 상징할 수 없는 한, 거의 없는 사람으로 보여진다. 이런 식으로 개인의 소비능력 보유는 성공 시스템에서 물러난 후에도 다음과 같이 받아들여진다. 이러한 소비를 통해, 경제에 없어서는 안 될 서비스가 제공되기 때문에, 성공을 대체할 적절한 수단이 된다.

이종현T의 독해 Point!

첫 두 문장의 I can only conclude that ~ 부분에서 소재를 잡으면 personalization이 될 수 있다. 그 문화에서 있는 것들에 대한 얘기가 핵심이고, 이게 쭉 이어진다고 볼 수 있다. 따라서 이게 들어간 선지를 찾으면 정답은 ④번이 된다.

4.⑤ 적어도 윤리적인 관점에서 기술이 어떻게 불가피할 수 있는 지, 어떻게 자율적일 수 있는지 알 수 없다. 어떤 사람들은 주어진 기술을 사용하기로 선택하지만, 다른 사람들은 그렇지 않다. 어떤 기술이든, 모든 개인이 사용하지 않기로 선택하는 경우가 될 수 있다. 경쟁자가 생기거나 도덕적 논쟁이 나타나 다수의 사람들이 더 이상 기술을 사용하지 않도록 설득할 수 있다. 그 기술은 개인의 결정으로 인해 구현되지 않는다. 따라서 기술 또는 적어도 구현이 불가피한 것은 아니다. 그것을 유지하기로 한 개인의 선택에 의존하는 한, 그것은 자율적이지 않다. 기술의 필연성과 자율성을 바탕으로 기술 윤리를 구현하려는 노력은 사람들이 선택을 하는 방식을 반영하지도 않고, 윤리적 의사결정을 내리지도 않으며, 개인과 기술의 전체 관계를 반영하지도 않는다.

이종현T의 독해 Point!

이 글은 개인의 선택과 기술의 관계에 관한 글이다. 이걸 두 번째 문장부터 생각해볼 수 있고, 중간에 That technology ~ 의 문장에서 확실하게 알 수 있다. 따라서 개인이 원인이고, 기술이 영향 받는다가 결과가 될 수 있는 선지를 고르면 ⑤번이 정답이 된다.

5.⑤ 물밀 듯이 밀려오는 외국태생과 토착태생, 백인, 흑인 등 다양한 인종, 소수만이 전문직 종사자였다. 사업가, 교사, 의사와 변호사, 성직자, 목사, 라비. 대부분의 사람들은 공장을 가득 채우고, 집을 짓고, 바닥을 닦고, 유복한 자들의 아기들을 돌보는 일꾼들이었다. 그러나 이 새로운 거주자들은 더 많은 것을 도시로 가져왔다. 그들은 그들의 종교, 정치, 제도, 예술을 가져왔다. 그들은 마을 잔치에는 거리를 가득 메웠고 속죄일에는 거리를 비웠다. 그들은 작은 가게 앞 교회와 공제조직을 만들었다. 그들은 유대 연예인들이 그들의 기술을 연마하는 보드빌 극장들과 래그타임 밴드들이 미국 음악의 경계를 허무는 게토 댄스홀로 서둘렀다. 그리고 그들은 도시의 공공의 생활에 나타났다.

이종현T의 독해 Point!

중간에 ~~~~, though. 가 들어간 문장에서 새로운 주민들이 많은 것을 도시로 가져왔다 가 핵심이 될 수 있다. 그 사람들이 가져온 것에 관한 이야기가 쭉 뒤로 이어진다. 따라서 이 새로 외국에서 온 사람들이 가져온 것들에 대한 얘기가 주제가 된다고 생각하면 정답은 ⑤번이 된다.

6.③ 배려의 표시로서의 사죄의 힘은 우리가 지금 공식적으로 보고 있는 진정한 사태의 핵심에 있다. 예를 들어, 정부는 1997년 미국이 의학 실험의 일환으로 매독 치료를 거부당한 흑인들에게 사과했을 때처럼 부당했던 집단에 대해 관심이 있다고 발표할 수 있다. 다른 나라에 사과를 하는 것은 향후 협력의 토대를 마련하는 효과적인 방법이다. 1990년대 후반, 체코는 유럽 국가 중 유일한 국가로 남아 있었다. 2차 세계 대전 동안 있던 나치에 박해에 있어 독일이 배상금을 제공하지 않은 유일한 국가는 체코다. 독일은 체코가 전후 Sudetenland에서 독일계 동포를 추방한 것에 대해 공식적으로 사과할 때까지 체코 피해자들에게 배상금을 지불하기를 거부했다. 체코 정부는 1997년 나토 가입에 대한 독일의 지원과 배상금을 모두 받기 위해 사과의 뜻을 밝혔다. 독일은 체코의 이익을 위해 기름을 마련하는 것으로 대응했고, 나토와 유럽연합은 체코를 그들의 멤버에 합류하도록 초청했다.

이종현T의 독해 Point!

이 글의 핵심이 apology가 될 수 있겠다는 생각은 첫 번째 문장에서 할 수 있고, '사과를 통해 서로 협력하게 된다'라는 얘기가 중간에 Offering ~이 들어간 문장부터 있다. 따라서 '사과를 통해 뭔가 협력하고 좋아지고'의 얘기가 되는걸 정답으로 찍으면 ③번이 된다.

7.⑤ 중요한 문제에 집중하고 있을 때 반복되는 방해만큼 신경계에 거슬리는 것은 없다. 최악의 실수 중 하나는 당신이 무엇을 하든 모든 전화를 받는 습관을 들이는 것이다. 전화를 다루는 좋은 방법은 오전 9시에서 10시 사이, 오후 4시에서 5시 사이 등 한 번에 통화를 집중시키는 것이다. 그 시간 동안 당신은 모든 전화를 받고, 당신에게 전화한 사람들에게 다시 전화해라. 바쁘다고 전화를 거절하는 건 무례한 행동이 아니다. 당신은 현명한 것이다. 만약 당신이 전화의 희생자라면, 전화 심사는 당신의 직장생활을 바꿀 수 있다.

이종현T의 독해 Point!

첫 번째 문장부터 반복되는 방해가 신경에 가장 거슬린다라고 나와 있다. 다음 문장에서도 뭘 하든 전화를 다 받는 것(즉 방해받는 것)을 하는 것이 문제라고 되어 있다. 따라서 뭔가를 할 땐 방해받는걸 하지 말라는 이야기도 될 수 있고, 그게 들어간 선지를 찍으면 정답은 ⑤번이 된다.

8.⑤ 경제체제의 내재적인 취약성이 그것이 더 안전하게 만들어질 수 없다는 것을 의미하지는 않는다. 많은 것들이 행해질 수 있고, 이미 행해졌고, 여전히 행해질 수 있습니다. 하지만 개혁을 설계할 때, 목표를 신중하게 선택하는 것이 중요합니다. 목표는

개별 은행이나 대형 기관의 실패 위험을 제거하는 것이 아니어야 한다. 실패에는 장점이 있다. 이는 올바른 인센티브를 창출하고 혁신을 촉진하며 효율성을 높이는 데 중요합니다. 오히려 정책입안자들은 더 넓은 금융 시스템의 탄력성을 강화하기 위해 노력해야 한다. 시스템이 극심한 스트레스를 받을 때도 결제, 재산권 처분 서비스 제공, 신용 제공, 리스크 이전 등의 기본적인 기능을 수행할 수 있어야 한다. 즉, 정책입안자들은 독특한 사건이 시스템적인 위기로 바뀌지 않는 시스템을 구축 하도록 노력해야 한다. 이는 재정적인 고통의 확률을 낮출 뿐만 아니라 실물경제가 그것으로부터 절연되어 있을 확률을 높이려는 것을 의미한다.

이종현T의 독해 Point!

중간에 Rather,부터 해야하는 것에 관한 얘기가 나오고, 더 넓은 금융 시스템의 탄력성을 강화시키기 위해 노력하고 등의 것들이 나온다. 그리고 그 결과가 마지막 문장에서 재정적인 고통의 확률을 낮추고 방어할 수 있다고 되어 있으므로 이게 들어간 선지를 찍으면 정답은 ⑤번이 된다.

9.③ 언어가 현대 인류의 주요 의사소통 체계로 발전한 후, 사람들은 음악을 통해 누구와 의사소통을 해야 하는지에 대한 질문을 남겨두었다. 음악은 결국 '음음음'의 파생물로서, 그 자체가 의사소통의 수단으로 진화했기 때문에 의사소통 기능은 쉽게 떨어질 수 없었다; 오늘날에도 여전히 존재하는 것처럼 현대 인간들 사이에는 음악과 의사소통해야 하는 강박 관념이 남아 있었다. 어떻게 이것이 실현될 수 있었을까? 다른 인간들과의 의사소통은 이제 언어 이전기의 유아들을 제외하고, 음악보다는 언어에 의해 훨씬 더 잘 성취되었다. 그러나 현대 인간들의 마음 속에는 이제 그들이 소통할 수 있고 소통해야 할 또 다른 유형의 실체인, 초자연적인 존재들이 있었다. 그래서 음악을 통해 의사소통을 하는 인간의 성향은 무당의 북을 치거나 바흐의 작품을 통해 초자연적인 것에 초점을 맞추게 되었다.

이종현T의 독해 Point!

두 번째 문장부터 음악의 의사소통 기능에 관한 얘기가 된다. 그리고 바뀌는 얘기가 없으므로 이 글의 핵심은 음악을 통한 의사소통이 될 수 있다. 따라서 정답은 ③번이 된다.

10.④ 5억1200만 명의 시민을 거느린 유럽연합은 최근까지 온실가스 제로 녹색 경제로 이끌었다. 14억에 가까운 인구를 가진 중화인민공화국은 탄소시대 이후로 전환하려는 계획으로 최근 몇 년간 이 분야에 뛰어들었다. 그리고 이제 미국은 3억 2천 5백만 명의 시민을 거느리고 이 무리에 합류할 태세이다. 세 마리의 코끼리 모두가 일치된 행진을 하고, 모범 사례를 공유하고, 공통의 코드, 규정, 기준, 인센티브를 제정하고, 나머지 인류를 무리로 끌어들이기 위해 함께 손을 뻗지 않는다면, 20년도 채 되지 않아 무탄소 문명화를 향한 경주에서 우리는 지고 말 것이다.

이종현T의 독해 Point!

EU, China, U.S.로 집단이 계속 바뀌면서 같은 맥락의 얘기이므로 여러 예시라고 할 수 있고, without ~의 문장부터 주제라고 할 수 있다. 따라서 '서로 공유하지 않으면 질 것이다'라고 되는 것이고, 우리는 '서로 공유해서 살아남아야 한다'가 이 글의 주제가 된다. 따라서 이게 들어간 선지를 찾으면 ④번이 된다.

11.① 전통적으로, 연구는 목표 추구를 단독적인 노력으로 다루어 왔다. 하지만 일상적인 경험은 우리의 관계가 우리의 발전을 촉진하거나 방해할 수 있다는 것을 보여준다. 만약 여러분이 매일 아침 일찍 일어나고 싶다면, 여러분은 밤 10시에 침대 옆 램프를 끄는 배우자와 함께 있는 것이 더 좋습니다. 만약 여러분이 채식주의자가 되고 싶다면, 두부 대 스테이크에 대한 여러분의 배우자의 감정이 아마도 영향을 미칠 것입니다. 현재 연구원들은 그 영향을 조사하고 있다. 워싱턴 대학의 한 연구는 매우 양심적이고 체계적이며 신뢰할 수 있는 배우자와 결혼하는 것이 미래의 직업 만족도와 더 높은 수입을 예측한다는 것을 발견했다. 독일 쾰른 대학의 Wilhelm Hofmann에 의한 연구는 높은 관계 만족도가 목표 추구를 통제하는 감정에 긍정적으로 영향을 미친다는 것을 보여준다. 호프만은 행복한 관계의 안정성이 집중하는 것을 더 쉽게 만든다고 가정한다. 호프만에 따르면, "사람들의 일상이 안정적이고 예측 가능하다고 느낄 때, 그들은 목표를 추구하는 능력을 더 잘 통제한다고 느낀다."

이종현T의 독해 Point!

중간에 Now부터 연구자들의 연구가 나오고, 그 연구 결과가 주제라고 한다면, 연구 결과는 '체계적이며 신뢰할 수 있는 배우자와 결혼해야 → 미래 직업 만족도와 수입이 올라간다'이다. 따라서 이게 들어간 선지를 찾으면 정답은 ①번이 된다.

12.④ 미국에서 풍차는 매년 최소 4만 5천 마리의 새와 박쥐를 죽일 것으로 추정된다. 그것은 많은 수의 새와 박쥐처럼 들린다.

그 숫자를 원근법에 넣기 위해, 주인의 집을 드나드는 것을 허용하는 애완 고양이들이 고양이 한 마리당 평균 300마리 이상의 새를 죽이는 것으로 측정되었다고 생각해 보라. 만약 미국의 야외 고양이 개체 수가 약 1억 마리로 추산된다면, 미국에 서는 풍차에 의해 연간 4만 5천 마리의 새와 박쥐가 죽는 것에 비해, 고양이는 최소한 300억 마리의 새를 죽이는 것으로 계산될 수 있다. 그 풍차의 희생자 수는 단지 150마리의 고양이의 일과 맞먹는다.

이종현T의 독해 Point!

첫 번째 문장부터 세 번째 문장까지 보면 풍차가 죽이는 새의 수와 고양이가 죽이는 새의 수를 비교하고 있고, 고양이가 죽이는 새의 수가 더 많다는 것이 핵심이므로 이게 들어간 선지를 찍으면 정답은 ④번이 된다.

13.⑤ 1967년 이후, 인플레이션을 감안한 미국의 중간 가계 소득은, 가장 부유한 미국인들의 부와 소득이 급증했음에도 불구하고, 인구의 하위 60퍼센트에 대해 정체되어 왔다. 유럽의 변화는 덜 극명하지만 같은 방향을 가리키고 있다. 기업의 이익은 1960년대 이후 최고 수준이지만 기업들은 점점 더 그러한 이익을 투자하기보다는 저축하는 쪽을 택하고 있어 생산성과 임금을 더욱 떨어뜨리고 있다. 그리고 최근 이러한 변화들은 민주주의의 공동화와 세계화된 엘리트들에 의한 테크노크라테스의 통치로 대체되는 것을 동반하고 있다.

이종현T의 독해 Point!

지문의 중간에 yet부터 문제점이 나온다고 보면 되고, 유럽 경제의 문제점에 대한 얘기가 쭉 나오는 글이 된다. 이게 들어간 선지를 찾으면 정답은 ⑤번이 된다.

14.② 지금 2번가와 3번가 사이에 있는 마을 동쪽에 있는 내 개인 병실에 누워 침대의 유리한 지점에서 찌르레기를 보고 있다. 민주당원 3명 : Harry Truman(타임즈의 케케묵은 사본) Adlai Stevenson(하퍼스) Dean Acheson(그의 당을 바라보는 한 민주당원이라고 불리는 책)이 나와 함께 침대에 누워 있다. 민주당원들은 닥스훈트가 부족하기 때문에 나와 함께 잠자리에 드는데, 사실 이런 경우에 나는, 몇 년 동안 죽어가고 있는 나의 닥스훈트인 Fred의 유령이 방문할 것을 거의 확신 한다. 인생에서 Fred는 항상 병자를 간호했고, 어떤 음란한 늙은 의사처럼 환자와 함께 침대로 바로 올라갔으며, 나쁜 상황을 더 악화시켰다. 이 어두운 아침 내내, 나는 구겨진 담요 위에서 마지못해 그를 즐겁게 해주었고, 그의 강압적인 몸무게를 느꼈으며, 그의 사기 보고를 들었다. 그는 살아있을 때 불편한 침대 동료였다, 죽음은 별로 나아지지 않았다 – 나는 여전히 붐비고, 그의 타고난 무례함과 그의 가식을 왜 참아냈는지 여전히 궁금하다.

이종현T의 독해 Point!

중간에 I am almost certain부터 새로운 인물인 Fred가 등장하고, 이 Fred를 중심으로 쓴 얘기를 본다고 생각하면 Fred가 어땠는지에 대해 생각하는 글이다. 따라서 Fred에 대해 생각한 글 같은 표현을 찾겠다고 생각하면 ②번이 된다.

15.④ 이혼 통계는 종종 가족 분열의 척도로 사용되며, 현재 높은 이혼율은 미국 가정이 심각한 어려움에 처해 있다는 증거로 인용된다. 그러나 과거보다 오늘날 이혼율이 높아진 것이 전적으로 더 많은 가정 불행의 결과인 것은 아니다. 초기 세대에는, 많은 커플들이 그들의 결혼 생활이 불행했음에도 불구하고 이혼을 피했다. 그들은 그것이 사회적 배척을 의미하거나, 여성의 경우, 그들이 잘 살 수 있는 기회가 거의 없기 때문에 가난을 피했다. 이혼 가능성이 높아지고 이혼이 쉬워지면서 불행한 부부들이 이 길을 택했다.

이종현T의 독해 Point!

첫 문장에서 이혼 통계에 관한 이야기라는 것을 알 수 있고, 중간에 However, ~부터 보면 이혼률이 높다고 더 가정이 불행해진 것은 아니다 라고 있으니, '이혼 통계를 통해 무조건 가정 불화는 아니다'라는 얘기가 이 글의 주제가 된다. 따라서 이게 들어간 선지를 찾으면 이혼 통계를 신중하게 해석하자는 ④번이 정답이 된다.

16.① 개발도상국의 대부분이 그렇듯이 유아 사망률이 높을 때, 부모들은 몇 명의 아이들이 성년기까지 살아남는 것을 보장하기 위해 아이를 많이 갖는 경향이 있다. 유아 사망률이 지속적으로 감소하기 전에 먼저 선행되지 않았던 출생률이 지속적으로 감소한 적은 없었다. 인구 통계학적으로 분류된 세계에서 가장 중요한 차이점 중 하나는 후진국의 유아 사망률이 높다는 것이다. 더 나은 영양 섭취, 개선된 건강관리, 간단한 경구 수분 보충 요법, 그리고 전염병 예방 접종은 유아 사망률을 획기적으로 감소시켰으며, 이는 대부분의 지역에서 출산율 하락을 동반했다. 쉽게 예방할 수 있는 전염병으로부터 매년 5백 만 명의 아이들의 목숨을 구하면 2000만 명 혹은 3,000만 명의 추가 출산을 피할 수 있을 것으로 추정된다.

이종현T의 독해 Point!

첫 문장부터 유아 사망률이 높은 것이 원인 → 사람들이 더 많은 수의 아이를 가지는 것이 결과가 되는 글로 시작한다. 그리고 그 얘기가 쭉 이어지므로 이 둘이 원인과 결과인 선지를 찾으면 정답은 ①번이 된다.

17.① 사람들은 걸으면서 말하고 또는 껌을 씹으며 지도를 읽는 것과 같은 두 가지 또는 그 이상의 것들을 한 번에 할 수 있지만, 컴퓨터처럼 우리가 할 수 없는 것은 두 가지에 동시에 집중하는 것이다. 우리의 주의력은 오락가락한다. 이것은 컴퓨터에게는 괜찮지만, 인간에게는 심각한 영향을 미친다. 두 대의 여객기는 같은 활주로에 착륙할 수 있다. 환자에게 잘못된 약을 투여한다. 갓난아기가 욕조에 방치되어 있다. 이 모든 잠재적 비극들이 공유하는 것은 사람들이 한꺼번에 너무 많은 일을 하려고 하고 그들이 해야 할 일을 잊어버리고 있다는 것이다. 두 가지를 동시에 하려고 할 때, 여러분은 둘 다 잘 할 수 없거나 잘 할 수 없을 거예요. 멀티태스킹이 더 많은 일을 할 수 있는 효과적인 방법이라고 생각한다면, 거꾸로 생각하는 것입니다. 그것은 일을 덜 할 수 있는 효과적인 방법이다.

이종현T의 독해 Point!

두 번째 문장의 but부터 문제점이 시작된다. 그리고 멀티태스킹의 문제점에 대한 글이고, 멀티태스킹의 문제점에 대한 얘기가 핵심소재라고 본다면 정답은 ①번이 된다.

18.⑤ 이 기회를 빌려 제 소개를 하고 여러분이 동네에 오신 것을 환영합니다. 제 아내 모니카와 저는 당신의 새 집에서 바로 길 위에 있는 19번지에 살아요. 우리는 지난 20년 동안 Meadow가에서 살아왔다. 아마도 제가 여기 있는 다른 사람들보다 나이가 많기 때문에, 저는 종종 이웃의 비공식적인 "시장"이라고 불리게 됩니다. 저는 몇몇 이웃들로부터 당신이 이사 온 이후 발생한 문제에 대해 그들의 바람을 전달해 달라는 요청을 받았습니다. 우리는 모두 음악을 사랑하고, 우리들 대부분은 10대들을 가졌고, 가질 것이다. 하지만, 너의 10대(자녀)들에게 볼륨을 줄여달라고 부탁해 주시면 감사하겠습니다.
당신이 제대로 정착이 된 후에 우리 모두는 당신을 만나 인사하기를 고대합니다.

이종현T의 독해 Point!

밑줄 마지막 부분에 though 부분부터 핵심이 나온다고 볼 수 있고 여기서 볼륨을 낮춰달라고 요청하고 있으니 이 얘기가 들어간 걸 찾으면 정답은 ⑤번이 된다.

19.① 웃음은 궁합에 대한 하나의 단서이다. 그것은 여러분이 장기적으로 얼마나 서로의 친구를 즐길지를 말해줍니다. 만약 여러분이 함께 웃는 것이 좋고 건강하며, 다른 사람들을 희생시키지 않는다면, 여러분은 세상과 건강한 관계를 맺게 될 것입니다. 웃음은 놀라움의 산물이다. 만약 여러분이 서로를 웃길 수 있다면, 여러분은 항상 서로를 놀라게 할 수 있습니다. 만약 여러분이 항상 서로를 놀라게 할 수 있다면, 여러분은 항상 여러분 주변의 세상을 새로운 것으로 유지할 수 있습니다. 웃음이 없는 관계를 조심하라. 진지함만을 바탕으로 한 가장 친밀한 관계조차도 우울해지는 경향이 있다. 시간이 지남에 따라, 세계에 대한 공통의 진지한 관점을 공유하는 것은 여러분을 같은 관점을 공유하지 않는 사람들에게서 멀어지게 하는 경향이 있고, 여러분의 관계는 함께 비판적이 되는 것에 바탕을 둘 수 있습니다.

이종현T의 독해 Point!

첫 번째 문장부터 웃음에 대한 글이라고 생각할 수 있고, 3번째 문장에서 웃음이 건강하면 그 결과 관계가 좋아진다고 되어 있다. 그러므로 이 글은 웃음을 통해(원인) → 관계를 좋아지게 만든다(결과)라고 볼 수 있고 이게 들어간 선지를 찾으면 정답은 ①번이 된다.

20.① 미국에서 어머니에 의해 조금이라도 양육된 유아의 비율과, 그렇게 양육된 유아가 젖을 떼는 연령은 20세기 대부분 감소했다. 예를 들어, 1970년대까지 미국 아이들 중 5%만이 6개월의 나이에 양육을 받았다. 그와 달리, 농부들과 접촉하지 않고 경작된 식품을 이용하지 못한 수렵채집인들 사이에서, 유아는 6개월 이상 양육을 받는다. 왜냐하면 그들이 먹을 수 있는 적합한 유아식은 모유뿐이기 때문이다. 그 유아들은 젖소의 우유, 아기용 분유, 부드러운 음식 대체품에 접근할 수 없다. 7개 이상의 수렵채집인 집단에서 젖을 떼는 평균 연령은 약 3살이며, 이는 아이들이 충분히 딱딱한 음식을 씹어 마침내 영양공급을 스스로 할 수 있는 연령이다.

이종현T의 독해 Point!

미국의 환경과 수렵 채집인의 환경을 비교해주는 글이고 먹는 음식에 따라 weaning의 나이가 달라진다는 것이므로 둘이 인과관계가 되는 글을 찾으면 된다. 정답은 ①번이 된다.

21.④ 중국의 채권시장이 이렇게 폭풍우가 몰아치는 봄을 맞이한 적은 없었다. 이미 2분기에 채무 불이행 기록을 세웠다. 기업에 대한 신용비용은 급증했다. 심지어 사회기반 시설에 투자하는 신성불가침의 국영 기업들조차 위험해 보인다. 무엇이 잘못되었을까? 질문에 대한 답은 전혀 없다. 채무 불이행은 중국을 위한 발전이며, 이는 누적 부채의 잔고를 정리할 필요가 있다. 올해 피해액은 채권시장의 0.1%에 불과하다. 하지만 투자자들이 정부가 어려움에 빠진 큰 회사를 지원할거라고 할 때, 그것은 여전히 가까운 과거에 대한 향상이다.

이종현T의 독해 Point!

첫 문장부터 중국의 채권시장에 문제점에 대한 글인 것을 알 수 있고, 중간에 '무엇이 문제되었을까? 에 대한 답이 없다'이므로 채권 시장에 큰 문제가 없음을 알 수 있고, 이에 대한 선지를 찾으면 ④번이 된다.

22.⑤ 우리는 진귀한 지구에 살고 있는가? 다른 행성들이 기껏해야 단순한 미생물의 서식지가 될 때, 아주 이례적으로 생명체의 풍부한 다양성을 수용하는 거의 유일한 존재인가? 또는 우리가 거대한 우주 동물원의 일부로 존재하는 것을 의미하면서 여기에 존재하는 것들만큼이나 복잡한 생명체로 가득한 우주에 살고 있는가? 이에 관한 논쟁이 한창이지만, 우리는 후자가 매우 가능성이 높다는 것을 받아들일 때가 되었다고 말한다. 지금까지 우리는 적어도 3,700개의 외계행성에 대해 알고 있으며, 잠재적으로 거주할 수 있는 무수히 많은 외계행성들과 외계위성들이 우리 은하계 내에 그리고 그 너머에 존재하는 것 같다. 우리는 생명체가 보통 그 행성 위에서 어떻게 생겨나는지 모르지만, 많은 과학자들은 그것이 어떤 적합한 행성의 화학적이고 물리적인 특성에서 아마 생겨났을 거라고 생각한다.

이종현T의 독해 Point!

중간에 to date부터 오늘날 얘기이고, 이 오늘날 얘기가 주제문이라고 생각하면 3700개의 외계 행성이 있고, 우리가 거주할 수 있는 행성이 있다는 얘기가 핵심이 된다고 볼 수 있다. 따라서 이게 들어간 선지를 찍어주면 정답은 ⑤번이 된다.

23.③ 천주교는 신이 주신 유일한 천직은 사제직이라고 주장했지만, 개신교 신자들은 사람들이 세속적인 공예품이나 무역에 부름을 받을 수 있다고 생각했다. 그들이 신을 섬기고 있다는 믿음은 그들이 더 많은 상품을 생산하고 더 많은 돈을 벌도록 이끌면서 종교적 열정으로 일하도록 격려했다. Weber는 개신교 신앙이 필연적으로 자본주의 경제사회로 이어진다고 믿었는데, 왜냐하면 그것은 신자들에게 이윤 추구를 탐욕과 야망과 같은 도덕적으로 의심스러운 동기의 증거가 아니라 헌신의 증거로 볼 수 있는 기회를 주기 때문이다. 운명의 개념은 또한 신자들이 사회적 불평등과 가난에 대해 걱정할 필요가 없다는 것을 의미했다. 물질적인 부는 정신적인 부의 표시였기 때문이다.

이종현T의 독해 Point!

이 글의 뒤에 나오는 Protestants의 집단이 핵심이고, 이들은 종교를 통해 돈을 벌게 해주는 것이 핵심이므로 이게 들어간 선지를 찍으면 정답은 ③번이 된다.

24.③ 호기심, 허영심 아니면 아직까지 탐구되지 않은 이유에서든, 사람들은 여러 시대에 걸쳐 자신의 반사된 모습을 보고 싶어 했다. 기원전 2,500년 초기 이집트인들은 대개 청동이지만, 가끔 은이나 금으로 만들어진 아주 광이 나는 금속 거울을 지니고 있었다. 최초의 상업용 유리 거울은 1564년에 베니스에서 만들어졌다. 이 유리 거울은 입으로 불어 납작해진 유리로 만들었고 수은과 주석의 혼합물로 코팅되었다. 베니스인들은 유럽에 수세기동안 거울을 공급하면서 발전했다. 1840년이 되고 나서야 Justus Liebig라는 독일 화학자가 우리가 오늘날 사용하는 은도금 방식을 생각해 냈다. 이 기술에 의해, 은과 암모니아의 화합물이 전화당, 로셀염, 포르말알데히드와 같은 불순물을 감소시키는 화학 반응을 거치게 되었고, 그 결과 금속성의 은이 매끄러운 판유리 뒷면에 고르게 발라졌다.

이종현T의 독해 Point!

유리의 발전에 대한 시간의 흐름을 보여주고 있으므로 이에 대한 선지를 찾아주면 정답은 ③번이 된다.

25.② 여러분의 개나 고양이가 행복한 잠에 웅크리고 있는 것을 보는 것보다 더 위안이 될 수 있는 것은 무엇일까요? 두 종 모두 거의 하루의 반을 어떤 형태의 수면에 몰두하며 보냅니다. 하지만 모든 것이 편안하다고 생각하는 것은 아니다. 나이든 동물들, 근육이나 관절에 문제가 있는 사람들, 또는 매우 활동적인 개들은 종종 속도를 내거나 자주 이동한다. 만약 여러분의 동료가 이러한 범주 중 하나에 들어맞는다면, 그는 치료용 침대의 혜택을 받을 수 있을 것입니다. 이 특화된 제품들은 일반 침대나 즉석에서 자는 장소와는 달리 지지와 편안함을 제공한다. 나이와 건강에 관계없이, 좋은 침대는 근골격계 건강을 증진시키고 추가

적인 회춘과 치유 효과를 제공한다.

이종현T의 독해 Point!

지문의 중간에 If절부터 he(강아지나 고양이)가 침대로 이득을 볼 수 있다고 되어있으니 이게 들어간 선지를 찾으면 정답은 ②번이 된다.

26.⑤ 행복은 살 수 없다. 당신은 가장 가까운 식료품점에 가서 당신이 버터 1파운드를 주문하는 것처럼 행복의 1파운드를 주문할 수 없다. 하지만, 행복은 내면에서 나오기 때문에, 여러분은 자신의 행동으로 행복의 척도를 확보할 수 있습니다. 당신은 불우한 동료들을 도와줌으로써 만족감을 찾을 수 있다. 그들과 함께 나누지 않는다면 불행으로 인해 행복한 크리스마스를 보내지 못하는 사람들을 도울 수 있습니다. 평화와 선의의 계절 동안, 어려움에 처한 사람들에게 우리의 눈으로 행복을 보도록 강요하지 말자. 오히려, 그들이 직접 눈으로 보고 행복을 찾을 수 있도록 돕자. 지역 사회의 불행을 살피자.

이종현T의 독해 Point!

앞 두 문장은 부정문으로 깔고가는 표현이고 2번째 줄의 But, since ~부터 하고싶은 주제가 나온다. 즉 '불우한 동료들을 도우면서 행복을 찾는다'가 핵심이 되는 것이고, 이게 들어간 선지를 찾으면 정답은 ⑤번이 된다.

27.④ 광산과 갑옷 기술의 중심은 독일의 Augsburg였는데, 그것은 우연의 일치가 아니었다. Augsburg는 유럽의 주요 철광석 매장 지역 중의 하나로, 갑옷을 입은 기사들로 군사력을 강화시킨 봉건 국가들의 금속 수요 때문에 광업이 호황을 이루고 갑옷 사업도 또한 빠르게 번창하였다. 봉건 유럽 전체가 짜증을 낼 정도로, 독일인들은 손님들이 다른 대안이 없다는 것을 알고 있었으므로, 매우 높은 가격을 책정했다. 독일의 갑옷은 세계에서 최고였고, 만약 손님들이 그 가격이 맘에 들지 않는다면, 그 손님은 다음 전쟁에서 막대기와 돌을 들고 앞으로 돌격 할 수밖에 없었다. 이렇듯 막대한 이익을 낸 독일의 갑옷 제조업자들은 광범위한 연구와 개발 노력을 할 수 있었다. 그것은 결과적으로 더 강력한 갑옷, 예를 들어 머리 전체를 덮으면서 움직이는 면갑이 있는 강철 투구를 만들어 냈다.

이종현T의 독해 Point!

독일 지역의 갑옷 기술에 대한 얘기이고 독일 지역에서 갑옷 산업이 발달했다가 핵심이 된다. 따라서 이게 들어간 선지를 찾으면 정답은 ④번이 된다.

28.① 흥정하기가 싫지요? 당신 혼자만 그런 것은 아니다. 전국적인 통계 조사에 따르면 과거 3년 동안 모든 재화와 용역에 대해 단지 48%의 쇼핑객들만이 더 나은 거래를 하기 위해 흥정을 시도했고, 그 수치는 2007년의 61%에서 감소된 것이다. 하지만 겁쟁이라면, 당신이 흥정에서 진 것이다. 흥정을 한 사람들 중 적어도 89%는 한번은 보상을 받았다. 성공적인 가구 흥정가들은 평균 300달러를 아꼈으며 의료비에 의문을 제기한 사람들도 마찬가지였다. 휴대폰 요금에 흥정을 시도했던 사람들은 80달러를 절약했다. 분명히 말하자면, 값을 흥정하지 않는 사람들은 테이블 위에 돈을 버리고 있는 것이다.

이종현T의 독해 Point!

흥정하지 않는 것이 문제, 흥정을 해야 좋은 결과를 낼 수 있다는게 해결책으로 제시된 글이다. 따라서 이게 들어간 선지를 찾으면 정답은 ①번이 된다.

29.① 혐오의 감정적 반응은 종종 어린 아이들이 특정 채소를 먹는 것을 완강히 거부하는 것과 관련이 있다. 아이들에게 영양가 있는 음식을 제공하기로 결심한 부모들에게는 그러한 혐오감이 불합리해 보일 수 있지만, 위생적인 행동에 관심이 있는 과학자들은 합리적인 설명을 한다. 이 이론은 사람들이 낯설고 어쩌면 해로운 물건에 대한 보호 메커니즘으로 혐오감을 발전시켰다고 주장한다. 최근의 한 연구는 혐오감이 위험한 물질의 섭취를 막을 뿐만 아니라 사람들이 잠재적으로 전염될 수 있는 상황에 들어가는 것을 단념시킨다는 것을 보여준다. 예를 들어, 이 연구의 대상들은 만원 철도 차량이 빈 열차보다 더 역겹고 말벌보다 머릿니가 더 역겹다고 선언했다.

이종현T의 독해 Point!

지문의 중간에 들어가는 scientists부터 집단이 바뀌게 되고, 이 집단이 바뀌게 된 부분부터 핵심이 등장한 거로 본다면 이 뒷 얘기의 핵심은 혐오감으로(원인) 나쁜 것을 막아준다(결과)가 된다고 할 수 있다. 따라서 이게 들어간 선지를 정답으로 찍으면 정답은 ①번이 된다.

30.② 과학자로서의 성공은 단순히 우리가 머리 속에 가지고 있는 아이디어의 질이나 손에 쥐고 있는 데이터의 함수일 뿐만 아니라, 그것을 묘사하기 위해 사용하는 언어의 함수이기도 합니다. 우리 모두는 "출판하느냐 망하느냐"가 현실이고 우리의 직업

적인 삶을 지배한다는 것을 이해한다. 그러나 "출판하느냐 망하느냐"는 성공이 아니라 생존에 관한 것이다. 논문을 발표한다고 해서 과학자로서 성공할 수는 없다. 그들을 인용함으로써 과학자로서 성공한다. 일이 중요한 것은 중요하다. 성공은 인쇄에 있는 페이지 수가 아니라 그 영향력에 의해 정의됩니다. 당신은 동료들이 당신의 일을 이해하고 그것을 그들 자신의 일에 동기를 부여하는 데 사용할 때 성공한다.

이종현T의 독해 Point!

첫 번째 문장에서 과학자로서의 성공에 대한 얘기가 나오고, 중간 부분에 과학자로서 성공하는 방법에 대한 얘기가 나온다. 즉 성공은 영향력으로 정의가 된다는 것이 핵심이고, 과학자로서의 성공은 영향력이 결정해준다는 얘기를 찾으면 정답은 ②번이 된다.

31.⑤ 여러분은 건강한 습관의 장수 이점을 얻기 위해 채식주의자가 되거나, 운동 예찬에 충성을 맹세하거나, 전업 명상가가 될 필요가 없습니다. 최근의 과학은 정반대의 사실을 보여주고 있는데, 사실 건강한 수명을 연장하는 것은 특별히 어렵지 않은 몇 가지 작은 변화만으로도 우리 중 많은 사람들에게 달성 가능하고 여러분을 비참하게 하지 않을 것이라는 것이다. 연구원들은 예를 들어, 체육관에 가는 시간이 장기간 앉아 있는 부정적인 영향을 대응할 수는 없지만 몸을 조금씩 움직이는 단순한 동작만으로도 가능하다는 것을 알아냈다. 그들은 또한 여러분이 먹는 양을 줄이는 것이 고통스러울 필요는 없으며, 그것이 더 오래 살 수 있는 기회를 향상시킬 수 있다는 것을 발견했다.

이종현T의 독해 Point!

중간에 있는 The latest science is showing quite the opposite부터 핵심이 나온다고 볼 수 있고, 다음 문장에 어렵지 않게 수명을 연장할 수 있다를 핵심으로 볼 수 있다. 따라서 이게 들어간 선지를 찍어주면 정답은 ⑤번이 된다.

32.③ 과체중일 때 건강관리를 시작하면 추가로 비용이 든다. 2013년 Duke의 연구에서, 연구원들은 체질량 지수(BMI) 수치에 따라 드는 건강관리 비용을 조사했다. 저체중인 체질량 지수(BMI)가 19인 사람의 평균 연간 비용은 2,541달러였다. 과체중이라고 생각되는 체질량 지수(BMI)가 25인 사람은 2,893달러였다. 비만이라 여겨지는 체질량 지수(BMI)가 33인 사람은 3,439달러로 비용이 가장 높았다. "정상 체중의 하단부에서부터 병의 위험도는 이미 증가하기 시작한다."고 대표 연구원인 Truls Ostbye는 말한다. 추가 비용은 진료실에서만 끝나지 않는다. 2010 McKinsey 연구는 비만인 미국인들이 추가로 옷을 사는데 들어가는 비용이 총 300억 달러에 이를 것으로 추산했다. 또한 비만인 40세 남성이 생명 보험에 내는 비용이 두 배에 이를 것으로 추산했다.

이종현T의 독해 Point!

첫 번째 문장부터 과체중일 때의 문제점에 관한 이야기이고 문제점에 관한 얘기로 끝나고 있으므로 이게 들어간 선지를 찾아주면 정답은 ③번이 된다.

33.③ 자동차 사다리를 오르는 일은 힘들며, 정상을 유지하기란 더욱 힘들었다. 매년 오래된 관행에 따라 Chevrolet는 전체를 새롭게 디자인하고, 보통 더 큰 모델을 출시했다. 어제 최신식이었던 자동차는 내일은 작고 쑥스럽고 구식처럼 보였다. 상상하는 것처럼, 이 모든 것이 미국 사회 전반에 걸쳐 불안감을 야기했다. 그런데 1959년에 외견상으로 어디선지 모르게, 단순한 전면 신문 광고가 "작게 생각하라."는 헤드라인과 아무런 장식이 없는 Volkswagen사의 Beetle 자동차 이미지와 함께 실리기 시작했다. 그 광고는 자동차가 크지 않고 효율적이라는 것을 제외하고는 그 이상 말하지 않았고, 심지어 Beetle 자동차를 고물덩어리라는 당시 속어인 'filiwer(싸구려 소형 자동차)'라 불렀다. 사람들은 그 광고가 깜짝 놀랄 만큼 솔직하고 재미있으며, 마케팅 담당자들이 수년 동안 그들 마음속에 품어왔던 남모르는 불안감을 공개적으로 표출했다고 생각했다. 내가 사다리 꼭대기에 올라가야만 하는가? 누가 상관하겠는가?

이종현T의 독해 Point!

중간에 Then in 1959부터 시점이 바뀌고 여기부터 핵심을 잡겠다고 생각하면, 이 때 생겼던 광고에 대한 얘기가 핵심이고, 크게 보지 않고 작게 봤다는 것이 핵심이다. 따라서 이게 들어간 선지를 찍어주면 정답은 ③번이 된다.

34.⑤ 비록 우리가 그들의 문화를 공유하지는 않지만, 바흐와 베토벤의 동시대 사람들에게 흥미로웠던 음악은 여전히 흥미롭다. 비록 비틀즈가 불행히도 해체되었지만 초기 비틀즈의 노래들은 여전히 흥미진진하다. 마찬가지로, 수백 년 전에 작곡되었을 벤다 노래들도 여전히 나를 흥분시킨다. 우리 중 많은 사람들은 일본의 코토 음악, 인도의 시타르 음악, 초피 실로폰 음악 등에 열광한다. 나는 우리가 연주자들과 정확히 같은 방식으로 음악을 받는다고

말하지는 않지만, 우리 자신의 경험은 문화 간 의사소통의 가능성이 있다는 것을 암시한다. 저는 이것에 대한 설명이 음악 속 깊은 구조의 수준에는 인간의 정신에 공통적인 요소들이 있다는 사실에서 발견될 것이라고 확신합니다. 비록 그것들이 표면 구조에서는 나타나지 않을지라도요.

이종현T의 독해 Point!

중간에 similarly부터 핵심이 나온다고 볼 수 있고, 수백 년 전의 음악이 나를 흥분시킨다는 것이 핵심이므로 과거의 음악에 열광한다는 얘기가 될 수 있는 선지를 찾으면 정답은 ⑤번이 된다.

35.③ 우리는 종종 사람들을 고무시키고 놀라운 성공에 대한 이야기를 봅니다. 우리들 중 일부는 벽에 그들의 사진을 붙이거나 그것들로부터 주목할 만한 인용구를 오려냅니다. 하지만 영감을 주는 사람이 우리가 결코 할 수 없거나 결코 할 수 없는 일을 했다면 우리에게 어떤 도움이 될까요? 우리들 중 많은 사람들에게 역할 모델의 선택은 비교를 유도하고, 우리의 능력과 결과가 측정되지 않는다면, 역할 모델은 영감이 아니라 좌절과 패배의 원천으로 작용한다. 여러분이 성취할 수 있는 것과 성취하고 싶은 것을 성취한 사람을 여러분의 역할 모델로 고르세요. 유명한 운동선수, 지도자, 역사적인 인물보다는 존경하는 동료나 가족을 사용하는 것이 큰 가치를 지닌다. 그들은 큰 성공을 경험했지만 당신의 경험과 공통점이 적은 사람들이다.

이종현T의 독해 Point!

중간에 But ~부터 문제점이 시작이 되고, 그 밑에 Choose ~ 로 시작하는 문장부터 해결책이 나온다고 할 수 있다. 성취할 수 있는 것을 성취한 사람을 롤모델로 삼으라는 것이 해결책이 되므로 이게 들어간 선지를 찾으면 정답은 ③번이 된다.

36.③ 최근에 나는 브리티시 콜롬비아 해안에서 멸종 위기에 처한 회색 곰에 대해 읽고 있었다. 저자들은 아기들이 어떻게 먹이를 찾고 소비하는 어미의 기술을 예리하게 관찰하는지 강조했다. 어미들의 모형제작에 의해 아기들이 배운 것은 삶과 죽음의 문제였다; 그런 지식이 없었다면 아기들은 아마 살아남지 못했을 것이다. 우리에게도 같은 원칙이 적용된다. 우리가 쥐꼬리만한 삶을 살 때, 어떻게 우리의 아이들은 그렇지 않을 것이라고 믿을 수 있을까? 우리가 무의식적으로 습득하고 소비할 때, 우리의 아이들이 어떤 식으로든 그들의 사물과의 관계에서 절제하고 의미를 알게 될 것이라고요? 만약 제가 카운터에서 받은 여분의 거스름돈을 돌려주지 않거나, 주인을 찾으려고 노력하지 않고 돈을 챙기는 것과 같은 사소한 것들을 정기적으로 속인다면, 나는 아이들에게 그런 행동을 가르치고 있습니다.

이종현T의 독해 Point!

중간에 The same principle applies to us.부터 우리에 관한 공통비교 얘기가 시작되고, 그 뒷 부분 내용을 보면 우리가 하는 행동을 아이들이 배운다는 얘기가 된다. 따라서 우리의 행동을 아이들이 배운다는 내용이 들어간 선지로 찍어주면 정답은 ③번이 된다.

37.⑤ 최초의 로빈 후드 연가는 1450년에 인쇄되었으며, 대중문화에서 알고 있던 멋진 영웅으로 묘사되지는 않았다. 그는 자작농이었으며 때로는 거칠고 잔인했다. 그 전설은 부자들로부터 훔친 돈을 지키고 가끔 가난한 사람들을 도왔던 강도에 더 바탕을 두고 있다. 그는 숲속에서 이상 사회를 건설하기를 원치 않았다. 로빈 후드와 그의 부하들은 주로 사회적 불평등을 바로잡고 잘 살기위해 노력했다. 로빈 후드는 17세기까지 매우 유명해져서 사람들은 그의 이름을 따서 배나 장소에 붙였다. 19세기까지 많은 이야기와 노래가 로빈 후드 전설에 주요한 변화를 가져왔다. 그의 자작농 태생은 사라졌고, 그는 점차 가난한 사람들의 권리를 대변하는 Sherwood 숲의 영웅적 범법자가 되었다.

이종현T의 독해 Point!

earliest부터 과거부터 현재까지의 흐름을 생각해볼 수 있고 계속 시간에 따른 변화를 나타내주고 있다. 따라서 로빈 후드의 변화로 써있는 ⑤번이 정답이 된다.

38.② 한 연구에서 100명의 남녀는 누군가와 상호작용할 때마다 혈압을 측정하는 장치를 착용했다. 그들이 가족이나 즐거운 친구들과 함께 있을 때, 그들의 혈압은 떨어졌다; 이러한 상호작용은 즐겁고 위로가 되었다. 그들이 골치 아픈 사람과 함께 있을 때, 혈압 상승이 있었다. 그러나 가장 큰 증가는 그들이 반대 감정을 느끼는 사람들, 즉 고압적인 부모, 변덕스러운 연인, 또는 경쟁적인 친구와 함께 있는 동안 일어났다. 변덕스러운 상사가 전형적이라고 볼 수 있지만, 이 역학은 우리의 모든 관계에서 작용한다.

이종현T의 독해 Point!

두 번째로 나오는 when절인 when they were with someone who was troublesome,부터 문제상황 또는

새로운 상황이 나온다고 볼 수 있고, 이 때 결과가 핵심이 된다. 따라서 이게 들어간 선지를 찾으면 정답은 ②번이 된다.

39.⑤ 관찰 연구는 엄마들이 아이들 주변에서 하는 일들 중 일부에 대한 정보를 제공하지만, 아이들, 보육, 그리고 그들 자신에 대한 그들의 감정, 생각, 신념에 대해서는 거의 제공하지 않는다. 어머니들은 형식심리학의 견해와 반드시 일치하지 않는 자녀와 양육에 대한 다양한 견해를 가지고 있으며, 이러한 견해는 자녀들이 자녀들과 어떻게 상호작용하는지에 영향을 미칠 수 있다. 어떤 엄마들은 자녀들에게 민감하게 반응하는 것이 쉽게 다가오지 않는다는 것을 알게 된다. 이것은 그들이 자녀들과 쉽게 관련될 수 없거나, 우울하거나 고립되어 있거나, 또는 감수성이 자녀들과의 관계의 중요한 부분이라고 믿지 않기 때문일 수 있다. 어떤 엄마들은 그들의 행동과 감정과 심리 이론에 의해 규정된 것 사이에 불일치가 있을 수 있고; 그리고 그들 자신의 욕구와 그들의 아이들의 욕구 사이에 충돌이 있을 수 있다.

이종현T의 독해 Point!

2번째 줄제 Mothers ~ 부분의 문장을 보면 엄마들의 양육에 대한 의견과 심리학과 맞지 않는다는 것을 알 수 있고, 두 입장이 비교/대조가 되는 글이다. 따라서 두 집단의 의견차가 있다는 얘기를 찾아주면 정답은 ⑤번이 된다.

40.③ 알렉산더 대왕은 기원전 332년에 이집트의 그리스-로마 시대를 시작했다. 서남아시아의 일부 지역을 정복한 후, 마케도니아 장군은 이집트에서 수백 년간의 소요와 외부인들에 의한 점령 후에 정치적으로 지친 사람들에 의해 환영을 받았다. 여전히 풍요로운 이집트의 문화와 그리스의 (그리고 후에 로마의) 영향력의 결합은, 지중해 주변에 일게 된 사회적이고 종교적인 변화를 가져왔다. 이러한 활기를 띤 새로운 시기에, 그리스와 로마의 신화에서 이집트의 신과 반신반인이 그들과 대응하던 것들과 섞인 반면에, 이집트인들의 의복과 조각품의 방식은 서서히 그리스와 로마까지 나아갔다. 많은 그리스-로마 신들과 영웅들이 이집트 전역의 신전에서 기림을 받는 동안, 지모신 이시스는 결국 시저스의 땅에 신전을 지었을 것이다.

이종현T의 독해 Point!

2, 3번째 줄을 보면 이집트의 문화와 그리스의 문화가 결합했다는 얘기가 나온다는 것을 알 수 있고, 그 얘기가 계속 이어지는 글임을 알 수 있다. 따라서 이게 들어간 선지를 찾아주면 정답은 ③번이 된다.

41.④ 실수는 여러분이 바꾸려고 노력했던 오래된 행동을 시작하는 하나의 사건입니다. 과실을 극복하는 열쇠는 교통 체증과 도로 건설이 고속도로에서 여러분을 지연시킬 수 있는 것처럼 때때로 그것들을 예상하는 것이다. 지난번에 장거리 여행에 나섰을 때를 생각해 보세요. 여러분은 도중에 속도를 늦추는 무엇인가를 만났을 가능성이 있지만, 포기하지 않고, 차를 돌려 집으로 향했다. 예상보다 시간이 조금 더 걸릴 수도 있지만, 여전히 목적지에 도착했습니다. 개인적인 변화도 마찬가지입니다. 여러분이 과일이나 채소를 더 넣으면서 음식의 균형을 맞추고 있었지만, 갑자기 패스트푸드 햄버거를 먹고 싶은 충동에 굴복했다고 가정해 봅시다. 당신은 방금 실수를 했어요.

이종현T의 독해 Point!

두 번째 문장부터 실수를 극복하는 열쇠인 해결책이 나오고, 이 해결책으로 나온 것이 '지체될 수 있다는걸 아는 것이다'라고 나와 있다. 즉 실수를 하고 그래서 조금 늦을 수도 있다 가 핵심이고, 목적지로 가는 과정에서 실수는 할 수 있다는 얘기가 될 수 있는 선지로 찾아주면 정답은 ④번이 된다.

42.① 당신은 Cross-Continent Enterprise(CCE)의 과정을 따르고 공급자 선정에 맞추어 내부 통제구조를 고수해야 한다. 공급자 선정은 절대 선물이나 접대 혹은 보답을 받는 것에 근거를 두 면 안 된다. 공급자 선정이 제품이나 서비스의 공급을 위한 공식적이고 구조화된 제안(종종 '입찰'이라곤 불리는)일 때, 우리가 내부통제를 뒷받침하는 문서를 지키는 것이 가장 중요하다. 공공 부문에서, 공금의 사용을 위한 경쟁이 공개적이고 공정하며 부패로부터 자유롭다는 것을 보장하기 위해서 그러한 입찰 과정은 법률적으로 상세하게 요구되고 결정될 것이다. 관련 계약을 위한 경쟁은 입찰에 맞춰 처리되어야 한다는 조건하에 입찰 과정에는 안건을 제출하는 다른 관계자들을 모집 하는 것이 포함되며, 어떤 관계자도 계약을 두고 따로 사전에 비공개로 진행된 협상에 대한 부당한 혜택을 갖지 않으며, 입찰 과정은 자격이 있는 모든 입찰자에게 공개되고 봉인입찰은 정밀조사를 위하여 공개되며 가격과 품질을 기준으로 하여 선택된다.

이종현T의 독해 Point!

첫 번째 문장에서 CCE와 system of internal controls around suuplier selection을 따르는게 핵심이라고 잡을

수 있고, 뒤에 반대말 없이 계속 그 얘기가 이어지므로 이게 들어간 선지를 찍으면 정답은 ①번이 된다.

43.① 빛이 지구의 대기에 부딪힐 때, 다른 색깔이 다양한 방식으로 반응을 보인다. 일부 색깔은 기체 분자들에 의해서 흡수되는 반면에, 그렇지 않은 것도 있다. 단파장의 색깔(보라색과 파란색처럼)은 기체 분자에 의해 흡수되는 반면에, 대부분의 장파장 색깔(빨간색이나 오렌지색처럼)은 대기권을 곧장 통과하여 영향을 받지 않는다. 왜냐하면 이러한 (단파장) 색깔들의 파장 (즉, 각 파동의 골 사이의 거리)의 크기가 산소 원자의 지름과 비슷하기 때문이다. 기체 분자가 이러한 색깔들을 발산시키고 하늘에 흩뿌려서 하늘이 파랗게 보인다.

이종현T의 독해 Point!

첫 문장에서 빛에 따라(원인) 색깔 반응이 달라진다(결과)를 잡을 수 있다. 그리고 그 light에 대한 얘기가 뒷부분에 because절에 wavelength로 표현되어 있다. 따라서 wavelength에 따라(원인) 색깔 반응이 달라진다(결과) 라고 할 수 있으므로 이게 들어간 선지를 찍어주면 정답은 ①번이 된다.

44.③ 낙관주의가 여러분을 살아있게 하거나 적어도 암을 예방할 수 있다는 믿음은 1979년 랜싯 의학 저널에 유방암 환자의 회복에 대한 연구가 발표된 후 설득력을 얻었다. 그 이후로, "투지 정신"을 가진 환자들이 절망감을 느끼는 환자들보다 더 낫다는 것이 가정적인 생각이 되었다. 그러나 최근 몇몇 대규모 메타 분석에서는 낙관론이 암환자들의 생명을 연장시킨다는 설득력 있는 증거가 부족하다는 것을 발견했다. 명확한 자료가 부족함에도 불구하고, 긍정적인 사고의 힘에 대한 믿음이 너무 널리 퍼져서 실제로 해를 끼칠 수도 있다. 암 환자들은 정신이 혼미할 때에도 낙관적으로 행동하거나, 위안이나 치료를 찾는 대신 절망을 감추거나, 병이 진행되면 스스로를 탓할 수 있다.

이종현T의 독해 Point!

지문의 중간에 However,부터 앞선 연구에 관한 반박하는 연구 얘기가 나오고, 그 얘기는 낙관론이 별로 도움이 되지 않는다는 얘기이다. 따라서 이게 들어간 선지를 찾아주면 정답은 ③번이 된다.

45.① 사모스 섬에게 해의 아리스타르코스는 처음에 지구와 다른 행성들이 태양 주위를 움직였다고 제안했는데, 이것은 코페르니쿠스가 2,000년 후에 다시 제안하기 전까지 천문학자들에 의해 거부된 생각이었다. 코페르니쿠스 이후, 덴마크 천문학자 Tychö Brahe는 발트해 섬 Hveen에 있는 그의 천문대에서 화성의 움직임을 관찰했다; 그 결과 요하네스 케플러는 화성과 지구 그리고 다른 행성들이 태양 주위를 타원형으로 움직이는 것을 보여줄 수 있었다. 그 후 아이작 뉴턴은 그의 만유인력의 법칙과 운동의 법칙을 제안했고, 이것들로부터 태양계 전체에 대한 정확한 설명을 도출할 수 있었다. 이것은 그 후 몇 세기 동안 몇몇 위대한 과학자들과 수학자들의 마음을 사로잡았다.

이종현T의 독해 Point!

인물들이 계속 바뀌고 있으므로 이럴 땐 마지막 인물에 집중하는 것이 좋다. 마지막에 뉴턴이 나오고 뉴턴이 태양을 이해하려고 했으므로 이게 들어간 선지를 찾으면 정답은 ①번이 된다.

46.① 교환을 기초로 하는 상업 사회에서 모든 사람은 '어느 정도 상인이 된다.' 노동 분업과 다른 사람들에게 결과를 초래하는 의존성과 함께, 시장에서 사리사욕을 추구하는 것은 사람의 행동을 다른 사람들의 기대에 맞추게 이끈다. 그러므로 시장 그 자체는 훈육하는 기관이다. Adam Smith가 아래와 같이 쓰길, "노동자에게 행사되는 실질적이고 효과적인 훈육은 그의 기업에 대한 훈육이 아니라, 그의 고객에 대한 훈육이다. 그것은 속임수를 억제하고 그의 부주의를 바로잡는 실직에 대한 두려움이다." 다른 사람들과의 경제적 교환에 성공하기 위해서 개인은 Smith가 "예의"이라고 부르는 적정 수준의 자제를 발전시키게 된다. 시장이 장려하는 특징은 사리분별과 장기적 이익을 위해 단기의 만족감을 뒤로 미루는 능력을 포함한다.

이종현T의 독해 Point!

첫 문장에서 상업 사회라는 상황이 소재임을 알 수 있고, 모든 사람이 상인이 된다는 말이 다음문장에서 어떻게 쓰여있는지를 찾으면 된다. 다다음 문장에 결과로 시장은 훈육하는 기관이라고 되어 있으므로 상업 사회에선 시장에 교육을 받는다는 얘기가 된다. 따라서 이게 들어간 선지를 찾으면 정답은 ①번이 된다.

47.② 열에서부터 홍역, 간질까지 다양한 질병을 치료하는 것으로 알려진 코뿔소 뿔은 수천 년 동안 한약의 중요한 성분으로 여겨져 왔다. 뿔을 찾고 있던 흰 코뿔소의 개체 수는 1910년까지 남아프리카에서 100마리로 떨어졌다. 오늘날, 1977년에 코뿔소 부품 판매를 금지했음에도 불구하고, 아프리카의 코뿔소들은 다시

한 번 멸종 위기에 직면해 있습니다. 이 금지가 코뿔소들을 불법 밀렵으로부터 보호할 수 없었기 때문에, 아이러니하게도, 코뿔소 뿔에 대한 고도로 규제된 거래를 합법화하는 것은 결국 코뿔소들을 구할 수 있다. 코뿔소의 뿔은 동물들을 다치게 하지 않고 자르거나 깎을 수 있고, 다시 자랍니다. 만약 중앙집권화된 단일 조직에 의해 엄격히 통제된다면, 압수된 암시장 뿔과 자연사한 코뿔소에서 채취한 뿔과 함께 법적 뿔을 잘라 현재의 수요를 충족시킬 수 있다.

이종현T의 독해 Point!

이 글에서의 핵심은 중간에 Today부터 시작해서 오히려 코뿔소 뿔의 거래를 합법화하는 것이 코뿔소를 지킬 수 있다는 얘기가 나온다. 따라서 이게 들어간 선지를 찾으면 정답은 ②번이 된다.

48.④ 갑부들은 그들의 재산을 모은 후 자선 활동으로 시선을 돌릴 때 종종 가난한 학생들을 위해 장학금을 대고, 의료 서비스를 향상시키는 데 애를 쓰고, 또는 예술에 기여한다. Chang Yung-Fa의 임무는 다름 아닌 바로 사회적 가치를 '재조직'하는 것이다. 5년 전 그는 만화 잡지 〈Morals〉를 시작했는데, 이것은 매월 발간되어 타이완과 전 세계에서 사람들의 도덕성 향상을 추구한다. 그가 돈을 벌든지 잃든지 간에, 도덕성은 85세의 Chang이 행하는 많은 것을 뒷받침한다. 그는 그의 Evergreen Group – 세계에서 4번째로 큰 운송 회사, 호텔, EVA 항공과 섬의 주요 공항으로 가는 장거리 버스를 포함하는 – 이 회사의 도덕적 문화를 배경으로 하는 마음이 통하는 직원 관계 때문에 더욱 번창한다고 믿는다.

이종현T의 독해 Point!

첫 문장에 나온 상황부터 갑부들이 자선활동을 활용하는 상황에 대한 얘기이고, 이 얘기가 쭉 이어지는 글이다. 따라서 갑부들은 도덕적으로 좋은 활동을 활용한다는 얘기로 끝나는 글이고, 이게 들어간 선지를 찍어주면 정답은 ④번이 된다.

49.② 아마도 달 (탐사) 프로그램을 다시 일으키는 것에 가장 흥분한 과학자들은 달 전문가가 아니라, 넓은 범위의 대상을 연구하는 천문학자들일 것이다. 그런 과학자들은 달의 건너편에 지름 30미터의 거대한 망원경을 설치하는 새로운 임무를 좋아할 것이다. 망원경이 최적의 작동을 하기 위해 필요한 두 가지는 극심한 추위와 아주 적은 진동이다. 달의 온도는 어두운 쪽에 있는 분화구에서 섭씨 영하 200도 정도만큼 몹시 추울 수 있다. 달에는 진동 활동이 없기 때문에 달은 안정된 기반이다. (달의) 영구적인 어둠은 망원경을 지속적으로 사용할 수 있다는 것을 의미한다. 지지자들은 이러한 상태에서 달에 설치된 망원경은 Hubble 망원경이 10년 동안 성취해 낸 것을 대체로 17일 정도에 많은 것을 성취할 수 있다고 주장한다.

이종현T의 독해 Point!

마지막 문장에 Proponents claim that 절이 이 글의 주제문이라 할 수 있고, 달에 설치된 망원경이 많은 것을 관찰할 수 있다는 얘기가 핵심이 된다. 따라서 이게 들어간 선지를 찾으면 정답은 ②번이 된다.

50.④ 자유를 옹호하는 일부 사람들이 중요하게 생각하지 않는 배려라는 것이 있다. 어른들의 간섭 없이 남겨진 아이들의 공동체에는 대부분의 어른들의 폭정보다 훨씬 더 잔인한 강자들의 폭정이 있다. 만약 두세 살짜리 두 아이가 함께 놀도록 내버려 둔다면, 그들은 몇 번의 싸움 후에 누가 반드시 승리할 것인지 알게 될 것이고, 다른 아이는 노예가 될 것이다. 아이들의 수가 더 많은 곳에서, 한 두 명은 완전한 지배력을 얻고, 다른 사람들은 어른들이 약하고 덜 반항적인 사람들을 보호하기 위해 간섭했을 때보다 훨씬 더 적은 자유를 가진다. 대부분의 아이들과 함께 타인에 대한 배려는 자발적으로 일어나지 않고, 가르쳐야 하며, 권위의 행사 외에는 거의 가르칠 수 없다. 이것은 아마도 어른들의 퇴위에 반대하는 가장 중요한 논쟁일 것이다.

이종현T의 독해 Point!

자유를 옹호하는 사람들이 중요하지 않게 생각하는 문제점에 대한 얘기가 첫 번째 문장에서 시작된다. 다음 문장에서 나오는 문제점은 어른들의 간섭이 없을 때 아이들에게 생기는 문제점에 대한 얘기라고 볼 수 있고, 중간 부분에 비교급으로 어른들이 간섭하지 않았을 때 간섭했을 때보다 더 적은 자유를 가진다 라고 되어 있으므로 이 글에서 필자가 말하는 해결책은 어른들이 간섭해야한다는 것임을 알 수 있다. 따라서 이게 들어간 선지를 찍으면 정답은 ④번이 된다.

51.④ 질병을 유발하는 간접흡연의 장소는 수년 동안 연구되어 왔다. 서부 주에 있는 한 중간 규모의 도시가 예기치 않게 데이터에 추가되었다. 공공장소와 직장에서의 흡연이 금지되었고 6개월 후에 금지령이 해제되었다. 공공장소에서 흡연이 금지되었던 기간 동안, 심장마비의 병원 입원율은 24였다. 전형적으로

6개월 동안, 그 비율은 40명이다. 연구원들은 그 방울이 간접흡연의 부정적인 효과의 증거라고 믿었다. 간접흡연은 심장박동수를 높이고 혈관의 확장 능력을 감소시킴으로써 심장마비에 기여한다.

이종현T의 독해 Point!

첫 문장에서 연구가 나오고 그 연구 결과를 찾으면 된다. 마지막 문장에 나오는 연구 결과는 간접흡연(second smoke)가 원인 → 심장병 문제가 결과이므로 이게 들어간 선지를 찾으면 정답은 ④번이 된다.

52.④ 만약 쓰레기 위기 문제가 존재한다면, 그것은 바로 우리가 쓰레기를 있는 그대로, 즉 확실히 복잡하긴 하지만 처리 가능한 도시의 문제로 다루는 것이 아니라, 환경적인 위협으로 간주하고 있다는 것이다. 비록 많은 오래된 도시의 쓰레기 매립지가 수용 용량에 근접하고 있지만, 안전한 쓰레기 매립을 위한 공간은 이 나라 안에 얼마든지 있고, 또 앞으로도 항상 존재할 것이라는 것이 현실이다. 그러나 우리는 지금까지 쓰레기를 관리 차원의 문제로 보지 않고 도덕적 위기 문제로 보아 왔다. 그 결과 (쓰레기) 재활용은 비용 편익 분석의 조사와는 거리가 먼, 비난할 수 없는 미덕으로 여겨지고 있다. 하지만 현실의 세계에서, 지방자치단체들이 재활용에 지출하는 돈은 학교와 도서관, 병원, 경찰에는 지출될 수 없다. 현실 세계에서, 많은 도시와 마을들이 도입한 대규모 재활용 프로그램 같은 것들은 부족한 정부 자금을 가장 효율적으로 사용하는 방법이 아닐지도 모른다.

이종현T의 독해 Point!

중간에 ~~~, however, ~~~가 들어간 문장부터 문제점이 시작된다. 즉, 도덕적 문제로만 봤다는 것이 문제라는 것이다. 그리고 다음 문장에서 문제점으로 제시되는 것이 비용, 편익 등을 분석하지 않는다는 것이다. 따라서 이 비용, 편익을 고려하지 않는다는 문제점에 대한 얘기가 들어간 선지로 찾으면 정답은 ④번이 된다.

53.③ 지구에 도달하는 햇빛의 양은 1950년대 초기에서 1990년대 초기 사이에 10퍼센트 감소했다. 과학자들은 태양의 문제가 아니라는 사실을 알아냈다. 그 어떤 기구로도 태양 광선이 어두워졌음을 기록하지는 못했다. 문제는 태양과 지구의 사이에 있는 것 같다. 환경오염이 방해가 되고 있는 것이다. 미립자로 된 오염 물질은 햇빛을 우주 밖으로 반사시킨다. 환경오염은 또한 공기의 응축 증가를 유발한다. 이 응축은 더 두껍고, 더 어두운 구름을 형성한다. 과학자들은 그들의 이론을 증명하기 위해 오염이 아주 없거나 적은 지역을 지목한다. 그러한 장소에서 (관측) 기구는 햇빛이 여느 때와 같이 밝다는 것을 보여 준다.

이종현T의 독해 Point!

중간에 The problem appears to ~부터 환경 오염이 문제다 라는 얘기가 시작된다. 그리고 환경 오염 물질이 햇빛을 우주 밖으로 반사시키는 것이 문제가 된다. 따라서 이게 들어간 선지를 찾으면 정답은 ③번이 된다.

54.④ Walter Benjamin은 무엇인가 이야깃거리를 가지고 방랑으로 부터 돌아온 여행가뿐만 아니라 고향에 근간을 둔 채 전통을 지키는 사람들도 전통적인 구비문학(이야기)과 동일하다고 여긴다. 중세 시대에는 지역에 거주하는 장인과 여행 중인 기술자들이 같이 작업장에 모이게 되는 수공업의 구조로 인하여, 두 종류의 구비문학은 서로 밀접한 연관성을 갖게 되었다. 하지만 '역사의 세속적이고 생산적인 강요'에 의한 작업을 통해, 이야기란 살아 있는 대화의 범주에서 배제되어 갔다. 구비문학과 대척점에 있으며, 그것을 완전하게 대체하고 있는 과정 중에 있는 것은 바로 소설로, 소설은 인쇄 기술의 발명과 책의 개념과 밀접하게 연관되어 있다. 소설가는 필연적으로 고립되고 눈에 보이지 않으며, 동료와의 대화에는 끼어들 수 없는 숨어 있는 신과 같은 존재이며, 따라서 훌륭한 조언이 되는 지혜도 전달할 수 없다.

이종현T의 독해 Point!

이 글은 구전 문학(storytelling)과 novel이 비교대조 되고 있는 글이고, storytelling이 소설로 대체되고 있다는 것이 이 글의 주제가 된다. 따라서 이게 들어간 선지를 찍어주면 정답은 ④번이 된다.

55.③ 현대 심리학은 '대학 2학년 학생들의 행동에 관한 과학'이라고 불린다. 1960년대에서 1970년대 사이에, 몇몇 심리학자들은 4개의 학술지를 분석하여 58%에서 96%에 달하는 논문이 대학생들에 대한 연구를 근거로 했다는 것을 알아냈다. 더욱 최근인 1991년에, 나는 그 학술지 중 2곳에 수록된 논문 들을 분석해 77%는 대학생들을 대상으로 수행된 연구를 발표한 것이라는 사실을 알아냈다. 미시간 대학의 심리학자이자 연구 대상이 되었던 학술지 중 한 곳의 편집자이기도 한 Melvin Manis는 편리함은 다른 분야에서 연구 대상을 선택할 때도 영향을 준다고 말했다. 그는, "코끼리에 대해 이루어지는 유전자 연구는 거의 없어요. 초파리의 수명이 더 짧을 뿐만 아니라 훨씬 더 저렴하기 때문에

대부분은 초파리에 대해 연구가 이루어집니다."라고 말했다. 그것은 코끼리와 초파리가 비슷한 유전적 체계를 지니고 있다면 문제가 없다. 하지만 대학생들이 대학생이 아닌 동료들이 하는 것처럼 생각하고 행동하며 느낄 수 있을까? 또는 그런 문제에 대해서 성인이 하는 것처럼 할 수 있을까? 이 두 가지 질문에 대한 정답은 "아니다" 이다.

이종현T의 독해 Point!

끝 부분에 But부터 college students들에 관한 결과가 나오고, college students들은 다르다, 즉 college students들에 관한 결과는 앞 부분의 결과와 다르다는 얘기가 핵심이 된다. 따라서 이게 들어간 선지를 찾아주면 정답은 ③번이 된다.

56.② 사냥꾼들은 자연의 일부인 들판과 숲에서 일생을 보내는 독특한 의미에서 철학자나 시인보다 추격하는 동안 그녀를 관찰하는 데 더 호의적인 기분을 느끼는 경우가 많습니다. 심지어 기대감을 가지고 접근하는 철학자나 시인보다 더 많습니다. 그녀는 그들에게 자신을 드러내는 것을 두려워하지 않습니다. 초원의 여행자는 자연스럽게 사냥꾼입니다. 여행자일 뿐인 그는 중고로, 반쪽씩만 배우고 권위가 떨어집니다. 과학이 그 남자들이 이미 실질적으로 또는 본능적으로 알고 있는 것을 보고할 때 가장 관심이 많은데, 그 이유는 그것만으로도 진정한 인류애, 즉 인간 경험에 대한 설명이기 때문입니다.

이종현T의 독해 Point!

첫 문장의 결과가 자연을 알고 인식한다는 얘기가 된다. 다음 문장 부터는 중간 논리가 되고, 그 방법에 대한 글로 끝났으니 이게 들어간 선지를 찍으면 정답은 ②번이 된다.

57.③ 다음 대통령의 가장 큰 자산은 아마도 전 세계가 미국이 위대해지거나 적어도 영감을 주기를 바라는 것일 것입니다. 마찬가지로 미국인들은 대통령이 위대해지거나 적어도 존경받을 수 있기를 원합니다. 모든 반대와 절망에도 불구하고 미국인들은 아직 냉소적이지 않으며 열정을 잃지 않았습니다. 유권자들은 한 사람이 임무에 동등하다는 미국의 가정을 받아들일 뿐만 아니라 국민에 대한 책임감과 책임감을 가질 수 있는 인물인 대통령 영웅을 찾고 있습니다. 그들은 그들을 찾을 수 있을까요? 현재의 분야가 훌륭해 보이지 않는다면 역사는 대통령도 군주처럼 권력을 잡아야만 진정한 자질을 보여준다는 것을 증명합니다. 어쨌든 이상적인 인물을 찾거나 적어도 이상적인 인물을 찾는 데 있어 유권자들은 궁극적으로 작은 이유와 많은 본능, 그리고 운명이라고도 알려진 많은 행운에만 의존할 수 있습니다.

이종현T의 독해 Point!

첫 문장의 결과는 미국 대통령에게 원하는 결과가 미국을 위대하고 영감을 주게 한다는 것이다. 이 내용의 결과의 결과로 나오는 것이 없으니 이 결과가 핵심 결과가 된다. 따라서 정답은 ③번이 된다.

58.④ 개념적 틀로서 기호학은 학생들에게 설득력 있고 잘 뒷받침되는 해석을 수립하도록 가르칩니다. 기호학은 가정과 언어가 세상에 대한 우리의 이해를 형성하는 방식을 조사하는 것을 강조합니다. 또한 기호학은 단순히 신념을 판단하거나 평가하는 것보다 사회적, 정치적 맥락에서 신념이 어떻게 형성되는지에 초점을 맞추기 때문에 민감하거나 정치적으로 중요한 문제를 논의하는 데 이상적입니다.

문학, 미디어 및 커뮤니케이션 연구, 인류학, 예술 및 디자인 과정, 사회학, 법학, 시장 연구(일부 더 두드러진 분야 응용 사례만 언급하자면)에서 사용되는 접근 방식인 기호학은 다양한 전공과 분야의 학생들로 구성된 글쓰기 수업에 이상적일 정도로 다양한 분야에 걸쳐 매력적인 접근 방식을 가지고 있습니다. 기호학은 매우 기술적이거나 이론적인 것으로 유명합니다. 이 책은 학생이나 강사가 기호학에 대한 기술적 지식을 갖출 필요가 없으므로 안심하세요.

이종현T의 독해 Point!

마지막에 this book이 앞 내용 전체를 받아준다. 그리고 이 책을 읽는데 필요한 능력에 대한 원인의 원인으로 나왔으니 이 부분이 핵심이 된다. 따라서 이 내용을 받은 선지를 찾으면 정답은 ④번이 된다.

59.⑤ 니콜라스 골드버그는 모든 영어 전공자들이 어디로 갔는지 묻습니다. 대답은 간단합니다: 그들은 항상 가왔던 곳으로 갔습니다. 아마도 교사나 변호사가 될 것입니다. 많은 인문학 전공자들이 스스로에게 묻고 있는 질문은 다음과 같습니다: 결국 교사가 되려면 왜 '고순위' 대학에 다니면서 빚을 지게 되었을까요? 결국 캘리포니아 주립대학교 학교는 캘리포니아주 최고의 교사 준비 대학입니다. 변호사가 되기로 결심한 인문학 전공자들도 비슷한 질문을 하고 있을지도 모릅니다: '고순위' 대학에서 빚을 지고 실제로 로스쿨에 다닐 돈이 있는 대신 주립대에 다니는 것이 더 나았을지도 모릅니다. '고순위' 학부에 입학하는 것은 자랑할

만한 권리이지만 좋은 교사는 여전히 좋은 교사이고, 좋은 변호사는 어떤 대학에 다녔든 여전히 좋은 변호사입니다. 골드버그의 질문에 답하기 위해 영어 전공자들은 잘 지내고 있습니다.

이종현T의 독해 Point!

첫 문장의 질문이 모든 영어 전공자들이 어디로 갔는지 이니까 이것이 결과이다. 사실 그리고 그 다음부턴 결과 고정이고 다른 결과의 결과는 없으니 이 답변으로 마지막에 나온 모든 영어 전공자들은 괜찮다는 것이 핵심 결과가 된다. 따라서 이게 들어간 선지를 찾으면 정답은 ⑤번이 된다.

Unit 2. 일치/불일치/추론 유형

1~2. 기후 변화는 생태계, 경제, 인간의 삶에 깊고 예측할 수 없는 방식으로 영향을 미치는 다양한 결과를 초래했습니다. 해수면 상승으로 인해 전체 해안 지역 사회가 이주하는 상황이 발생하고 있으며, 기후 난민 인구가 증가하고 있습니다. 기후 패턴의 변화로 인해 농업 시스템이 혼란에 빠지면서 이미 빈곤과 싸우고 있는 지역의 식량 부족과 취약성이 증가하고 있습니다. 또한 지구 온도 상승으로 인해 많은 종들이 서식지 손실이나 급변하는 환경에 적응하지 못해 멸종 위기에 처하면서 생물 다양성의 상실이 가속화되고 있습니다. 예를 들어 산호초는 대규모 백화 현상을 겪고 있으며, 이는 해양 생태계와 산호초에 의존하는 수백만 명의 생계를 위협하고 있습니다.

기후 변화는 생태적 영향을 넘어 허리케인, 가뭄, 산불과 같은 극한 기상 현상의 빈도와 심각성을 심화시켜 자연 경관과 인적 인프라를 광범위하게 파괴하고 있습니다. 정부와 지역사회가 재난 대응, 복구 및 완화 노력에 점점 더 많은 자원을 할당함에 따라 경제적 비용이 증가하고 있습니다. 이러한 상호 연결된 효과는 기후 변화의 복잡성을 강조하며, 이는 다양한 방식으로 나타나며 어떤 부문도 손상시키지 않습니다. 그 여파는 즉각적인 피해를 넘어 전 세계 시스템에 연쇄적인 영향이 파급되어 국가와 개인의 효과적인 대응 능력에 도전하고 있습니다.

이종현T의 독해 Point!

1.B 첫 문장의 결과를 보면 climate change 때문에 생기는 여러 결과다. 즉 불특정 결과가 나왔으므로 climate change 때문에 생기는 여러 결과가 중간 논리로 나오게 된다. 이렇게 되면 그냥 첫 문장의 논리가 주제가 된다. 결국 끝까지 그렇게 나오고 있으므로 첫 문장 그대로 선지에서 찾으면 정답은 B가 된다.

2.D 첫 문장에 여러 결과로 간다는 불특정 결과를 썼으므로 '결과가 하나밖에 없다'라고 쓴 선지는 불일치가 된다. 따라서 정답은 D가 된다.

3~4. '디지털 디톡스'를 지지하는 일부 사람들은 기술로부터의 장기적인 단절이 정신 건강에 필수적이며, 더 큰 창의성, 집중력, 정서적 웰빙을 촉진한다고 주장합니다. 그들은 끊임없는 알림과 온라인 방해로부터 단절함으로써 개인이 시간을 되찾고 세상과

더 의미 있게 다시 참여할 수 있다고 주장합니다. 그러나 이러한 관점은 기술과 정신 건강의 관계를 지나치게 단순화하여 현대 생활에서 기술의 미묘한 역할을 설명하지 못합니다.

예를 들어 과도한 화면 시간이 번아웃이나 주의력 저하로 이어질 수 있다는 것은 사실이지만, 기술은 스트레스 해소와 생산성을 위한 중요한 도구이기도 합니다. 많은 사람들이 안내 명상, 시간 관리 또는 가상 치료 세션에 앱을 사용하는데, 이는 정신 건강 결과를 개선하는 것으로 나타났습니다. 또한 디지털 플랫폼은 의미있는 연결을 촉진하고 고립감을 느낄 수 있는 사람들을 위한 지원 시스템을 제공할 수 있습니다. 완전한 '디톡스'는 현대 사회에서 기술이 대처하고 번영하는 데 필수적인 자원이라는 현실을 무시하는 것입니다.

디지털 디톡스에 대한 주장은 개인의 변동성의 중요성도 간과하고 있습니다. 모든 사람이 기술 사용으로 인해 같은 정도의 피해를 경험하거나 단절로 인해 모두가 동등하게 혜택을 받는 것은 아닙니다. 일부 사람들에게는 디지털 도구를 적당히 사용하는 것이 금욕보다 훨씬 더 효과적입니다. 의도적인 휴식은 실제로 도움이 될 수 있지만, 보편적으로 필요하다고 생각하는 것은 경험의 다양성과 기술이 웰빙에 미칠 수 있는 긍정적인 기여를 고려하지 못합니다.

이종현T의 독해 Point!

3.B 디지털 디톡스에 대한 한 관점에 대해 문제점을 제시하는 문제점 반박의 논리에 대한 글이다. 따라서 이걸 그대로 담은 선지를 찾으면 정답은 B가 된다.

4.D 반박의 논리가 있는 글이기에 '항상/모든/어떤 ~도 ~한다'처럼 가는 논리는 기본적으로 불일치가 된다. 따라서 정답은 D가 된다.

5~6. 도서관의 역할은 수세기에 걸쳐 사회적 요구와 기술 발전에 따라 크게 변화해 왔습니다. 고대에는 학자, 사제, 왕족과 같은 엘리트만 접근할 수 있는 독점적인 지식 저장소 역할을 했습니다. 예를 들어 알렉산드리아 도서관은 지적 권력을 상징하며, 소장품은 가치 있는 소수를 위해 보호되고 큐레이팅 되었습니다. 15세기 인쇄기의 발명과 함께 도서관은 민주화되기 시작했고, 도서가 더 저렴하고 널리 보급됨에 따라 엘리트 기관에서 공공 자원으로 전환되었습니다. 19세기까지 공공 도서관의 설립은 교육과 평등에 대한 사회적 강조가 커지면서 각계각층의 사람들이 지식에 접근할 수 있게 되었습니다.

디지털 시대에 도서관은 다시 한 번 변화하여 관련성을 유지하기 위한 기술을 수용하고 있습니다. 이제 도서관은 디지털 데이터베이스, 전자책, 온라인 학습 플랫폼에 대한 접근성을 제공하며, 종종 기술 문해력의 허브 역할을 합니다. 그러나 이러한 변화는 물리적 책과 전통적인 도서관 공간의 미래에 대한 논쟁을 불러일으켰습니다. 도서관은 계속해서 적응하고 있지만, 그 핵심 임무는 방법과 매체가 진화하는 동안에도 지식의 민주화에 뿌리를 두고 있습니다. 이러한 궤적은 시대의 요구를 충족시키기 위해 끊임없이 재구성되어 온 도서관의 유동적인 특성을 강조합니다.

이종현T의 독해 Point!

5.B 이 글은 도서관이 시간에 따라 어떻게 역할이 바뀌어 왔는지에 대한 글이다. 따라서 이걸 답은 선지를 찾으면 정답은 B가 된다.

6.D 도서관이 시간에 따라 역할이 변했다는 것이 핵심이므로 이걸 반대로 쓴다면 시간이 흘러도 똑같다는 논리의 선지가 불일치가 된다. 따라서 이것부터 찾으면 정답은 D가 된다.

7~8. 경외심을 불러일으키는 자연 경관인 조류의 이동 현상은 잘 문서화되어 있지만, 이러한 행동을 유발하는 정확한 메커니즘은 여전히 파악하기 어렵습니다. 매년 수백만 마리의 새가 수천 마일을 이동하며 대륙을 놀라운 정확도로 항해합니다. 이러한 놀라운 능력이 먹이에 대한 접근성과 유리한 번식 조건을 보장한다는 것은 분명하지만, 새가 이러한 업적을 어떻게 달성할 수 있는지에 대한 문제는 아직 해결되지 않았습니다. 연구자들은 자기장, 천체 신호, 유전자 프로그래밍 등 여러 요인이 작용할 수 있음을 확인했습니다. 일부 연구에서는 새가 지구의 자기장을 감지할 수 있는 자기 수용체를 가지고 있다고 제안하는 반면, 다른 연구에서는 기억과 학습 경로의 역할을 강조합니다. 그러나 이러한 설명 중 어느 것도 철새가 처음 발견하는 경우에도 신뢰성과 정확성을 완전히 설명하지 못합니다.

미스터리에 더해 모든 종에 걸쳐 이동 패턴이 균일하지는 않습니다. 어떤 새는 엄격하고 선형적인 경로를 따르는 반면, 어떤 새는 목적지에 도달하기 전에 불규칙하게 방황합니다. 기후 변화와 같은 환경 변화와 혼란으로 인해 이러한 행동을 지배하는 주요 요인을 파악하기가 더욱 어려워졌습니다. 수십 년간의 연구에도 불구하고 본능, 학습된 행동, 환경적 영향의 정확한 조합이 이동을 가능하게 하는 것은 생물학의 지속적인 수수께끼 중 하나로 남아 있습니다.

이종현T의 독해 Point!

7.B 새들의 움직임에 대해서 그 방법에 대해선 정확하게 알 수 없다는 Mystery 논리의 글이다. 따라서 정답은 B가 된다.

8.D Mystery 논리의 글이므로 확실하게 알았다는 내용의 선지는 기본적으로 불일치가 된다. 따라서 정답은 D가 된다.

9.③ 우리의 불필요한 관찰자가 본능 자체가 없고 일반적인 본능과 특히 공격성이 모두 유산될 수 있는 방식을 알지 못하는 순수한 이성의 존재라고 가정한다면, 그는 역사를 어떻게 설명해야 할지 전혀 모를 것입니다. 역사의 끊임없이 반복되는 현상이 "인간 본성"이라는 일반적인 표현에 의해 발생한다고 말하는 것은 흔한 일입니다. 비합리적이고 비합리적인 인간 본성은 두 나라가 경쟁하게 만들지만, 경제적 필요성이 그렇게 강요하지는 않습니다. 이는 놀랍도록 유사한 구원 프로그램을 가진 두 정당이나 종교가 서로 격렬하게 싸우도록 유도하고, 알렉산더나 나폴레옹이 자신의 영지 아래 세상을 통합하려는 시도에서 수백만 명의 목숨을 희생하도록 강요합니다. 우리는 이러한 부조리와 유사한 부조리를 저지른 일부 사람들을 존중하여 '위대한' 사람으로 간주하는 법을 배웠습니다. 우리는 책임자들의 정치적 지혜에 굴복하지 않으며, 이러한 현상에 너무 익숙해져서 대부분의 사람들이 인류의 역사적 집단 행동이 실제로 얼마나 끔찍하고 어리석고 바람직하지 않은지 깨닫지 못합니다.

이종현T의 독해 Point!

이 글의 핵심 논리는 ⇒ 인간은 비합리적이고 ⇒ 그래서 서로 싸우고 갈등하게 되고 ⇒ 그 사이에서 권력자, 정복자들이 위대한 사람이 된다는 논리가 된다. 따라서 이 핵심 논리를 담고 있는 선지를 제일 먼저 찾는다면 정답은 ③번이 된다.

10.④ 우리 대부분은 유통기한에 의존하여 식료품이 아직 신선한지 여부를 알 수 있습니다. 하지만 영국의 산업 디자이너 솔리비가 팍슈타이트는 대중교통 프로젝트를 위해 시각장애인들과 인터뷰했을 때 알 수 있듯이 눈에 보이지 않으면 그 날짜를 읽을 수 없습니다. 이 사실을 알게 된 23세의 여성은 식품 포장에 젤라틴 층으로 코팅된 일련의 돌출부인 범프 마크를 디자인하게 되었습니다. 젤라틴 단백질이 부패하면 돌출부가 눈에 띄게 됩니다. 그때 음식이 전성기를 지났다는 것을 알 수 있습니다. 이는 동물 발굽으로 만든 젤라틴이 스테이크, 생선 필레 또는 샐러드 봉지와 거의 같은 속도로 만들어지기 때문입니다. 이 기술의 잠재력은 생각보다 훨씬 큽니다. 인쇄된 날짜는 식품 부패의 실제 지표가 아닌 가이드라인에 불과하기 때문에 완벽하게 좋은 식품을 많이 낭비합니다. (영국에서는 식료품점과 소비자가 매년 총 1,200만 톤의 식품을 버립니다.) 범프 마크가 실제 부패율을 측정하기 때문에 이를 해결하는 데 도움이 될 수 있습니다. 팍슈타이트는 현재 젤라틴에서 식품으로의 부패율의 정확도를 높이기 위해 시장 조사, 제조 연구, 실험실 테스트를 진행하고 있습니다. 신선한 아이디어에서 나온 신선한 식품입니다.

이종현T의 독해 Point!

The revelation inspired the 23-year-old to design the Bump Mark, a series of raised bumps coated with a layer of gelatin on food packaging. As the gelatin protein decays, the bumps become tangible. That's when you know the food is past its prime. This works ⇒ 여기까지가 결과이고, because부터 그 결과가 생긴 이유가 된다. 즉 gelatin이 steak와 같은 속도로 썩는다는 것이 가능한 이유이므로 이걸 반대로 쓴 선지부터 찾으면 정답은 ④번이 된다.

11.③ 부유한 로마 가정에서 태어난 마르쿠스 테렌티우스 바로는 길고 모험적인 삶을 살았습니다. 저명한 학자 루시우스 아엘리우스 스틸로 밑에서 공부한 후 철학을 공부하기 위해 아테네로 향했습니다. 바로는 카이사르가 결국 승리한 권력 투쟁 중 하나에서 패배한 쪽에 맞서 싸우기 위해 돌아왔습니다. 그는 용서를 받고 카이사르의 보호 아래 두각을 나타냈으며, 기원전 43년 안토니우스 휘하에서 급격히 몰락했습니다. 바로는 죽음을 피했지만 개인 도서관이 파괴되는 고통을 겪었습니다. 그는 인생의 후반부를 읽고 쓰기 위해 은퇴했으며, 89세의 나이로 세상을 떠났습니다. 추정치는 다양하지만 일부 기록에 따르면 그는 620권의 책을 출간했는데, 대부분의 로마 서적이 현대 챕터의 길이라는 점을 인정했습니다. 바로는 천문학, 지리학, 농업, 수학, 법학, 역사, 철학, 언어 등 거의 모든 주제에 대해 글을 썼습니다. 또한 시, 연설, 편지도 남겼습니다.

이종현T의 독해 Point!

이 글의 논리는 바로가 권력을 얻었는데 ⇒ Antony에서부터 내려갔다는 것이 핵심 논리이다. 따라서 이걸 반대로 쓴 ③번 선지가 불일치가 된다.

12.⑤ 형사 문제와 직접 관련된 사안의 경우, 실질적인 수사의 대부분은 경찰이 대부분의 관할권에서 검시관의 역할이 거의 없는 형사 사법 시스템을 대신하여 수행합니다. 이러한 상황에서 병리학자가 실제로 경찰 수사관을 위한 서비스를 수행하고 있다고 결론지을 수 있는 실질적인 근거가 있습니다. 실제로 범죄 수사는 여러 단계를 포함합니다. 전통적으로 법의학 병리학자는 사망 또는 부상에 초점을 맞춘 수사 단계, 특히 부상자나 사망자의 성격과 원인을 확인하기 위한 조사에 관여했습니다. 그러나 실제로 법의학 병리학자는 범죄 수사에서 더 넓은 역할을 합니다. 예를 들어, 그들은 사망 장면의 조사나 피해자에게 상해를 입혔을 가능성이 있는 용의자의 조사에 관여할 수 있습니다. 그들은 의학적 목적으로 의료 기록을 평가하고, 의학적 문제와 관련된 다른 증인의 진술을 검토할 수 있습니다. 따라서 실제로 법의학 병리학자는 의심스러운 사망을 다루는 것보다 더 넓은 역할을 합니다. 법의학 병리학자들이 수행하는 대다수의 부검은 사회가 조사하고 확인할 것을 요구하는 확인되지 않은 자연사와 관련이 있습니다. 의심되지 않는 자연사, 치명적 사고, 자살로 인한 사망 및 기타 형태의 고의적 및 비의도적 부상으로 인한 사망에 대한 조사가 그들의 사례 대부분을 차지합니다.

이종현T의 독해 Point!

법 의학 병리학자들이 수행하는 일은 의심스러운 죽음에 대해서 조사하는 것보다 훨씬 더 많은 것을 한다는 논리 추가의 표현이 핵심 논리에 해당하므로 이걸 반대로 쓴 선지를 찾으면 정답은 ⑤번이 된다.

13.③ 18세기 후반까지 자연사 분야는 이른바 파슨-자연주의자들, 즉 비카, 파슨스, 수도사, 수도사들이 정원을 가꾸고 식물과 동물 표본을 수집하여 신성한 창조의 경이로움을 섬겼지만, 일반적으로는 근본적인 가정에 의문을 제기하지 않았습니다. 그 결과 이 분야는 독특한 왜곡을 겪었습니다. 식물과 동물 종의 분류학이 번성하면서도 생물의 기원에 대한 탐구는 금지된 방관으로 밀려났습니다. 자연사는 역사없이 자연에 대한 연구로 전환되었습니다. 다윈이 문제를 삼은 것은 바로 이러한 정적인 자연관이었습니다. 자연사학자는 자연의 상태를 원인과 결과의 관점에서 설명할 수 있어야 한다고 다윈은 추론했습니다. 마치 물리학자가 공중에서 공의 움직임을 설명할 수 있는 것처럼 말이죠. 다윈의 파괴적 천재성의 본질은 자연을 사실이 아닌 과정, 진행, 역사로 생각하는 그의 능력이었습니다.

이종현T의 독해 Point!

파슨 자연주의자와 반대될만한 집단으로 다윈이 나오고, 둘의 핵심적인 차이는 생명체의 근원에 대해서 고민하는 것을 금지했던 것이 파슨이고 다윈은 그것을 고민했으므로 이걸 반대로 쓴 선지를 찾으면 정답은 ③번이 된다.

14.⑤ 프랑스 철학자 가스통 바슐라르는 자신이 공간의 시학이라고 부르는 것에 대한 분석을 쓴 적이 있습니다. 그는 집의 내부는 실제든 상상이든 친밀감, 비밀, 보안, 현실이든 상상이든 적절한 경험으로 인해 형성된다고 말했습니다. 집의 모퉁이, 복도, 지하실, 방의 객관적인 공간은 시적으로 부여된 공간보다 훨씬 덜 중요한데, 이는 보통 우리가 이름을 짓고 느낄 수 있는 상상력이나 비유적 가치를 지닌 특성이기 때문입니다. 따라서 집은 유령이 될 수도 있고, 집처럼 될 수도 있으며, 감옥처럼 될 수도 있고, 마법처럼 될 수도 있습니다. 따라서 공간은 일종의 시적 과정을 통해 감정적이고 이성적인 감각을 습득하며, 이를 통해 비어 있거나 익명의 거리가 우리에게 의미로 전환됩니다.

이종현T의 독해 Point!

이 지문의 핵심 결과는 공간의 시적인 뿐이고 ⇒ 다음 문장에서 원인으로 경험으로 형성된다고 나와 있다. 그러니 이 논리를 잘못 쓴 선지가 반대 선지이고, 5번 선지는 내 경험에 따라 만들어진다는 것이 아니고 객관적인 것에 따라 만들어진다는 것이니 논리가 잘못되었으므로 불일치이다. 따라서 정답은 ⑤번이 된다.

15.③ 스위스 목사 요한 캐스퍼 라바터는 턱이 사람의 힘을 상징한다고 자신 있게 썼습니다. 그는 "재민하고, 잘 정돈된, 확고한 사람"에게는 각진 턱이나 뒤로 물러나는 턱이 거의 발견되지 않는다고 주장했습니다. 또한 그는 "풍부하고 선명한 가로 눈썹은 항상 이해력, 냉정함, 계획을 세울 수 있는 능력을 전달한다"고 주장했습니다. 놀랍지 않게도 그는 유럽의 얼굴 관상이 다른 사람들보다 뛰어나다고 생각했습니다. 흥미로운 점은 비글호의 지휘관인 피츠 로이가 라바터의 팬이었다는 점입니다. 비글호는 다윈이 증거를 수집하기 위해 전 세계를 돌아다니게 한 배

로, 이후 진화론을 발전시켰습니다. 다윈은 자신의 전기에서 선장이 다윈의 코를 가진 사람이라면 "항해에 충분한 에너지와 결단력을 가지고 있지 않다"고 의심했다고 썼습니다. 물론 다윈의 진화론에 영감을 준 것은 바로 이 코 때문이었습니다.

이종현T의 독해 Point!

이 글은 외모의 특징에 따른 성격 차이를 비교하면서 중간논리로 보여주고 있으므로 외모의 특징에 따라 성격을 다르게 봤다를 반대로 쓴 것은 핵심 논리를 반대로 쓴 선지이다. 이게 없다면 특징별 성격을 잘못 연결한 선지가 불일치하는 선지가 된다고 판단하면 된다.
핵심 논리를 반대로 쓴 선지는 없으므로 특징별 성격을 잘못 연결한 선지를 찾으면 정답은 ③번이 된다.

16.② 사회학 분야에서 방법론적 자연주의에 강하게 반대하는 역사주의는 사회학과 물리학의 심오한 차이로 인해 물리학의 일부 특징적인 방법을 사회과학에 적용할 수 없다고 주장합니다. 물리 법칙, 즉 '자연의 법칙'은 물리 법칙이 어디서나 항상 유효하다는 것을 알려줍니다. 물리 세계는 공간과 시간에 걸쳐 불변하는 물리적 균일성의 시스템에 의해 지배되기 때문입니다. 그러나 사회학적 법칙 또는 사회생활의 법칙은 장소와 기간에 따라 다릅니다.

역사주의는 정기적인 재발이 관찰될 수 있는 일반적인 사회적 조건이 많다는 것을 인정하지만, 사회 생활에서 감지할 수 있는 규칙성이 물리적 세계의 불변하는 규칙성의 성격을 가진다는 것을 부인합니다. 이 규칙들은 역사와 문화의 차이에 따라 달라집니다. 이 규칙들은 특정 역사적 상황에 따라 달라집니다. 따라서 예를 들어 경제 법칙에 대한 추가적인 자격 없이 말할 것이 아니라 봉건 시대나 초기 산업 시대의 경제 법칙 등을 언급해야 하며, 항상 문제의 법칙이 승리했다고 가정되는 역사적 시기를 언급해야 합니다.

역사주의는 사회 법칙의 역사적 상대성 이론이 대부분의 물리학 방법을 사회학에 적용할 수 없게 만든다고 주장합니다. 이러한 견해의 근거가 되는 대표적인 역사주의적 논거는 일반화, 실험, 사회 현상의 복잡성, 정확한 예측의 어려움, 방법론적 본질주의의 중요성에 관한 것입니다.

이종현T의 독해 Point!

이 글의 핵심 논리는 물리학적 방법과 사회 과학은 관련이 없다는 것이 핵심 논리이다. 따라서 이걸 인과관계인 것처럼 쓴 선지가 기본적으로 불일치가 된다. 2번 선지가 사회학 적 역사 상대성으로 ⇒ 과학적 법칙을 알 수 있다라는 선지이니 핵심 논리 반대가 된다. 정답은 ②번이다.

17.① 일단 움직이는 물체에 부여된 속도는 가속도나 지연의 외부 원인이 제거되는 한 엄격하게 유지되며, 이는 수평면에서만 발견되는 조건입니다. 아래로 기울어지는 평면의 경우 이미 가속도의 원인이 있으며, 위쪽으로 기울어진 평면에서는 지연이 발생합니다. 이를 통해 수평면을 따라 움직이는 운동은 영구적이며, 속도가 균일하다면 속도를 줄이거나 느슨하게 할 수 없고, 훨씬 덜 파괴될 수 있기 때문입니다.

이종현T의 독해 Point!

속도를 통해서 외부의 힘이 작용하는지 아닌지를 알 수 있는 것이 아니고, 속도의 변화가 있는지 아닌지에 따라 알 수 있는 것이므로 원인이 잘못된 선지가 ①번이 된다.

18.② 언어학자들은 노동자 계급과 교육 수준이 낮은 중산층 구성원들이 더 단순하거나 거친 언어를 구사한다는 신화에 반복적으로 부딪힙니다. 이는 대화의 용이성에서 비롯된 악의적인 착시 현상입니다. 색각이나 걷기와 같은 일반적인 말하기는 사용자가 패널 뒤에 숨겨진 복잡한 기계를 모른 채 결과를 당연하게 여길 정도로 잘 작동하는 공학적 우수성의 패러다임입니다. 그는 어디로 갔을까요? 그리고 제가 만난 사람은 스스로 목숨을 끊었고, 이는 영어 사용자라면 누구나 자동으로 단어를 배열하여 의미를 표현합니다. 수십 년간의 노력에도 불구하고 길거리에서 사람을 복제하는 데 근접한 인공적으로 설계된 언어 시스템은 없습니다.

이종현T의 독해 Point!

노력했지만 일상 언어와 거의 비슷한 시스템은 없다고 했으므로 우리가 복잡한 체계를 알고 있다고 하는 2번 선지는 핵심 논리의 반대 선지이다. 정답은 ②번이다.

19.③ 찌르레기는 그물에서 먹이를 주는 장소로 날아가서 풀밭을 탐사하여 부리로 가득 찬 가죽 재킷을 찾고, 그 다음 둥지로 데려갑니다. 찌르레기의 문제는 언제 포기해야 하는가 입니다. 찌르레기는 너무 일찍 포기하면 작은 짐을 얻기 위해 많은 시간을 여행하고, 너무 오래 버리면 비효율적인 탐색에 시간을 보내는데, 이는 집에 가서 짐을 버리고 다시 시작하는 것이 더 나을 수 있습니다. 비슷한 문제는 꿀벌이 꿀로 꿀 작물을 채우는 꽃에서

꽃으로 날아가면서 벌통으로 돌아가는 과정에서 발생합니다. 꿀벌은 종종 최대 운반량보다 적은 짐을 싣고 벌집으로 돌아오는데, 이는 찌르레기와 유사한 모델로 설명할 수 있습니다. 그러나 중요한 차이점이 있습니다: 꿀벌은 수확물의 꿀이 더 많은 꽃을 빨아들일 수 없게 하거나 자원 부족으로 인해 수확량이 감소하는 곡선을 경험하기 때문이 아니라 작물의 꿀 무게가 비행에 상당한 에너지 비용을 추가하기 때문입니다. 꿀벌이 작물에 짐을 많이 실을수록 집에 돌아가기 전에 연료로 더 많이 소모됩니다.

이종현T의 독해 Point!

이 글에서 나오는 starling의 문제는 너무 오래 머물러도 문제, 너무 짧게 머물러도 문제가 된다는 논리이다. 그러므로 핵심 논리의 반대 선지라면, 최대한 오래 머무르면 좋다. 또는 '최대한 짧게 머무르는 것이 좋다'라고 써 있는 선지가 핵심 논리의 반대가 되는 불일치 선지가 된다. 따라서 정답은 ③번이 된다.

20.④ 스피노자의 윤리학을 읽는 이유는 무엇인가요? 아마도 대학 과정에서 독서를 해야 할 것입니다. 어쩌면 여러분은 방치된 영역을 탐구하고 싶은 철학자일 수도 있습니다. 또는 현실의 본질, 마음, 인간 행동에 대한 호기심에 이끌리는 것일 수도 있습니다. 이러한 범주 중 하나에 속한다면 이 책, 그리고 실제로 스피노자의 윤리학 자체가 여러분을 위해 쓰여졌습니다.

스피노자의 윤리학이 17세기 철학계만큼이나 21세기 비전문가 독자들을 위해 쓰여졌다는 소식을 들으면 놀랄 수도 있습니다. 스피노자는 자신의 책이 당시의 철학적 전통에 깊이 빠져 있는 사람들에 의해 주로 읽힐 것이라고 예상했습니다. (철학적 배경이 있다면 플라톤, 아리스토텔레스, 스토아 학파, 데카르트, 홉스의 작품 속 메아리와 니체, 사르트르, 푸코, 들뢰즈에 대한 기대를 들을 수 있을 것입니다.) 하지만 스피노자는 300여 년 후 자신의 작품을 읽는 비전문가들을 알게 되어 기뻐할 것입니다. 그의 목표는 가능한 한 많은 사람들이 진실을 이해할 수 있도록 돕는 것입니다. 윤리학은 독자가 자신의 이해를 발전시킬 수 있도록 설계된 워크북입니다. 스피노자는 더 많은 사람들이 윤리학을 읽으면 인간 사이의 이성과 덕목이 증가하여 더 평화롭고 관용적인 사회로 이어질 것이라고 생각합니다.

그렇다고 해서 윤리학이 일종의 초기 자기계발 매뉴얼이라는 뜻은 아닙니다. 스피노자의 윤리학은 형이상학, 인식론, 윤리학의 풍부하고 복잡한 작품입니다. 의심할 여지없이 이 책은 여러분이 읽게 될 가장 어려운 철학 책 중 하나입니다. 익숙하지 않은 언어와 개념으로 씨름하고 깊이 동의하지 않을 수 있는 아이디어를 접하게 될 것입니다. 하지만 이 책은 지금까지 쓰여진 철학 책 중 가장 흥미로운 책 중 하나이기도 합니다. 스피노자는 우리에게 가능한 한 인간이 되기 위한 프로그램, 즉 누구나 얻을 수 있는 현실의 본질에 대한 깊은 이해를 바탕으로 한 프로그램을 제공합니다. 그는 우리가 무엇인지와 우주에서 우리의 위치에 대한 진실을 드러내는 여정으로 우리를 안내합니다. 우리 자신에 대한 진실을 이해하는 것은 긍정적인 인간 관계, 진정한 과학 지식, 좋은 정치 조직의 기초가 됩니다. 스피노자는 자신과 삶, 자연, 신, 자유, 윤리에 대해 다르게 생각하게 만들 수 있습니다. 스피노자의 윤리학을 읽는 가장 좋은 이유는 아마도 이것입니다: 바로 여러분의 삶을 바꿀 수 있는 책이기 때문입니다.

이종현T의 독해 Point!

이 글의 핵심 논리는 스피노자의 윤리학을 읽으면 ⇒ 많은 사람들이 진리를 알 수 있고 ⇒ 진리를 알게 되면 ⇒ 긍정적인 인간관계, 과학적 지식, 좋은 정치 조직을 만들 수 있고 ⇒ 우리의 삶을 바꿀 수 있다 가 된다.
이걸 가지고 쓴 선지들은 일치이고, 이걸 반대로 쓰면 불일치가 된다. 이 문제 같은 경우는 1, 2, 3번 선지가 정확하게 핵심 논리에 해당하는 선지이므로 일치이고 남은 선지인 4번이 불일치가 된다. 정답은 ④번이다.

21.③ 위기가 새로운 이론의 출현을 위한 필수 전제 조건이라고 가정하고 과학자들이 그 존재에 어떻게 반응하는지 다음으로 질문해 보겠습니다. 중요한 것은 과학자들이 심각하고 장기적인 이상 현상에 직면했을 때 결코 하지 않는 일을 먼저 언급함으로써 답의 일부를 발견할 수 있다는 점입니다. 그들은 신뢰를 잃기 시작하고 대안을 고려하기 시작하더라도 자신을 위기로 몰아넣은 패러다임을 포기하지는 않습니다. 과학 철학의 어휘에서는 이상 현상을 반례로 취급하지 않습니다. 부분적으로 이 일반화는 나중에 패러다임 거부에 대한 우리의 검토가 무엇을 더 완전히 드러낼지 암시하는 예를 바탕으로 한 역사적 사실의 진술일 뿐입니다: 패러다임의 지위에 도달한 후 과학 이론은 대체 후보자가 그 자리를 차지할 수 있는 경우에만 무효로 선언됩니다. 과학 발전에 대한 역사적 연구에서 아직 공개된 어떤 과정도 자연과의 직접 비교를 통한 위조라는 방법론적 고정관념과 전혀 유사하지 않습니다. 그렇다고 해서 과학자들이 과학 이론을 거부하지 않는다는 의미는 아니며, 그 경험과 실험이 과학 이론을 거부하는 과정에 필수적이지도 않습니다. 그러나 과학자들이 이전에 받아

들여진 이론을 거부하게 만드는 판단 행위는 항상 그 이론을 세상과 비교하는 것 이상에 기반한다는 것이 핵심입니다. 한 패러다임을 거부하는 결정은 항상 다른 패러다임을 받아들이는 결정이며, 그 결정에 이르는 판단은 두 패러다임을 자연과 서로 비교하는 것을 포함합니다.

이종현T의 독해 Point!

이 지문의 핵심 논리는 패러다임들과 자연적인 현상과도 비교를 하고, 패러다임들 끼리 비교도 하고 둘 다 해야 ⇒ '기존 패러다임을 버리고, 새로운 패러다임을 선택하는 결정을 하게 된다'라는 논리가 핵심 논리이다. 이걸 그대로 쓴 선지를 찾으면 정답은 ③번이 된다.

22.② 아이작 뉴턴은 그림자가 퍼지지 않고 날카로운 가장자리를 가지고 있기 때문에 빛이 마치 작은 입자의 흐름처럼 행동한다고 믿었습니다. 그는 붉은 빛이 가장 큰 입자와 가장 작은 보라색으로 구성되어 있다고 생각했습니다. 대신 후이겐스는 빛이 바다의 파도처럼 진공 상태에서 전파되는 파동처럼 행동하기 때문에 빛의 파장과 주파수에 대해 이야기한다고 주장했습니다. 회절을 포함한 빛의 많은 특성은 자연스럽게 파동 이론으로 설명되며, 그 후 몇 년 동안 후이겐스의 견해는 빛의 빔에 노출되면 금속에서 전자가 방출되는 광전 효과를 설명할 수 있음을 보여주었습니다. 현대 양자역학은 두 가지 아이디어를 결합하여 오늘날 빛을 어떤 상황에서는 입자의 빔으로, 다른 상황에서는 파동으로 행동하는 것으로 생각하는 것이 일반적입니다. 이러한 파동-입자 이원론은 우리의 상식과 쉽게 일치하지는 않지만, 빛이 실제로 실험에서 보여준 것과 매우 잘 일치합니다.

이종현T의 독해 Point!

인물들간의 차이가 나오고 있으므로 이 특징을 반대로 쓴 선지는 불일치가 된다. wave-particle duality = 뉴턴의 것이 아니고 현대 양자역학의 특징이므로 ②번이 불일치하는 선지가 된다.

23.② 다윈은 유전 이론이 진화 이론의 주변적인 것이 아니라 매우 중요하다는 것을 깨달았습니다. 갈라파고스 섬에서 자연선택에 의해 그로스비크 핀치의 변종이 나타나려면 모순되는 두 가지 사실이 동시에 사실이어야 했습니다. 첫째, 짧은 부리를 가진 "정상적인" 핀치는 때때로 괴물이나 괴물 같은 그로스비크 변종을 만들어낼 수 있어야 합니다. 둘째, 일단 태어난 그로스비크 핀치는 자손에게 동일한 형질을 전달할 수 있어야 하며, 이를 통해 향후 세대에 걸쳐 변이를 수정할 수 있어야 합니다. 두 가지 요인 중 하나가 실패하면 자연은 도랑에 빠져 진화의 톱니바퀴가 막히게 됩니다.

이종현T의 독해 Point!

유전 이론에서 변종이 나타나는 결과가 나오기 위해 필요한 원인 2가지가 있다. '첫 번째는 정상적인 것이 ⇒ 변종을 만들어내야 하고, 두 번째는 동일한 형질을 전달할 수 있어야 하고 ⇒ 그걸 통해서 변이를 수정해야 한다'가 된다. 둘 다를 충족시켜야 ⇒ 변종이 나타난다는 것이 핵심 논리가 된다. 2번 선지는 변종이 변화하지 않아도 괜찮다는 것이므로 불일치가 된다. 그리고 애초에 논리 자체가 A와 B 둘 다를 만족시켜야 하고 둘 중 하나만 만족시키지 못해도 안 된다는 논리이므로, 이건 괜찮을 수 있다는 논리의 2번 선지는 기본적으로 불일치가 된다. 정답은 ②번이다.

24.① 모든 물리 이론은 가설에 불과하다는 점에서 항상 잠정적입니다. 절대 증명할 수 없습니다. 실험 결과가 아무리 어떤 이론과 일치하더라도 다음 번에 그 결과가 이론과 모순되지 않을 것이라고 확신할 수는 없습니다. 반면에 이론의 예측과 일치하지 않는 하나의 관찰이라도 찾으면 이론을 반증할 수 있습니다. 과학철학자 칼 포퍼가 강조했듯이 좋은 이론은 원칙적으로 관찰에 의해 반증되거나 위조될 수 있는 여러 예측을 한다는 사실로 특징지어집니다. 새로운 실험이 관찰될 때마다 예측과 일치하는 이론은 살아남고 이론에 대한 신뢰도가 높아지지만, 새로운 관찰이 동의하지 않는 것으로 판명되면 이론을 포기하거나 수정해야 합니다.

이종현T의 독해 Point!

이 글의 핵심 논리는 '모든 물리 이론이 증명 불가 ⇒ 그래서 가설이다'가 핵심 논리가 된다. 따라서 1번 선지에서 쓴 관찰된 것과 예측이 딱 맞아야 한다 라는 내용은 증명이 되어야 한다는 내용이므로 핵심 논리를 반대로 쓴 선지가 된다. 따라서 정답은 ①번이 된다.

25.② 퍼스트 얼러트 브랜드 제품의 제조업체인 BRK Brands, Inc. ("BRK")는 구매일로부터 5년 동안 이 제품에 재질 및 제작상의 결함이 없음을 보증합니다. BRK는 보증 기간동안 이 제품 또는 결함이 발견된 제품의 모든 구성 요소를 수리하거나 교체합

니다. 교체는 새 제품 또는 재제조된 제품 또는 구성 요소로 이루어집니다. 제품이 더 이상 사용할 수 없는 경우 동일하거나 더 큰 가치의 유사한 제품으로 교체할 수 있습니다. 이는 귀하의 독점 보증입니다.

이 보증은 최초 소매 구매일로부터 원래 소매 구매에 대해 유효하며 양도할 수 없습니다. 원래 판매 영수증을 보관하세요. 이 보증은 제품의 부주의한 사용, 부적절한 전압 또는 전류 사용, 또는 BRK 이외의 사용 지침에 반하는 사용 등 부품의 정상적인 마모나 손상에 대해서는 보장하지 않습니다. 또한, 화재, 홍수, 허리케인 및 토네이도와 같은 신의 행위에 대해서는 보증이 적용되지 않습니다.

이종현T의 독해 Point!

이 글은 보증이 된다는 것이 핵심 논리이고, 그 보증이 되는 상황들이 중간 논리로 비교 대상처럼 제시가 되었다. 따라서 보증이 안된다고 쓴 선지가 핵심 논리를 반대로 쓴 선지가 되고, 이게 아니라면 상황에 따라 보증이 되고 말고를 잘못 쓴 선지가 불일치가 된다. 일단 보증이 안된다고 쓴 선지는 없으므로, 상황에 따라 결과를 잘못 쓴 선지를 찾으면 된다. 자연 재해 같은 현상에 대해선 보증하지 않는다고 했으므로 ②번은 불일치가 된다. 정답은 ②번이다.

26.③ 마키아벨리의 용서할 수 없는 죄는 위선적으로 공언된 것이 아니라 진정으로 실천된다면 기독교의 겸손, 사랑의 친절, 신뢰가 자신을 기리는 모든 국가에 파멸을 가져온다는 것을 드러내는 것이었습니다. 반면 마키아벨리가 비르투라고 부른 것은 시민의 영광과 위대함을 얻기 위해 필요한 모든 것을 하겠다는 이교도의 결의로 국가가 공화주의적 자치를 이룰 수 있게 해주며, 그는 이를 최고의 정치적 선으로 여겼습니다. 어떤 통치자도 적을 처리할 준비가 되어 있지 않으면 오랫동안 통치할 수 없습니다. 그러나 가면을 쓰지 않고 휘두르면 칼은 무딘 도구가 됩니다. 통치자는 권력을 승계한 귀족을 안내하기 위해 쓴 중세 '왕자를 위한 거울'에 묘사된 정의로운 주권자가 되어서는 안 됩니다. 대신 상황에 따라 세상에 제시하는 얼굴을 바꾸는 많은 페르소나를 가져야 합니다. 개인의 진정성은 감당할 수 없는 사치이며, 진실은 신중하게 사용해야 하는 무기입니다. 적을 제거할 준비가 되어 있는 만큼 통치자는 모방을 위해 끊임없는 연습이 필요합니다. 어떤 정치 프로젝트에서든 성공은 기독교가 악덕이라고 비난하는 특성에 달려 있습니다. 마키아벨리는 슬픔이나 후회없이 이러한 사실을 보고합니다. 환멸을 느낀 인문주의자의 나르시시즘적 고통에 대한 그의 글에는 흔적이 없습니다.

이종현T의 독해 Point!

이 지문에서 마키아벨리의 입장과 기독교의 입장은 서로 반대되는 입장이 된다. 그런데 ③번 선지를 보면 마치 마키아벨리의 입장과 기독교의 입장이 서로 같은 입장인 것처럼 썼으므로 이는 불일치가 된다.

27.③ 세계경제포럼이 노동과 생산성의 최신 혁신, 즉 근거리 로봇과 인공지능 혁신을 지칭하기 위해 처음 만든 별명인 4차 산업혁명은 디지털 기술이 데스크톱 컴퓨터의 한계에 갇히지 않는 시대를 말합니다. 사물인터넷은 거의 모든 물리적 제품에 컴퓨팅 기술을 도입할 것을 약속합니다. 정량화된 자아는 심박수와 홍조 반응부터 감정적 유창성 및 활동 추적에 이르기까지 모든 인간의 감각과 행동을 디지털로 포착할 수 있음을 시사합니다. 디지털과 물리적 감시가 결합하여 각 개인의 신체적 및 온라인 활동을 통합된 전체적인 그림으로 완벽하게 파악할 수 있습니다. 대규모 네트워킹은 정보가 풍부하게 융합되어 인구 통계 데이터, 구매 습관, 대출 불이행 가능성 등 포착이 불가능했던 2차 지식을 창출할 것을 약속합니다. 로봇 혁신은 노화와 부상에 대한 일반적인 개념을 위협하며, 인간과 기계가 물리적 세계에서 결합하는 방식을 바꾸는 외골격 및 기타 로봇 정형외과를 제안합니다.

이종현T의 독해 Point!

이 글의 핵심 논리는 4차 산업 혁명이 되면서 컴퓨터 기술이 실제 세상과 결합되고 실제 세상으로 기술이 나오는 것이 핵심 논리가 된다. 따라서 이를 담은 선지를먼저 찾으면 정답은 ③번이 된다.

28.③ 우리 뇌에서 뉴런은 몸, 수상돌기, 축삭을 가지고 있습니다. 한 뉴런의 신호는 축삭을 따라 이동하여 다음 뉴런의 수상돌기로 전달됩니다. 신호가 전달되는 연결을 시냅스라고 합니다. 뉴런 자체는 쓸모가 없습니다. 하지만 뉴런이 많으면 함께 작동하여 심각한 마법을 만들어냅니다. 이것이 딥러닝 알고리즘의 아이디어입니다! 관찰을 통해 입력을 받아 입력을 한 층에 넣으면 됩니다. 이 층은 출력을 생성하여 다음 층의 입력이 되는 등의 과정을 반복합니다. 이는 최종 출력 신호가 나올 때까지 계속해서 발생합니다. 입력 층을 감각으로 생각해 보세요: 예를 들어 보고, 냄새 맡고, 느끼는 것들입니다. 이는 하나의 관찰에 대한 독립적인 변수입니다. 이 정보는 컴퓨터가 사용할 수 있는 숫자와 이진

데이터의 비트로 나뉩니다. 이러한 변수는 동일한 범위 내에 있도록 표준화하거나 정규화해야 합니다. 뉴런은 특징 추출과 변환을 위해 여러 층의 비선형 처리 장치를 사용합니다. 각 연속적인 층은 이전 층의 출력을 입력에 사용합니다. 학습한 내용은 개념의 계층 구조를 형성합니다. 이 계층 구조에서 각 레벨은 입력 데이터를 점점 더 추상적이고 복합적인 표현으로 변환하는 방법을 배웁니다.

이종현T의 독해 Point!

이 글의 핵심 논리는 관찰이 ⇒ data로 바뀌고 ⇒ 그게 또 다른 층으로 넘어가고 ⇒ 그렇게 출력까지 간다는 논리가 된다. 따라서 이를 담고 있는 선지를 먼저 찾으면 정답은 ③번이 된다.

29.① 키스 해링의 예술에서 특히 매력적인 점은 그의 강렬한 그래픽 스타일과 많은 상상력을 결합하는 능력에 있습니다. 그의 인물과 형태는 지속적인 변화와 새로운 창작물에 의해 영향을 받으며, 그가 초안 작업자, 화가, 조각가로서의 자질을 지속적으로 증명합니다. 그의 작품 속에서 우리는 꾸준한 스타일적 진화를 목격합니다. 그의 끊임없는 새로운 도전에 대한 탐구는 어떤 표면에 그림을 그릴지에 대한 실험과 함께 이루어집니다. 벽, 의류, 자동차, 비행선 등 무엇보다도 종이, 캔버스, 미처리 면 또는 비닐에 그림을 그릴지 여부에 관계없이 해링의 특징은 실행의 완벽함입니다. 그의 공식적으로 계획된 프로젝트나 즉흥적인 벽화 디자인 모두 스케치나 연구를 기반으로 한 그의 대사가 아닙니다. 우리는 오류나 수정, 비례의 비대칭성을 식별할 수 없습니다. 자발성과 확신은 그의 작품의 뛰어난 속성입니다.

이종현T의 독해 Point!

이 지문의 핵심 논리는 키스 해링의 예술이 항상 새로운 도전/실험을 한다는 것이다. 즉 과거에 했던 것과는 다른 것을 도전한다는 것이 된다. 따라서 이 논리를 담구 있는 선지를 찾으면 정답은 ①번이 된다.

30.② 로마는 전통에 힘입어 성공을 거두었고, 이를 결합하여 로마만의 정체성을 만들었습니다. 그 중에는 절대 왕의 통치를 받지 않겠다는 결의도 있었습니다. 제국 시대에도 옛 로마 정부의 형태는 유지되었습니다. 로마 군단이 사용하는 표준에는 황제의 이름이 적혀 있지 않았지만 "로마의 원로원과 국민을 위한"을 뜻하는 SPQR이라는 글자가 적혀 있었습니다. 가족은 로마 생활의 핵심이라고 여겨졌으며, 저명한 가문의 이름은 로마 역사에서 수세기에 걸쳐 반복되었습니다. 가족의 명성을 높이기 위해서는 전쟁이나 시민 생활에서 성공을 거두는 것이 매우 중요했습니다. 또 다른 로마의 특징은 도시가 적들에게 굴하지 않는 방식이었습니다. 로마의 많은 적들이 전투에서 로마를 이겼지만 전쟁에서 그들을 물리칠 수 있는 적은 거의 없었습니다. 마침내 로마의 통치 체제는 야심 찬 사람들이 성공할 수 있도록 허용했습니다. 두 명의 집정관이 1년 동안 협력하여 근무한 영사 제도는 각 집정관에게 재임 기간 동안 성공할 수 있는 일을 하도록 장려했습니다. 이러한 제도는 종종 어리석은 실수로 이어졌지만 큰 성공에도 기여했습니다. 상원의원들이 자신의 지위를 지키려는 시도에도 불구하고 로마 제도는 결국 더 넓은 집단의 사람들이 정부에 참여할 수 있도록 허용했습니다.

이종현T의 독해 Point!

이 글의 핵심 논리는 로마라는 곳은 왕의 통치를 받지 않는다는 것이다. 이것이 로마의 정체성이다. 따라서 이 논리의 반대로 쓴 것부터 먼저 찾으면 정답은 ②번이 된다.

Unit 3. 지칭 추론 유형

1.③ 건축이 상징적으로 특히 중요한 정치적 발언이 되면서 로마 제국 시기에 건축가의 입지가 높아졌습니다. 키케로는 건축가를 의사와 선생님과 함께 분류했고 비트루비우스는 "이만큼 위대한 직업"이라고 말했습니다. 아우구스투스 카이사르 통치 기간 동안 실용적인 건축가였던 마르쿠스 비트루비우스 폴리오는 건축에는 실용적인 지식과 이론적 지식이 모두 필요하다는 것을 인식하고, 건축가 지망생이 배워야 한다고 생각하는 학문인 문학과 글쓰기, 초안 작성, 수학, 역사, 철학, 음악, 의학, 법학, 천문학 등 아직 추천할 것이 많은 커리큘럼을 나열했습니다. 그는 학문 없이 수작업 기술을 습득하려는 건축가들은 자신의 계획에 부합하는 권위 있는 위치에 도달하지 못했고, 이론과 학문에만 의존해 온 건축가들은 분명히 "실체가 아닌 그림자를 쫓고 있다"고 주장했습니다.

이종현T의 독해 Point!

이 글의 핵심 논리는 건축을 하려면 이론적 지식, 실용적 지식이 둘 다 있어야만 한다는 논리가 된다. 근데 밑줄 문장에서의 사람들은 only theories만 있는 사람들이므로 다른 것은 없는 사람들이 된다. 여기서 다른 것은 실용적인 지식이 되므로 실용적인 지식은 없는 사람들이 된다. 따라서 이걸 가지고 있는 선지를 찾으면 정답은 ③번이 된다.

2.④ 1890년 윌리엄 제임스는 주의력을 "여러 가지 동시에 가능해 보이는 대상이나 사고의 흐름 중 하나를 명확하고 생생한 형태로 마음이 소유하는 것"이라고 설명했습니다. 주의력은 매력적인 오프 - 램프 신호처럼 하나의 과제, 하나의 사고, 하나의 정신적 길에 머물기 위해 우리가 내리는 선택입니다. 이러한 선택을 하지 못하고 자주 길을 비켜주지 않으면 제임스가 주의력과 정반대라고 말한 "혼란스럽고 멍하며 흩어진 뇌 상태"에 빠지게 됩니다. 인터넷이 도착하고 온라인으로 독서의 많은 부분을 옮기면서 한 길에 머무는 것은 훨씬 더 어려워졌습니다. 모든 하이퍼링크는 오프 - 램프로, 우리가 조금 전에 선택한 것을 포기하라고 촉구했습니다. 니콜라스 카는 2010년 저서에서 한 길에 머물 수 있는 능력을 잃은 것을 슬퍼했습니다. 인터넷에서의 삶은 책을 읽으려는 - 밖에서도 그의 뇌가 정보를 찾는 방식을 바꿨습니다. 그는 이제 끊임없는 자극의 흐름을 갈망했기 때문에 집중하고 성찰하는 능력이 감소했습니다: "한때 저는 말의 바다에서 스쿠버 다이버였습니다. 지금은 제트 스키를 타는 사람처럼 수면을 따라 지퍼를 잠그고 있습니다."

이종현T의 독해 Point!

실제 이 글의 핵심 논리는 과거에 비해 오늘날 인터넷 시대로 오면서 한 길에 오래 머무르는 것이 어려워졌고, 성찰하는 능력도 줄어들었다는 것이다. 그리고 밑줄도 오늘날 어떤지에 대한 얘기이므로 하나를 깊게 파는 것이 어려워졌다는 의미가 밑줄의 내용이 된다. 따라서 이걸 담은 선지를 찾으면 정답은 ④번이 된다.

3.③ 20세기 초, 자연과학을 전공한 인류학자들은 인류 과학이 어떤 모습이어야 하며 사회과학자들이 문화 집단을 연구하는 데 어떻게 나아가야 하는지에 대해 새롭게 구상하기 시작했습니다. 이러한 인류학자들 중 일부는 연구 대상자들을 실제로 관찰하고 대화하는 데 최소한 상당한 시간을 할애해야 한다고 주장했습니다. 프란츠 보아스와 알프레드 코트 해든과 같은 초기 민족지학자들은 일반적으로 해당 사람들이 사는 외딴 지역을 여행하며 몇 주에서 몇 달 동안 그곳에서 시간을 보냈습니다. 그들은 식민지 관리, 선교사, 사업가 등 사람들과 그 지역에 익숙한 현지 서양 호스트를 찾아 그들을 통해 숙소를 찾았습니다. 때때로 가이드 없이 지역 사회에 진출하기도 했지만, 일반적으로 현지 사람들과 함께 시간을 많이 보내지는 않았습니다. 따라서 그들의 관찰은 주로 그들의 베란다에서 이루어졌습니다.

이종현T의 독해 Point!

이 글의 핵심 논리는 20세기 초에 사람들을 관찰할 때 직접 그 사람들과 함께 시간을 보내지는 않으면서 그 사람들에 대해서 봤다는 논리가 된다. 따라서 밑줄도 그 뜻이 될 것이라 생각하고 선지에서 찾으면 정답은 ③번이 된다.

4.① 즉흥 연기에서 배우들은 대화나 진행 방향을 통제할 수 없습니다. 배우들은 다른 배우의 말이나 비언어적 의사소통에만 반응할 수 있습니다. 이 때문에 배우들은 몸짓 언어를 읽고 말의 대사 사이를 읽는 전문가가 됩니다. 이렇게 하지 못하면 배우들은 어둠 속에 남겨져 공연이 무너집니다. 이는 일상적인 대화에도 적용되지만, 우리는 보통 너무 자기 - 중심적이어서 알아차리지 못합니다. 즉흥 연기자들이 대화의 빵가루를 알아차리는 데 능숙해지는 것처럼, 우리도 똑같이 해야 합니다. 사람들이 특정한 이야기를 하고 싶을 때는 거의 나와서 그냥 말하지 않습니다.

99%의 사람들은 "이봐, 지금 내 강아지에 대해 이야기하자. 그러니까..."라고 말하지 않을 것입니다. 대신 힌트를 줄 것입니다. 상대방이 즉흥적으로 주제를 꺼내거나 질문을 하면 그 주제에 대해 이야기하고 싶어합니다. 때때로 상대방이 이러한 신호를 포착하지 못하는 것 같으면 그 주제에 대해 계속 이야기를 그 특정 주제로 리디렉션합니다. 주제가 나올 때마다 흥분한 것 같으면 그 주제에 대해 이야기하고 싶어합니다.

이종현T의 독해 Point!

improv actors들이 하는 행동의 핵심이 밑줄의 의미가 된다. 이 사람들은 말의 대사 사이를 잘 읽는다는 것이 핵심이다. 따라서 이걸 담고 있는 선지를 찾으면 정답은 ①번이 된다.

5.② 폭(모두가 약간 소진된 느낌)과 깊이(일부는 너무 소진되어 더 이상 일을 할 수 없습니다)에 대한 필요성을 균형 있게 해결하려면 번아웃을 상태가 아닌 스펙트럼으로 생각해야 합니다. 번아웃에 대한 대부분의 공개 토론에서 우리는 "번아웃된" 노동자들에 대해 이야기하는데, 마치 그 상태가 흑백인 것처럼 말입니다. 그러나 흑백 관점으로는 번아웃 경험의 다양성을 설명할 수 없습니다. 전구처럼 번아웃과 번아웃 사이에 명확한 경계가 있다면, 번아웃이라고 말하지만 여전히 유능하게 일을 해내는 사람들을 분류할 좋은 방법이 없습니다. 번아웃을 스펙트럼으로 생각하면 이 문제가 해결됩니다. 번아웃을 주장하지만 번아웃으로 인해 쇠약해지지 않는 사람들은 단순히 부분적이거나 덜 심각한 형태의 번아웃을 겪고 있을 뿐입니다. 번아웃은 번아웃 없이 경험하고 있습니다. 번아웃은 마지막 단어를 가지고 있지 않습니다.

이종현T의 독해 Point!

번아웃이라는 것은 하나의 스펙트럼(정도)가 된다. 즉 하나로 딱 정해진 상태가 아니고 정도가 된다는 것이 이 지문의 핵심 논리가 되고, 마지막 줄의 의미도 그 뜻이라고 생각을 하고 선지에서 이에 대한 것을 찾으면 정답은 ②번이 된다.

6.⑤ 불을 끄고 작은 손전등의 광선을 한쪽 눈으로 향하세요. 시선을 위아래로 움직이면서 광선을 흔들어 보세요. 섬세한 가지처럼 보이는 것을 엿볼 수 있어야 합니다. 이 가지는 망막 위에 있는 혈관의 그림자입니다. 혈관은 빛이 눈으로 흐르면서 끊임없이 그림자를 드리우지만, 이러한 그림자는 움직이지 않기 때문에 뇌는 그림자에 대한 반응을 멈춥니다. 손전등 빔을 움직이면 그림자가 순간적으로 보일 정도로 그림자가 이동합니다. 이제 움직이지 않는 것을 응시하는 것만으로도 이미지가 희미해질 수 있는지 궁금할 수 있습니다. 하지만 시각 시스템이 눈 근육을 끊임없이 흔들기 때문에 세상의 이미지가 완벽하게 안정화되는 것을 방해하기 때문에 그럴 수 없습니다. 이러한 근육 움직임은 믿을 수 없을 정도로 작지만 그 효과는 엄청납니다. 눈을 고정한 후 얼마 지나지 않아 보이는 것을 조정하여 실명할 수 있습니다! 흥미로운 개념입니다: 완벽보다는 완벽에 가까운 것이 더 낫다는 것입니다.

이종현T의 독해 Point!

이 지문의 핵심 논리를 찾아보면, 움직이지 않고 있게 되면 ⇒ 반응을 안하고 보이지 않게 되지만 움직이게 되면서 ⇒ 그게 보이게 된다는 것이 된다. 따라서 이 논리가 핵심 논리라고 생각하고 선지에서 이 내용을 찾으면 정답은 ⑤번이 된다.

7.⑤ 이러한 인식은 시각적 및 청각적 정보와 같은 감각적 입력에 대한 인식만으로는 사실이 아닙니다. 만나는 사람, 먹는 음식, 심지어 구매하는 제품에 대한 인식과 같은 사회적 인식에도 해당됩니다. 예를 들어 와인을 연구한 결과, 와인을 블라인드로 맛본 경우 와인의 맛 등급과 가격 사이에는 상관관계가 거의 또는 전혀 없었지만, 와인에 가격을 표시했을 때는 유의미한 상관관계가 있었습니다. 피험자들이 - 가격이 높은 와인이 더 좋은 와인이어야 한다고 의식적으로 믿었기 때문에 그에 따라 의견을 수정했기 때문이 아니었습니다. 오히려 의식적 차원에서만 사실이 아니었습니다. 피험자들이 와인을 맛보는 동안 연구자들은 자신의 뇌 활동을 이미지화하고 있었고, 이미지를 통해 비싼 와인 한 잔을 마시는 것이 더 저렴하다고 표시된 같은 와인 한 잔을 마시는 것보다 즐거움을 위해 미각의 중심을 활성화하는 것으로 나타났습니다. 이는 위약 효과와 관련이 있습니다. 통증과 마찬가지로 맛은 단순히 감각 신호의 산물이 아니라 와인을 맛보는 것이 아니라 가격을 맛보는 등 심리적 요인에 따라 달라집니다.

이종현T의 독해 Point!

이 지문의 핵심 논리는 어떤 대상에 대한 경험이나 느낌은 감각적인 것에 따라 달라지기도 하지만 심리적인 요인에 따라서도 달라지게 된다는 것이다. 따라서 이걸 담고 있는 선지를 찾으면 정답은 ⑤번이 된다.

Unit 4. 빈칸 유형

1.① 우주에 우리만 존재할까요? 아마도 과학이 아직 답하지 못한 가장 심오한 질문일 것입니다. 하지만 지금까지 외계 생명체에 대한 탐색은 ____________만 발견했습니다. 하지만 앞으로 몇 년 동안 외계 생명체에 대한 탐색은 심각하게 증가할 것입니다. 지금까지 건설된 망원경 중 가장 강력한 망원경인 제임스 웹 우주 망원경은 3월 말부터 지구로 이미지를 다시 보내기 시작할 예정입니다. 이 망원경의 센서와 기술을 통해 과학자들은 그 어느 때보다 지구와 같은 외계 행성을 자세히 살펴볼 수 있게 될 것입니다. 2023년에는 칠레의 베라 루빈 천문대가 별을 관측하기 위해 셔터를 열 예정입니다. 이 망원경은 역대 가장 큰 카메라를 탑재하여 천문학자들이 전례 없는 세부 사항으로 우주를 지도화하고 목록화할 수 있게 해줄 것입니다. 하지만 새로운 기술에 관한 것은 아닙니다. 소수의 과학자들도 외계 생명체를 완전히 새로운 방식으로 찾기 위한 계획을 세웠습니다. 천문학자들은 신호나 생명체의 성분 흔적, 생물의 부산물을 찾는 대신 외계 기술이라는 더 크고 쉽게 찾을 수 있는 무언가를 찾아야 한다고 생각합니다. 공상 과학 소설처럼 들리지만 그 이면에는 심각한 과학이 숨어 있습니다.

① 그림자
② 기적
③ 청사진
④ 대피소
⑤ 피나클

이종현T의 독해 Point!

빈칸에 들어갈 내용을 찾는다면 ⇒ 빈칸 다음 문장부터 미래로 바뀌게 되고 미래가 되면서 ⇒ 더 외계인에 찾는 게 많아지는 것이 결과라고 본다면 이제까지는 제대로 찾은 것이 없다는 뜻이 된다. 따라서 빈칸에 들어갈 내용은 외계 생명체에 대해 제대로 잘 못 찾았다는 얘기가 들어가면 되고 이런 의미가 될 수 있는 선지는 ①번이 된다.

2.① 동물 해방론자들은 일반적으로 지각이나 감정의 경계에서 도덕적 고려의 선을 그립니다. 싱어에게 있어 이는 갑각류와 연체동물 사이의 어딘가에 위치한 것으로, 홍합은 메뉴에 포함되지만 게와 바닷가재는 제외됩니다. 반면 환경 윤리는 개별 유기체에 대한 강조는 훨씬 적지만 강이나 산과 같은 무생물에 대한 도덕적 고려를 요구하며 고통과 고통이 자연의 필수적인 부분이라고 가정합니다. 이러한 윤리적 갈등은 실질적인 결과를 초래하는데, 해방론자들은 일반적으로 ____________________ 인 반면, 생태철학자들은 특정 종의 폭발적인 개체 수가 지역 환경 전체를 위협할 경우 도태되어야 한다고 주장합니다. 이러한 갈등은 특히 외래 포식자나 파괴적인 초식동물이 취약한 생태를 위협하는 경우에 더욱 시급해졌습니다.

① 사냥에 반대하여
② 동물의 고통에 둔감한
③ 생물 공동체에 관심이 있는
④ 무생물에 집중하는 경향이 있는
⑤ 외국 포식자의 통제에 유리한

이종현T의 독해 Point!

빈칸의 근거는 해방론자들이 어떤 결과를 원하는지를 찾으면 된다. 이 입장은 뒤에 오는 생태 철학자들의 입장과 반대가 된다. 생태 철학자들의 입장은 특정 종(일부의 종)이 생태계를 위협하면 ⇒ 그것들을 좀 없애는 것은 된다는 논리가 된다. 그러므로 반대를 생각한다면 해방론자들은 절대 없애면 안된다는 논리가 된다. 따라서 이게 주관식이 되는 선지를 찾으면 정답은 ①번이 된다.

3.② 이제 어머니가 어두운 슬픔의 세계에 갇혀 계신 것 같지만, 그 당시에는 아버지뿐만 아니라 어머니도 잃었다는 것만 알고 있었습니다. 열한 살 때, 일곱 살이었던 여동생과 함께 저는 가장 자리를 맡게 되었습니다. 선택의 여지가 없었습니다. 저는 시장에서 음식을 사서 최대한 잘 요리하고 여동생과 저 자신을 잘 보이도록 노력했습니다. 만약 어머니가 더 이상 우리를 돌볼 수 없다는 사실이 알려졌더라면, 지역구는 어머니로부터 우리를 빼앗았을 것이고 ____________________________.
저는 학교에서 그 집 아이들을 보며 자랐습니다. 슬픔, 그들의 얼굴에 묻은 화난 손 자국, 어깨를 앞으로 웅크린 절망감. 이유를 알기도 전에 울고, 학교에 가기 전에 어머니의 머리를 빗고 땋아 준 그 행복한 사랑스러운 여동생을 절대 내버려둘 수 없었습니다. 아버지는 심의 모든 것에 묻은 석탄 가루 층을 싫어했기 때문에 매일 밤 면도 거울을 닦으셨습니다. 커뮤니티 홈은 그녀를 벌레처럼 짓밟을 것입니다. 그래서 저는 우리의 곤경을 비밀로 유지했습니다.

① 우리에게 스스로 일하라고 요청했습니다
② 커뮤니티 홈에 우리를 배치했습니다
③ 아버지의 유산을 구하는 것을 막았습니다
④ 우리에게 새로운 편안한 집을 제공했습니다

⑤ 여동생을 마을 학교에 보냈습니다

이종현T의 독해 Point!

빈칸에 들어갈 내용은 어머니에게서 멀어진 다음 생기는 결과가 된다. 다음 문장에서 그 집 아이들을 봤다고 되었으므로 그 집 = 어머니로부터 멀어진 다음 간 집이 된다. 따라서 빈칸에 들어갈 내용은 어머니로부터 멀어진, 즉 어머니가 없는 집에서 있는 내용이 들어가면 되고 정답은 ②번이 된다.

4.① 캘리포니아 대학교 데이비스 캠퍼스의 한 연구팀이 우주 비행사들이 ____________________을 예방하는 데 도움이 될 수 있는 유전자 변형 상추 균주를 개발했습니다. 일반 상추는 이미 국제우주정거장(ISS)에서 성공적으로 재배되었기 때문에 연구팀은 인간 부갑상선 호르몬(PTH)이라는 뼈 자극 화학 물질을 생성하는 식물 균주를 만들어 우주의 미세 중력에서 장기간 보내는 뼈 파괴 효과에 대응할 수 있는지 알아보기로 결정했습니다. 최근 NASA가 스콧 켈리와 크리스티나 코흐(ISS에서 1년을 보낸 최초의 두 명의 우주비행사)를 대상으로 실시한 연구에 따르면, 이들은 체류 기간 동안 매달 뼈 밀도의 1% 이상을 잃는 것으로 나타났습니다. 화성으로의 임무는 약 3년 정도 지속될 것으로 예상되는 가운데 과학자들은 이러한 효과에 대응할 수 있는 방법을 찾고 있습니다. 의학은 한 가지 가능성이고 음식은 더 실용적일 수 있는 또 다른 가능성입니다.

① 장거리 우주 여행 중 골밀도 감소
② 우주선을 더 효과적으로 제어하기
③ 뼈의 단단함을 검사하여 부작용을 확인하기
④ 배를 조종하는 동안 환각을 경험하기
⑤ 골수에서 알려지지 않은 돌연변이 획득

이종현T의 독해 Point!

빈칸에 들어갈 내용은 유전자 변형 상추 균주를 통해 ⇒ 할 수 있는 결과를 찾으면 된다. 따라서 이 연구의 결과를 뒤에서 찾으면 뒤에 뼈 밀도의 감소에 대한 얘기가 나온다. 즉 상추 균주를 통해 할 수 있는 결과는 뼈 밀도 감소를 막아주는 것이 된다. 이미 예방이라는 prevent는 지문에 있으므로 이제 빈칸에는 뼈 밀도 감소 라는 말만 들어가면 되고 정답은 ①번이 된다.

5.② 당시 모두가 알고 있듯이 2019년 메가 히트 영화 어벤져스: 엔드게임의 개봉은 역사상 가장 수익성이 높은 영화 프랜차이즈의 결말을 알리는 신호탄이 전혀 아니었습니다. 마블 시네마틱 유니버스는 실제 세계에 존재하는 우주처럼 끝이 보이지 않는 무한히 확장될 것을 약속합니다. 하지만 마야 필립스가 M.C.U.에 대한 미학적 접근 방식에서 언급했듯이, 이러한 광범위하고 상호 연결된 스토리 라인은 크리에이터에게 ____________를 제공하므로 전체 기업의 근간이 되는 오래된 만화와 신작 영화의 복잡한 상호 작용에 맞춘 비전통적인 서사 형식의 개발이 필요합니다. 결국 모든 것이 스스로의 무게로 무너질까요? 계속 지켜봐 주세요.

① 예술 매체
② 특별한 도전 과제
③ 예상치 못한 혜택
④ 관리 가능한 부담
⑤ 황금 같은 기회

이종현T의 독해 Point!

빈칸에 들어갈 얘기는 크리에이터가 뭘 해야하는지에 관한 얘기가 되고 뒤에서 그 핵심을 찾으면 된다. 뒤에 결론으로 무너진다는 얘기가 나오고 있으므로 크리에이터들이 하기 힘들다는 얘기가 들어가면 된다. 따라서 정답은 ②번이 된다.

6.② 과학이 항상 그 원인으로 효과를 추적할 수 있다고 정말 확신할 수 있을까요? 과학은 확실히 그렇게 하려고 합니다. 데카르트는 천체들 사이의 인력을 물리학의 중심 교리인 우주 규모의 도미노 효과로 설명하고자 했습니다. 마지막 분석에서 모든 현상은 기계적 접촉의 연쇄에 의한 것이라는 점을 설명하고자 했습니다. 달이 지구 궤도를 돌고 있는 이유는 무엇일까요? ______ ______________________________________을 위해서는 달과 지구 사이에 보이지 않는 물질인 에테르의 입자가 있고 지구를 정점으로 하는 거대한 소용돌이가 달을 가둔다는 가설만 세울 수 있었습니다.

① 그의 신념 체계를 재조정하기
② 그의 교리와 일치합니다
③ 받아들여진 이론들을 거부하기
④ 그의 동료들과 구별됩니다
⑤ 덜 인기 있는 아이디어를 구현하기

이종현T의 독해 Point!

빈칸은 결과 자리이고, 바로 앞에 의문문이 있으니 그 의문문의 결과로 고정이 된다. 그 상태에서 앞의 결과가 들어간다면 그의 이론에 대해 설명한다는 얘기가 빈칸에 들어가면 된다. 따라서 정답은 ②번이 된다.

7.⑤ 고통과 쾌락은 정의할 수 없는 단순한 개념입니다. 사람들은 감정에서 오해를 받을 가능성이 없지만, 그들이 주는 이름과 그들에 대한 추론에서 자주 틀립니다. 많은 사람들은 고통이 어떤 고통의 소멸이나 감소에서 비롯된다고 생각하기 때문에 고통은 반드시 어떤 쾌락의 제거에서 비롯된다고 생각합니다. 저는 오히려 가장 단순하고 자연스러운 방식으로 고통과 쾌락이 각각 긍정적인 성격을 띠고 있으며, 결코 ______________________________.

① 슬픔과 절망에 영향을 받아
② 동물적 존재의 본질적인 감정으로 정의됩니다
③ 그들만의 명칭과 의미에 구애받지 않는
④ 상호 작용으로 인한 변화와 무관한
⑤ 서로의 존재를 위해 의존하는

이종현T의 독해 Point!

앞 문장의 논리인 쾌락을 제거하면 ⇒ 고통이 된다는 논리를 반박하는 논리가 빈칸 문장이다. 이미 빈칸 문장에 by no means라는 부정문의 형태가 있으니 빈칸에 들어갈 내용은 다시 쾌락과 고통이 서로 관련이 있다는 얘기가 들어가면 된다. 정답은 ⑤번이 된다.

8.① 오즈의 마법사와 호커스 포커스의 샌더슨 자매의 착한 마녀 글린다는 화려한 옷장을 가지고 있었지만, 표준 마녀 의상의 기본은 일반적으로 검은색 드레스, 망토 또는 가운입니다. "역사적으로 치유하는 여성과 나중에 마녀라고 불리게 될 다른 사람들은 마을 공동체의 다른 사람들이 직접 만든 기능적인 옷을 입곤 했습니다."라고 라스베이거스 네바다 대학교의 영어 조교수 캐서린 워커는 말합니다. "중세 시대와 그 이후에는 이 옷에 망토나 후드가 등장했습니다. 따라서 처음에는 마녀가 ______________________"라고 말했습니다. 그러나 이러한 의상이 마녀와 연관되는 데는 그리 오래 걸리지 않았습니다. "특히 검은색 드레스와의 연관성은 르네상스 시대 내내 검은색과 악마 및 '검은 마법'이 연관되어 있었기 때문일 것입니다."라고 워커는 설명합니다.

① 이웃과 시각적으로 구별되는
② 이웃의 비판에 취약한
③ 이웃에게 해가 되도록 의도된
④ 이웃만큼이나 검소하게 여겨지는
⑤ 의상을 입은 이웃들과 동일합니다

이종현T의 독해 Point!

however 뒤부터 마녀가 상황이 변하면서 옷과 관련이 있다 고 되어 있으므로 however 앞 문장은 옷과 관련이 없다는 얘기가 되면 된다. 빈칸 문장에 not이 있으므로 다시 관련이 있다는 얘기를 찾으면 정답은 ①번이 된다.

9.⑤ 20세기에 들어서야 비유럽 문화는 진정한 글로벌 비전을 채택했습니다. 이는 유럽 패권의 붕괴를 초래한 중요한 요인 중 하나였습니다. 따라서 알제리 독립 전쟁(1954~62)에서 알제리 게릴라는 압도적인 수치, 기술, 경제적 우위를 점하며 프랑스 군대를 물리쳤습니다. 알제리는 글로벌 반식민지 네트워크의 지원을 받았고, 프랑스 자체의 여론뿐만 아니라 전 세계 미디어를 자국의 대의에 활용하는 방법을 고민했기 때문에 승리했습니다. 작은 북베트남이 미국 거상에게 가한 패배도 비슷한 전략에 기반했습니다. 이러한 게릴라 세력은 ______________________________.

① 그들의 전략은 적에게 노출되었습니다
② 이전 침략에서 교훈을 얻지 못했습니다
③ 그들은 잘 훈련된 엘리트 부대가 없었습니다
④ 그들은 격렬한 전투에서 적과 교전했습니다
⑤ 지역 투쟁이 전 세계적인 원인이 되었습니다

이종현T의 독해 Point!

지문의 핵심 논리를 넣겠다고 생각하면 된다. 게릴라 세력이 지원을 받게 되면 큰 세력도 이길 수 있다는 논리가 들어가면 된다. 따라서 정답은 ⑤번이 된다.

10.⑤ 면접이든 임시 업무 과제든 하이테크의 벽 안에 있을 때 염두에 두어야 할 한 가지가 있습니다. 주로 자신의 태도에 따라 판단됩니다. 하이테크 사람들은 열정적이고 보여주는 사람들을 좋아합니다. 그게 진부하게 들린다면 죄송하지만 사실입니다. 긍정적인 태도, 미소, 유머 감각은 입사할 때 놀라운 일을 할 수 있습니다. 면접을 볼 때 채용 담당자뿐만 아니라 채용 담당자를 볼 수도 있고, 일반적으로 입사 후 동료가 될 3~6명의 다른 사람들도 면접을 볼 수 있습니다. 이 사람들 각각은 주로 "적합"이라는 것으로 저를 판단할 것입니다. 네, 똑똑해야 하고, 직무를 이해하고 수행할 수 있음을 입증해야 합니다. 하지만 이 모든 것을 수행하면서도 여전히 "적합"이라는 질문에 대해 반박할 수 있습니다. 면접 중 태도와 태도는 ______________________________.

① 미래 직장에서 얼마나 잘 수행할 것인가

② 상사에게 정중하게 응답하는 방법
③ 직장에서 얼마나 유머러스한지
④ 까다로운 작업에 얼마나 열정적으로 임하십니까
⑤ 그룹에 얼마나 잘 어울릴 수 있을까요

이종현T의 독해 Point!

면접 중 태도와 태도를 통해 알 수 있는 결과가 빈칸에 들어가면 된다. 앞에서 그 결과를 찾으면 회사의 사람들이 당신에 대해 좋게 평가할 것이라는 얘기가 빈칸에 들어가면 정답은 ⑤번이 된다.

11.② 우리는 지구 이외의 조건에서는 생명체가 존재할 수 없으며, 다른 세계는 우리와 비슷하다는 조건에서만 사람이 살 수 있다고 상상하는 경향이 있습니다. 하지만 지구 자연 자체는 이러한 사고방식의 오류를 우리에게 보여줍니다. 우리는 물속에서 죽습니다: 물고기는 물속에서 죽습니다. 다시 말하지만, 근시안적인 자연주의자들은 바다 밑바닥에서 생명체가 불가능하다는 것을 단호하게 주장합니다: 첫째, 완전한 어둠 속에 있기 때문입니다; 둘째, 끔찍한 압력으로 인해 어떤 유기체도 폭발할 수 있기 때문입니다; 셋째, 모든 움직임이 불가능하기 때문입니다. 이러한 깊이에는 빛이 없습니다: 그들은 자신의 인광으로 그것을 만듭니다. 다른 조사자들은 지하 동굴을 방문하여 ______________________________에 의해 장기가 변형된 동물과 식물을 발견합니다.

① 엄청난 물의 압력
② 우울한 환경에 적응하기
③ 다양한 종에 걸친 교배 경향
④ 해양 생물의 자연스러운 성향
⑤ 갑작스러운 환경 변화

이종현T의 독해 Point!

동물들의 장기가 변형된 원인이 빈칸에 들어가면 된다. 환경에 따라 변하게 된다는 것이 핵심 논리이므로 환경에 대한 것을 찾으면 2, 5번 중 하나이고, 그 중 어두운 환경을 찾으면 ②번이 된다.

12.② 프톨레마이오스는 별들의 움직임에서 별들이 거대한 지구 내부에 붙어 있는 밝은 점이라는 결론에 도달했습니다. 이 지구의 움직임은 지구가 중심을 차지하고 있다는 가정과 일치했을 뿐입니다. 태양, 달, 별들이 나날이 떠오르며 찬란한 끝없는 행렬을 이루며 하늘을 가로질러 움직였고, 정해진 경로가 실행되었을 때 정식으로 설정되었다는 명백한 사실은 몇 가지 설명을 요구했습니다. 고정된 별들이 해마다, 그리고 나이에서 나이에 이르기까지 상호 거리를 유지했다는 정황은 프톨레마이오스에게 그 별들이 포함된 영역이 매일 한 번씩 지구 주위를 완전히 돌고 있다는 것을 증명하는 것처럼 보였습니다. 따라서 프톨레마이오스는 ______________________________.

① 별의 별자리는 지구에 영향을 미칩니다
② 지구는 정지해 있었습니다
③ 태양은 우주의 중심입니다
④ 우리의 지구는 태양 주위를 돌고 있습니다
⑤ 우리의 지구는 역동적이었습니다

이종현T의 독해 Point!

프톨레마이오스의 핵심 논리는 지구를 중심으로 별들이 돈다는 것이었다. 따라서 지구는 가만히 있고 그 주위를 별들이 돈다는 논리를 찾으면 정답은 ②번이 된다.

13.② 토지 윤리의 진화를 방해하는 가장 심각한 장애물은 아마도 우리의 교육 및 경제 시스템이 토지에 대한 강렬한 의식이 아닌 곳으로 향하고 있다는 사실일 것입니다. 오늘날 사람들은 많은 중개인과 수많은 물리적 장치에 의해 토지와 분리되어 있습니다. 그들에게는 중요한 관계가 없으며, 농작물이 자라는 도시 사이의 공간입니다. 땅에서 하루 동안 농작물을 풀어놓고 골프 링크나 '풍경한' 지역이 아니라면 지루할 수밖에 없습니다. 농작물을 농사 대신 수경 재배(수경 재배)로 재배할 수 있다면 매우 적합할 것입니다. 목재, 가죽, 양모 및 기타 천연 토지 제품의 합성 대체품이 원래보다 더 잘 어울립니다. 요컨대, 토지는 ______________________________입니다.

① 그들이 모방하고자 하는 모델
② 그들이 토지보다 더 크게 자란 것
③ 유기농 제품을 판매할 수 있는 장소
④ 어쨌든 그들에게 이익이 되는 것
⑤ 중재자의 도움으로 재배하는 것

이종현T의 독해 Point!

땅에 대한 핵심 결과를 찾으면 사람들은 이제 땅보다 훨씬 더 올라가서 땅과 별 관련이 없어졌다는 것이므로 이걸 빈칸에 넣으면 정답은 ②번이 된다.

14.⑤ 하이데거에 따르면, 존재와 시간의 전체는 하나의 질문, 즉 존재의 의미에 관한 질문에 관심을 가지고 있습니다. 하지

만 그가 '존재'라는 용어를 의미하는 것은 무엇일까요? 만약 그렇다면, 그것은 무엇을 의미할까요? 하이데거가 이 질문에 대해 명확하고 간단한 답을 제공하지 않는 것은 우연이 아닙니다. 하이데거가 보기에, 적어도 그의 책 전체가 우리가 일관되고 잠재적으로 유익한 방식으로 질문을 할 수 있는 지점에 도달하는 데 필요할 것이기 때문입니다. 그럼에도 불구하고, 그는 또한 존재에 대해 ______________________________ ______________________________에 대한 일정하고 예비적인 이해를 가지고 있으므로, 이 초기 단계에서도 적어도 우리의 사고에 대한 초기 방향을.

① 우리 대부분의 행동 방식에 부재합니다
② 의미 있는 방식으로 완전히 결여되어 있습니다
③ 그의 사고방식을 추구하는 데 있어 중요하지 않습니다
④ 그의 궁극적인 질문에 명확한 답을 제공하지 않습니다
⑤ 인간의 모든 말과 행동에 암묵적입니다

이종현T의 독해 Point!

Nevertheless 앞 부분 논리는 그는 존재에 대해 병확하게 답을 하지 않았다고 나와 있다. 그리고 그 반박이 된다면 어느 정도는 답을 했다가 되는 것이고, 이렇게 되는 의미를 찾으면 정답은 ⑤번이 된다.

15.④ 예술이란 정말 무엇이며 왜 인간이라는 것이 무엇을 의미하는지와 그렇게 밀접하게 연관되어 있는 것처럼 보이는 걸까요? 우리는 예술을 생산하는 유일한 포유류 종이며, 예술이 우리에게 중요하지만 신체적 생존을 위해 결코 필요하지 않습니다. 그럼에도 불구하고 인간이 예술적으로 표현할 권리를 위해 어떻게 목숨을 걸고 희생했는지에 대한 사례는 무수히 많습니다. 예술은 산문과 시를 담은 문학부터 조각과 그림, 영화 제작, 음악 작곡뿐만 아니라 춤과 같은 신체 표현까지 다양한 형태로 존재합니다. 하지만 우리가 예술을 통해 표현하고자 하는 열망은 무엇일까요? 천 년 동안 다양한 예술 작품을 연구함으로써 인간의 상태와 영혼의 존재 및 유사한 신비로운 현상을 포함한 삶과 죽음에 대한 불안한 숙고를 표현하는 몇 가지 주제가 계속 등장합니다. 이러한 주제는 일반적으로 현대적인 환경에서 묘사되며, 때로는 의도한 청중과 공감할 수 있는 은유를 통해 변형되기도 합니다. 예술의 많은 표현은 시간, 문화, 지리에 따라 다양한 형태와 형태를 취하며 적어도 과거에는 ______________________.

① 연극 예술 준수 의무
② 문화적 내러티브 기대에 대한 지침
③ 운동 능력 평가 기준
④ 미적 최소 기준 요구 사항
⑤ 환경 지속 가능성 계획을 위한 조건

이종현T의 독해 Point!

우리는 예술에 대해 과거에도 약간의 기준은 가지고 있었다는 얘기가 앞 부분의 오늘날의 반대로 들어간다고 생각하면 정답은 ④번이 된다.

16.① 도덕, 효용, 또는 최대 행복 원칙의 기초로 받아들이는 신조는 행동이 행복을 촉진하는 경향이 있는 만큼 비례하여 옳고, 행복의 반대를 초래하는 경향이 있는 만큼 잘못되었다고 주장합니다. 행복은 의도된 쾌락이고, 고통의 부재는 불행, 고통, 쾌락의 프라이버시에 의해 이루어집니다. 이론이 설정한 도덕적 기준을 명확하게 이해하려면 훨씬 더 많은 것을 말해야 합니다. 특히 고통과 쾌락의 개념에 무엇이 포함되어 있는지, 그리고 이것이 어느 정도까지 열려 있는지는 여전히 의문으로 남아 있습니다. 그러나 이러한 보충 설명은 이 도덕 이론의 근거가 되는 생명 이론, 즉 쾌락과 고통으로부터의 자유가 목적으로서 바람직한 유일한 것이라는 것, 그리고 모든 바람직한 것들(다른 어떤 계획에서처럼 공리주의적인 것들도 많음)이 그 자체로 내재된 쾌락을 위해 또는 ______________________________을 위해 또는 수단으로서 바람직하다는 것입니다.

① 쾌락 증진과 통증 예방
② 부의 획득과 빈곤 탈출
③ 지식 추구와 무지 회피
④ 권력의 획득과 억압으로부터의 해방
⑤ 덕목의 함양과 도덕적 우수성의 성취

이종현T의 독해 Point!

빈칸에 들어갈 내용은 바람직한 것들을 통해 얻는 결과에 대한 얘기가 들어가야 하고 앞에 들어가는 것은 쾌락은 올리는 것이고 고통은 내린다는 얘기가 들어가면 된다. 따라서 정답은 ①번이 된다.

17.① 7월 군주제 기간(1830~48) 동안 루이-필립의 보다 비공식적인 생활 방식과 왕실 부모의 자녀에 대한 헌신에 영향을 받아 가족 생활의 이상은 대중의 상상력을 강하게 사로잡았고 부르주아 사회의 핵심이 되었습니다. 자녀의 돌봄과 교육, 유아 인격의 발달은 큰 관심사가 되었습니다. 이러한 가족에 대한 집착과 자녀의 역할은 나폴레옹 3세(1852~70) 치하의 제2제국 시기에도 계속되었으며, 나폴레옹 3세는 그의 아내 외제니 황후와

함께 ______________의 이미지를 배양했습니다. 빅토리아 여왕과 핀스 알버트가 자손과 함께 노는 모습을 담은 판화가 많은 가정의 벽을 장식한 영국에서도 같은 현상이 발생했습니다. 1850년 이후의 이 시기는 경제적 번영, 시민 개선, 부르주아 자기 확신으로 주목받았으며, 19세기 아동 문학 발전에서 가장 결실이 많은 시기로 여겨질 수 있습니다. 가정 현실주의 소설 또는 가족 소설은 세기 전반기의 도덕적 이야기에서 발전하여 성인을 위한 현실주의 소설의 발전을 반영했습니다.

① 가족 간의 친밀감
② 행복한 어머니
③ 지배적인 가족
④ 번영하는 그룹
⑤ 중산층의 욕구

이종현T의 독해 Point!

가족에 대한 집착과 자녀의 역할을 통해 알 수 있는 결과가 빈칸에 들어가면 된다. 빈칸에 들어갈 결과도 가족들 간의 애정에 대한 얘기가 들어가면 되고 정답은 ①번이 된다.

18.④ 콜럼버스 신화는 백인 미국인들이 그들의 '이야기'에 대한 용기 있는 개방을 선언할 수 있게 해주었습니다. 이 신화는 미국에서 널리 퍼져 있는 영향력 있는 기원의 꿈 신화의 일부였습니다. F. 스콧 피츠제럴드의 위대한 개츠비는 아메리칸 드림의 힘과 살아있는 경험 속에서 꿈을 찾는 문제를 모두 인식하고 있습니다. 끝없는 진보, 자기 창조, 성취와 성공의 이상 - 콜럼버스 정신에 반영된 __________ 은 닉 캐러웨이의 눈을 통해 본 제이 개츠비의 모습으로 펼쳐집니다. 소설은 정체성 문제와 특히 '잃어버린 기원'으로 돌아가고자 하는 '꿈'을 믿고자 하는 유혹에 관한 것으로, 개츠비가 과거에 결혼할 뻔했던 여성 데이지 뷰캐넌이 '잃어버린 기원'으로 돌아가고자 하는 열망에서 나타납니다.

① 좌절된 계획
② 충족된 계획
③ 달성할 수 없는 목표
④ 결실 없는 그리움
⑤ 신화 속 꿈

이종현T의 독해 Point!

빈칸에 들어갈 뒤에 들어갈 결과를 찾으면 게츠비가 열망했다는 얘기가 있으므로 빈칸에도 열망에 대한 얘기가 들어가면 정답은 ④번이 된다.

19.⑤ 문학은 독자들에게 길러주는 __________ 때문에 언어 학습 과정에 도움이 될 수 있습니다. 핵심 언어 교육 자료는 언어가 규칙 기반 시스템과 사회적 의미 시스템으로서 어떻게 작동하는지에 집중해야 합니다. 학습 과정은 본질적으로 분석적이고 단편적이며 성격 수준에서는 상당히 피상적인 경우가 많습니다. 문학에 상상력 있게 참여하면 학습자는 외국어 시스템의 보다 기계적인 측면을 넘어 관심의 초점을 전환할 수 있습니다. 소설, 연극 또는 단편 소설이 일정 기간 동안 탐구되면 독자는 텍스트를 '습관화'하기 시작합니다. 그 결과 독자는 책에 끌리게 됩니다. 개별 단어나 구절이 무엇을 의미하는지 정확히 파악하는 것이 이야기의 전개를 추구하는 것보다 덜 중요해집니다. 독자는 사건이 전개될 때 어떤 일이 일어나는지 알아내기를 열망하며, 특정 인물과 가까워지고 감정적인 반응을 공유합니다. 언어는 '투명'하게 되며, 소설은 전체 사람을 자신의 세계로 끌어들입니다.

① 언어적 통찰
② 예술적 상상력
③ 문학적 감성
④ 대안적 관점
⑤ 개인적인 개입

이종현T의 독해 Point!

빈칸이 원인이고 ⇒ 그 결과가 언어 학습 과정에 도움이 된다는 것이다. 따라서 뒤에서 언어 학습 과정에 도움이 되는 원인을 찾게 되면, 뒤에 참여한다고 되어 있다. 즉 참여를 통해 학습에 도움을 준다는 것이므로 이게 들어간 선지를 찾으면 정답은 ⑤번이 된다.

20.③ 교육은 기껏해야 단순한 지식 이상의 것을 가르칩니다. 비판적 사고, 즉 행동하기 전에 멈추고 생각하고 감정적 압력에 굴복하지 않는 능력을 가르칩니다. 이것은 사고 통제가 아닙니다. 바로 그 반대입니다: 정신적 해방입니다. 아무리 진보된 지식인이라도 이 기술에는 완벽하지 않을 것입니다. 하지만 '자극 중심'이라는 불완전한 소유조차도 즉각적인 환경, 가장 밝은 색상 또는 가장 큰 소리에 끊임없이 반응합니다. 본능과 감정에 의해 항상 살아가는 휴리스틱한 반응에 이끌리는 것은 여러 면에서 매우 쉬운 삶의 방식입니다: 특히 경험이 없는 사람들에게는 생각이 노력적입니다. 하지만 감정도 지치고 단기적인 반응은 장기적으로 건강과 생존에 가장 유익하지 않을 수 있습니다. 편의를 위해 햄버거를 찾는 것처럼 언젠가 죽을 수도 있는 동맥 지방을 저장하면 감정에 대한 의존도가 큰 해를 끼칠 수 있습니다.

① 사람들의 위험을 강화합니다

② 우리의 이해를 높입니다
③ 사람을 부담에서 해방시킵니다
④ 우리가 피할 수 없는 것을 받아들일 수 있게 해줍니다
⑤ 경험이 필요합니다

이종현T의 독해 Point!

빈칸에 들어갈 결과는 앞의 결과를 넣어주면 된다. even이 들어간 문장이기 때문이다. 앞에 들어갈 결과는 mental liberation이므로 이게 들어간다면 정답은 ③번이 된다.

21.② 우리는 세계에서 가장 크고 수익성이 높은 비즈니스가 제 관심을 소비하는 주의 경제 시대에 살고 있는 것으로 유명합니다. 광고 산업은 말 그대로 제 삶의 의식적인 시간을 포착하여 다른 사람에게 판매하는 데 전념하고 있습니다. 이렇게 많은 흥미롭고 유용한 소프트웨어 시스템을 무료로 사용할 수 있다는 것이 마법처럼 보일 수 있지만, 이제는 무료로 보이는 것에 누가 비용을 지불하는지 볼 수 없다면 ________________________. 다른 사람들과의 창의적인 소통은 닉 시버가 캡톨로지라고 부르는 과정을 통해 우리의 주의를 사로잡고, 개인 탐구의 자유를 알고리즘 생성 재생 목록이나 알고리즘 생성 예술로 대체하도록 설계된 AI 기반 추천 시스템에 의해 중재됩니다.
① 당신의 모든 관심은 이미 소진되었습니다
② 판매되는 진짜 제품은 바로 당신입니다
③ 귀하의 개인정보가 침해되고 있습니다
④ 대중이 여러분을 후원할 수 있습니다
⑤ 친구 AI 덕분에 혜택을 누릴 수 있습니다

이종현T의 독해 Point!

빈칸에 들어갈 결과는 어떤 경우에도 판매는 되고 있다는 결과가 들어가면 된다. 따라서 정답은 ②번이 된다.

22.⑤ 중앙 집중식 공식 규칙은 ________________. 야구 규칙은 단순히 선수들의 행동을 규제하는 것이 아니라 게임을 하는 행동을 결정합니다. 규칙은 사람들이 야구를 하는 것을 방해하지 않으며, 사람들이 야구를 할 수 있는 바로 그 관행을 만듭니다. 음악 악보는 규칙을 부과하지만, 사람들이 음악을 제작할 수 있는 행동 패턴을 만들기도 합니다. 기업을 설립하고, 의지와 신탁을 사용하며, 협상 가능한 도구를 만들고, 모든 계약 관행을 확립하는 법적 규칙은 개인에게 새로운 기회를 창출하는 관행을 만듭니다. 그리고 판사, 신탁자, 파트너, 후견인 등 법 체계 내에서 개인이 수행하는 역할을 확립하는 법적 규칙이 있습니다. 사실, 이러한 역할을 확립하는 법적 규칙은 자신을 점유하는 개인의 행동을 제한할 뿐만 아니라 규칙 자체도 역할을 만들어냅니다. 규칙이 없다면 개인은 그 역할을 점유할 기회를 갖지 못할 것입니다.
① 자신의 행동 패턴을 합법적이고 생산적인 방식으로 분류하기
② 사람들이 사회에서 자신의 역할과 관행을 재평가하도록 이끌기
③ 창의적인 아이디어를 촉진하는 새로운 사고 방식을 장려합니다
④ 법적 및 확립된 맥락에서 자신의 행동을 강화합니다
⑤ 역할과 관행을 확립하여 생산적인 활동을 촉진합니다

이종현T의 독해 Point!

규칙을 통해 할 수 있는 결과가 들어가면 된다. 규칙을 통해 역할을 만들어낸다는 결과가 빈칸에 들어가면 되므로 이게 들어간 선지를 찾으면 ⑤번이 된다.

23.① 어느 정도 과학 기술 발전을 이룬 후에는 추가 발전이 더 쉬워지나요, 아니면 더 어려워지나요? 직관적으로 두 가지 경쟁 효과가 있기 때문에 어느 쪽이든 갈 수 있을 것 같습니다. 한편으로는 "거인의 어깨 위에 서 있다", 즉 이전 발견이 미래의 발전을 더 쉽게 만들 수 있다는 것입니다. 다른 한편으로는 "-hanging이 적은 과일을 따다", 쉬운 발견을 먼저하기 때문에 남아 있는 발견은 더 어렵습니다. 바퀴는 한 번만 발명할 수 있고, 한 번 발명하면 비슷한 중요한 발명품을 찾기가 더 어려워집니다. 이 두 가지 효과 모두 중요하지만 데이터를 살펴보면 후자의 효과 ________________. 전반적으로 과거의 발전은 미래의 발전을 더 어렵게 만듭니다. 혁신의 역사를 보면 이를 질적으로 쉽게 알 수 있습니다. 물리학을 생각해 보세요. 1905년 알버트 아인슈타인은 'miracle의 해'에 광전 효과, 브라운 운동, 특수 상대성 이론, 유명한 방정식인 $E=mc^2$를 설명하며 물리학에 혁명을 일으켰습니다. 당시 그는 스물여섯 살이었고 특허 사무원으로 일하면서 이 모든 일을 해냈습니다. 아인슈타인의 시대와 비교하면 물리학의 발전은 이제 훨씬 더 어려워졌습니다.
① 우세한
② 산란
③ 다양합니다
④ 사라지다
⑤ 페이드

이종현T의 독해 Point!

빈칸에 들어갈 결과는 후자가 좀 더 중요하다는 얘기가 들어가면 된다. 둘의 차이점이 되는 부분이다. 따라서 정

답은 ①번이 된다.

24.② 행동은 대부분 유전자와 뇌 신경 경로의 산물입니다. 살아있는 유기체가 움직이고, 생각하고, 행동하고, 행동할 때 직장에서 일어나는 우아한 화학 작용을 고려하세요. 물론 환경은 우리가 행동하는 방식에 영향을 미칠 수 있기 때문에 여기서 환경은 중요한 요소입니다. 비유를 통해 이를 적절히 설명할 수 있습니다. 환경을 가솔린으로, 우리 몸을 엔진으로 생각해 보세요. 실제로 엔진은 가솔린 없이 작동하지 않지만 엔진의 모든 복잡한 부품은 가솔린이 주입되기 훨씬 전에 반응성 목적으로 설계되고 조립된 물리적 아키텍처의 산물입니다. 더 많은 가스를 주입하면 엔진이 가속, 덜 가속, 느려집니다. 유기체도 마찬가지입니다. 행동은 환경에 대한 반응입니다. 우리에게는 '자유 의지'가 있지만 그 반응의 궁극적인 특성은 유전자와 뇌의 구조와 관련해서만 작용할 수 있습니다. 즉, 환경은 잠재적인 행동을 효과적으로 가속하거나 늦출 수 있지만 ______________________________ ______________________________, 따라서 환경은 촉매제일 뿐입니다.

① 올바른 입력에도 오작동
② 이미 구축되어 있으며 기능적입니다
③ 주기적으로 종료되는 경향이 있습니다
④ 예측할 수 없는 방식으로 실행됩니다
⑤ 예고 없이 변경될 수 있습니다

이종현T의 독해 Point!

빈칸에 들어갈 결과는 환경의 결과이다. 다음 문장에 환경은 결과를 발생시키는 촉매제일 뿐이다라고 되어 있으므로 빈칸에는 결과를 만들어낸다는 얘기가 들어가면 된다. 정답은 ②번이 된다.

25.② 1세 때의 사회적 - 인지 혁명은 유아들이 생후 2년차를 맞이하는 계기가 되며, 모든 종류의 도구, 유물, 상징의 사용을 모방적으로 배우기 시작합니다. 예를 들어, Meltzoff(1988)의 연구에서 14개월 된 - 아이들은 성인의 허리가 구부러지고 머리가 패널에 닿는 것을 관찰하여 불이 켜지는 것을 관찰했습니다. 그들도 그 뒤를 따랐습니다. 유아들은 단순히 손으로 패널을 누르는 것이 더 쉽고 자연스러웠음에도 불구하고 다소 특이하고 어색한 행동을 보였습니다. 이러한 행동에 대한 한 가지 해석은 유아들이 성인이 빛을 밝히는 목표가 있다는 것을 이해한 다음 가능한 다른 수단 중 하나를 선택했으며, 같은 목표를 가지고 있다면 동일한 수단을 선택할 수 있다는 것입니다. 마찬가지로 Carpenter 등(1998)은 16개월 된 - 유아들이 의도적으로 보이는 행동만 복잡한 행동 순서에서 모방적으로 학습하고 우발적으로 보이는 행동은 무시한다는 사실을 발견했습니다. 어린 아이들은 단순히 다른 사람의 팔다리 움직임을 모방하는 것이 아니라 ______________________________.

① 가족들의 눈에 어색해 보이지 않기
② 세상에서 다른 사람의 의도된 행동을 재현하기
③ 도움이 되는 우연한 사건의 가치를 인정합니다
④ 다른 사람들이 놓친 전례 없는 방식으로 행동합니다
⑤ 자신의 목표와 일치하지 않는 모든 목표를 약화시킵니다

이종현T의 독해 Point!

아이들이 하는 행동의 결과를 찾으면 된다. 그 결과는 사람들이 의도적으로 하는 행동을 따라하는 것이므로 이게 들어간 선지를 찾으면 ②번이 된다.

26.② 지적 탐구의 이상이자 지식의 발전을 위한 전략으로서 과학적 방법은 본질적으로 오류의 유용성을 보여주는 기념비입니다. 우리 대부분은 자신의 신념을 증명하려는 노력에 끌리며, 그 타당성을 전혀 조사하지 않습니다. 그러나 과학자들은 개인은 아니더라도 공동체로서 자신의 신념을 반증하려고 노력합니다. 따라서 가설의 정의적 특징은 틀렸다는 것이 증명될 가능성이 있다는 것이며(따라서 검증 가능하고 검증 가능해야 한다는 것), 이론의 정의적 특징은 아직 틀렸다는 것이 증명되지 않았다는 것입니다. 하지만 중요한 부분은 아무리 많은 증거가 확인되더라도, 아무리 많은 전문가들이 지지하더라도, 아무리 대중적인 지지를 받더라도 그것이 틀렸다는 것입니다. 사실, 주어진 이론이 틀렸다는 것을 증명할 수 있을 뿐만 아니라, 조만간 증명될 가능성도 있습니다. 그리고 그렇게 되면 과학의 실패가 아니라 성공을 알리는 계기가 될 것입니다. 이것이 과학 혁명의 중요한 통찰이었습니다: 지식의 발전은 현재의 이론 ______________________________ ______________________________.

① 시간적 및 공간적 제약에 관계없이 참을 유지하기
② 새로운 통찰과 발견 앞에서 무너짐
③ 과학자들의 명성 추구에 따라 변화하기
④ 대중에게 노출되고 인기를 누리기
⑤ 오류와 실패의 기회를 남기지 않기

이종현T의 독해 Point!

지식이 발전되는 원인이 빈칸에 들어가면 된다. 현재의 이론이 틀리게 되면 ⇒ 발전하게 된다는 것이 핵심 논리

가 된다. 따라서 원인 자리엔 현재의 이론이 틀렸다는 것이 들어가면 된다. 정답은 ②번이 된다.

27.② 나방이 빛에 끌리는 이유에 대해 많은 논의가 있었습니다. 나방은 ________________에 비해 빛에 그다지 끌리지 않는다는 것이 일치하는 것 같습니다. 빛은 곤충의 방향을 틀어 고정 패턴으로 보내주는 감각 과부하가 됩니다. 마하 밴드 이론이라는 가설에 따르면 나방은 광원 주변의 어두운 영역을 보고 광원이 빛을 벗어나기 위해 향한다고 합니다. 또 다른 이론에 따르면 나방은 광원에서 나오는 빛을 중앙에 어두운 점이 있는 확산 헤일로로 인식한다고 합니다. 나방은 빛을 피하려고 시도하다가 상상한 '포털'을 향해 날아가 광원에 더 가까이 다가갑니다. 빛에 가까워질수록 기준점이 바뀌고 포털에 도달하기 위해 절망적으로 빛을 돌립니다. 나방이 현관 조명을 도는 것은 누구나 잘 알고 있습니다. 나방의 비행은 목적이 없는 것처럼 보이지만, 빛의 끌어당김을 피하려고 하는 것으로 여겨집니다.

① 따뜻한
② 갇힌
③ 표적
④ 보호
⑤ 거부된

이종현T의 독해 Point!

나방은 빛에 끌리는 것이 아니고 빛에 있을 수밖에 없다는 얘기가 들어가면 되고, 빛과 함께 있다는 얘기가 될 수 있는 표현은 ②번이 된다.

28.② 통신 기술의 사용을 결정하는 요인 중 하나는 장비와 인력에 대한 투자의 종류, 누가 투자하고 그 대가로 무엇을 기대하느냐입니다. 투자가 반드시 ________________의 형태로 이루어질 것이라는 보장은 없습니다. 투자 자금의 소유권은 상업 조직의 손에 있는 경향이 있기 때문에 통신 인프라의 현대화는 잠재적인 수익성을 기반으로만 이루어집니다. 예를 들어, 아프리카 대륙 전역에 광섬유 통신 케이블을 설치하는 것을 들 수 있습니다. 여러 아프리카 국가들이 개발에 참여하고 있지만, 그 운영 구조는 접근 비용을 지불할 수 있는 국가들을 대상으로 할 것입니다. 교육 및 정보에 사용하고자 하는 많은 국가들은 이를 너무 비싸게 여길 뿐만 아니라 단순히 이용할 수 없게 될 수도 있습니다. 개발이 지역 사회의 수요보다는 투자 기회에 의해 주도되었다는 것은 의심의 여지가 없습니다.

① 유지 관리에 최소한의 비용과 노력이 필요합니다
② 대부분의 사람들에게 가장 적합합니다
③ 현재 표준 및 글로벌 규범에 부합합니다
④ 가장 진보된 기술을 사용합니다
⑤ 기업의 상업적 이익 증진

이종현T의 독해 Point!

투자가 많은 사람들에게 기회를 주는 것은 아니라는 핵심 결과가 빈칸에 들어가면 된다. 이미 아에 no guarantee 라는 부정문이 있으니 많은 사람들에게 기회를 준다는 얘기가 빈칸에 들어가면 되고 정답은 ②번이 된다.

29.① 도시의 질은 선택적 활동에 매우 중요하기 때문에 머무르는 활동의 정도는 종종 도시의 질뿐만 아니라 공간의 질을 측정하는 도구로 사용될 수 있습니다. 도시의 많은 보행자가 반드시 좋은 도시의 질을 나타내는 것은 아니며, 걸어 다니는 사람들이 많다는 것은 종종 교통 옵션이 부족하거나 도시의 다양한 기능 사이의 거리가 멀다는 신호일 수 있습니다. 반대로, 많은 사람들이 걷지 않는 도시는 종종 좋은 도시의 질을 나타낸다고 주장할 수 있습니다. 로마와 같은 도시에서는 걷기보다는 광장에 서 있거나 앉아 있는 많은 사람들이 눈에 띕니다. 그리고 그것은 필요성 때문이 아니라 ________________. 도시 공간에서 머물고 싶은 유혹이 너무 많은 상태에서 계속 움직이기는 어렵습니다. 반면에 많은 사람들이 지나가지만 정차하거나 머무는 경우는 거의 없는 새로운 숙소와 단지도 많이 있습니다.

① 도시의 품질이 매우 매력적입니다
② 공공장소는 이미 사용 중입니다
③ 대중교통 이용 불가
④ 주요 관광지가 도보 거리에 있습니다
⑤ 도시의 행정 건물이 밀집해 있습니다

이종현T의 독해 Point!

사람들이 광장에 서 있거나 앉아 있는 이유가 들어가면 된다. 다음 문장에 유혹이 너무 많은 것이 이유이므로 이게 들어간 선지를 찾으면 정답은 ①번이 된다.

30.③ 사람들에게 다른 사람이 필요하다는 것은 거의 새로운 소식이 아니지만, 루소에게 이러한 의존은 동반자나 심지어 사랑을 넘어 인간이 되는 과정에 이르기까지 훨씬 더 확장되었습니다. 루소는 사람은 태어나는 것이 아니라 모든 개인이 다른 사람의 적극적인 참여를 필요로 하는 잠재력의 묶음으로 만들어졌다고

믿었습니다. 자기 개발은 사회적 과정입니다. 자급자족은 불가능한 환상입니다. 루소는 대부분 열정적으로 그렇지 않기를 바랐습니다: 로빈슨 크루소는 가장 좋아하는 책이었고, 그는 사회 생활의 고통과 불확실성에서 벗어나기를 갈망했습니다. 그러나 그의 글은 __________________________. 우리의 가장 달콤한 존재는 상대적이고 집단적이며, 우리의 진정한 자아는 전적으로 우리 안에 있지 않습니다. 루소가 피티에의 루브릭 아래 분석한 친절은 '연민'으로 번역되지만 흄과 스미스가 정의한 '공감'에 훨씬 더 가깝습니다. 이것이 바로 이 집단적 존재의 핵심입니다.

① 인간 본성을 이해하기 위한 철학적 연구의 필요성
② 문학 작품을 통한 자급자족의 발전
③ 감정적 애착에 의한 개인의 형성
④ 투쟁을 통해 자기 reliant 인간을 만들기
⑤ 다른 사람을 진심으로 신뢰하는 것의 어려움

이종현T의 독해 Point!

그의 글에 생긴 결과를 찾으면 공감에 가깝다는 얘기가 빈칸에 들어가면 된다. 따라서 정답은 ③번이 된다.

Unit 5. 장문 유형

1~3. '형식이 수익을 따라 간다'는 것이 우리 시대 미학의 원리이다. 따라서 오늘날 설계기술은 가장 빠른 시간에 최소의 투자로 가능한 한 가장 큰 구내공간을 만들어 낼 수 있는 건축가의 능력에 따라 평가된다. 현재 빌딩의 설계를 결정하는 요인들은, 총면적 대비 임대가능 면적으로 환산할 경우 최대의 경제적 효과, 벽과 바닥의 비율, 그리고 최소의 층고이다. 그 결과는 변함없이 껍질이 얇은 상자의 형태로 된 쇼핑센터, 사무실 빌딩, 아파트 건물들과 같은 단일 활동의 건물인데, 이런 건물에는 비영리적인 공공의 면적이 없고, 표현적이거나 혁신적인 구조상의 특징도 없고, 그리고 확실히 건축술을 기념하는 공간도 없다. 아케이드, 정원, 그리고 발코니, 심지어는 움푹 들어간 창들은 임대 가능한 면적을 침해하고 그리고 수익의 원칙과 양립할 수 없는 것으로 간주된다. 그리고 개발업자들과 그들의 주주들은 자신들의 투자에 대한 빠른 회수를 원하기 때문에, — 증권 중개사들과 회계사들의 시야는 후대까지 미치지 않는다 — 가장 저렴한 자재들을 사용해야 한다. 일부 고객들은 심지어 나무를 심는 것도 거절한다. 도토리 열매는 재산의 임대 가능한 가치를 증가시키지 못할 것이다. 그리고 어떤 투자자도 참나무를 기다리지 않을 것이라는 이야기를 우리는 듣는다. 그러므로 대부분의 현대 건축은 디자이너의 작품이라기보다는 순전히 경제적 요소의 산물이다. 건축은 수익의 측면에서 환경을 보는 사회가 만들어내는 논리적인 산물을 나타낸다.

이종현T의 독해 Point!

1.① 빈칸에 지문의 핵심 소재가 들어간다고 생각하면 이 글에서의 핵심은 건물 디자인이 경제적인 요인에 따라 된다는 것이므로 빈칸에는 경제적 원인에 대한 표현이 드어가면 된다. 따라서 정답은 ①이 된다.

2.② 지문의 5번째 줄에 a thin-skinned box라는 표현이 있으므로 box 형태에 해당하는 선지를 찾아주면 정답은 ②가 된다.

3.③ 이 지문에서의 핵심은 경제적 요인이 건축에 주는 영향이므로 이게 들어가 있는 선지를 찾아주면 정답은 ③이 된다.

4~7. 파리와 캘리포니아 San Bernardino에서의 테러리스트의 공격의 여파로, 더 많은 시리아 난민들을 수용하려는 미국의 지원은 시들해졌다. 공화당의 대통령 후보인 Donald J. Trump는 우리가 극단적 이슬람들과 전쟁중이라고 말하면서 모든 이슬람인들이 미국으로 들어오는 것을 막기를 요구했다. 절박한 이 사람들을 미국에 받아줘야하는지 말아야하는지에 집중하는 것은 난민 위기의 더 큰 문제를 모호하게 만들어 버린다. 대다수의 4백만이 넘는 난민들은 일단 전쟁이 끝나면 시리아로 돌아가기를 원한다. 그러한 이유로, 대부분은 유럽으로 이주하거나 미국에 들어오기를 시도하는 것 보다는 종종 레바논과 조단 지역에 캠프에 몇 년 동안 지내면서 그 지역에 머무른다, 이러한 사람들은 1951년 난민 협약에 따르면 국제 사회의 책임이다. 미국과 그 협약에 서명한 모든 다른 협약국들은 난민과 그들의 건강을 보호해줄 의무를 지니고 있다, 그리고 그것은 필요한 경우엔 재정착을 의미한다. 그런데 난민은 점차 증가하는 부담을 마주하고 있다. 레바논과 조단 지역 둘 다 그들이 일하는 것을 허락하지 않고 있다. 레바논은 매 6달마다 부담되는 재등록 비용을 요구한다. 국제 커뮤니티가 제공해야만 하는 난민 지원에 대한 기금은 비참할 정도로 부족해졌다. 결과적으로, UN의 세계 식략 프로그램은 레바논에 있는 시리아 난민들에 대한 음식 배급을 반으로 줄여서 한달에 사람당 13.5달러만을 제공했다. 어떻게 누구라도 하루에 음식에 대해 50센트 이하만을 가지고 살아나갈 수 있겠는가? (누구도 그렇게는 살 수가 없다.) 그것은 많은 사람이 그 캠프(레바논과 조단 지역의 캠프)를 떠나 유럽으로 위험한 이동을 한다. 꽤나 단순하게, 세계는 중동에 있는 난민 위기를 지원해주지 않음으로써 이동의 위기를 조장하는 것을 도왔다. 미국은 우리가 난민 위기에 지원해줬던 정도에 대해 자부심을 갖고 있지만, 우리는 EU에 뒤쳐진다. 사람당을 기준으로 보면, 우리는 훨씬 더 작은 국가들에도 순위가 뒤처지고, 그렇게 우리보다 순위가 높은 유럽 국가들 중엔 영국, 노르웨이, 스웨덴, 그리고 덴마크가 있다. United Nations Appeal의 최대치의 자금 제공은 난민의 흐름을 막는데 어느정도 도움을 줄 것이다. 미국 혼자서 최소 5억 달러 이상을 United Nations Appeal에 매년 제공할 수 있다. 이번에, 테러에 대한 증가된 걱정이 수백만의 난민의 곤란과 섞였을 때, 우리들 중에는 조치를 취하기에 충분히 머리가 좋은 리더와 보통의 시민들이 있어야 한다. 실제로, 그렇게 하지 않는 것의 비용은 너무 크다.

이종현T의 독해 Point!

4.⑤ 빈칸에는 난민들이 일을 못하게 한다는 맥락의 내용이 들어가야 하므로 비용이 높다는 얘기가 들어가야 한다. 따라서 정답은 ⑤가 된다.

5.④ stem이 타동사로 막다 라는 뜻이 있으므로 정답은 ④가 된다.

6.② 핵심적인 문제로 지적되는 것이 시리아 난민의 원인이 돈의 문제라는 것이므로 정답은 ②가 된다.

7.④ 이 지문은 문제점과 해결책을 제시해주는 글이다. 따라서 문제점에 대한 얘기가 아니라 해결책에 대한 얘기가 정답이 된다. 따라서 정답은 ④가 된다.

8~11. 저명한 물리학자인 스티븐 호킹은 최근에 AI가 인간의 지능을 능가하면 AI는 인간 문명의 존재에 위협을 야기할 수 있다는 것을 경고했다. 만약 AI가 현존하는 위협이 된다면, 이것은 첫 번째 위협이 아닐 것이다. 1950년대 민방위 훈련 동안에 제가 책상 아래에 앉아있는 아이였을 때 인류는 현존하는 위협에 노출되었다. 그 때 이후로 우리는 생화학무기 테러리스트가 인류가 어떤 방어체계도 가지고 있지 않은 새로운 바이러스를 만드는 것과 같이 그에 상응할만한 무서운 것을 마주해왔다. 불은 항상 우리를 따뜻하게 해주면서 또한 우리의 마을을 불태운 이후로 기술은 항상 양날의 검이어왔다. 보통의 반 이상향적인 미래주의 영화는 하나 또는 두 명의 사람이나 그룹이 AI의 통제권을 얻기 위해 싸우게 한다. 아니면 우리는 AI가 세계 지배를 위해 인간과 싸우는 것을 본다. 그런데 이것은 AI가 오늘날의 세상에 통합된 방법이 아니다. AI는 하나 또는 두 사람의 손에 있는 것이 아니라 이것은 10억 또는 20억 명의 손에 있다. 스마트폰을 가진 아프리카에 있는 아이는 20년 전의 미국 대통령보다 지식에 더 많은 접근이 가능하다. AI가 지속적으로 더 똑똑해지면서, AI의 사용은 오로지 증가할 것이다. 사실상 모든 사람의 정신적인 능력은 10년 안에 이 AI에 의해 강화될 것이다. 오늘날의 AI는 병의 진단을 발전시키고, 치료법을 찾고, 깨끗한 재생가능한 에너지를 개발하고, 환경을 치우는걸 돕고, 세계에 있는 사람들에게 높은 수준의 교육을 제공하고, 몸이 불편한 사람들을 도와주고(호킹스의 목소리를 제공해주는 것을 포함해서) 수많은 다른 방식으로 기여한다. 우리는 앞으로 몇 십년 안에 인간의 엄청난 어려운

것들을 해결하는 것에 있어서 주요한 발전을 할 기회를 가지고 있다. AI는 이러한 발전을 성취하는데 있어서 중요한 기술이 될 것이다. 우리는 위험을 통제하면서 이 가능성을 깨달을 도덕적 의무를 가지고 있다. 우리가 이것을 하는데 성공하는 것은 처음이 아닐 것이다. (이렇게 하는데 성공할 것이다 라는 의미)

이종현T의 독해 Point!

8.④ 낫 트루 문제는 주제랑 반대가 되는 표현을 찾는 것이 기본이다. 따라서 이 지문은 좋은 점과 나쁜 점을 동시에 보여주면서 좋은 점을 강조하는 글이므로 ④번은 주제와 반대가 된다.

9.② access의 동의어로 될 수 있는 것은 admittance이므로 정답은 ②가 된다.

10.② 핵심 소재가 들어간 표현을 정답으로 찍어주는 것이 중요하다. 이 지문에서 기술이 핵심 소재가 아니라 AI가 핵심 소재이기 때문에 AI가 들어간 ②번이 정답이 된다.

11.② 필자는 호킹 박사의 주장에 반박하고 AI가 좋다는 얘기가 핵심이므로 정답은 ②가 된다.

12~14. 역사는 현재의 사건들을 설명하는 것을 돕기 때문에 필요하다. 문화가 어떻게 흥하고, 어떻게 망하는가? 역시는 유리에게 답을 주지 않을 것이지만 그러나 역사는 우리의 문제와 오늘날 세상에서 작용하고 있는 힘들의 이해에 초점을 맞추는 것을 분명히 도울 것이다.

물론 역사가 쉽게 조작된다는 사실이 실재 발생한 사건을 우리들이 아는 것을 훨씬 더 중요하게 만들지라도, 역사는 쉽게 조작된다. 우리는 지도자들과 미디어의 현혹을 알아내기 위해 역사의 지식을 필요로 하다. 유권자와 시민으로서, 우리는 이러한 위험한 왜곡을 꿰뚫어 볼 수 있어야 한다. 뿐만 아니라, 역사는 흥미가 있고 — 혹은 흥미가 있어야 한다. 세부 사항이 매혹적인 것처럼, 원인과 결과의 연쇄관계도 매혹적이다. 역사에 관한 훈련을 받지 못한 많은 교사들은 이것을 회피하면서 자연적으로 수세적인 태도를 취하며, 자신들의 과목이 학생들을 지루하게 할지 모른다고 두려워한다.

나는 역사가들이나, 역사교사들이 도덕적인 역할을 갖고 있다고는 결코 주장하지 않을 것이다. 그들의 주된 의무는 시대의 정신을 이해하고 그 이해를 전해주는 것이다. 그들은 도덕적인 효과를 위하 역사를 단순화시켜도 안 된다. 역사는 도덕적인 사례와 도덕적인 딜레마의 상상할 수 있는 가장 풍부한 원천을 제공하며, 그 자체가 위대한 소설의 본질, 위대한 드라마, 그리고 삶 자체의 원천이 된다. 역사에 대한 이해가 없다면, 우리는 정치적으로, 문화적으로, 그리고 사회적으로 빈곤하게 된다.

이종현T의 독해 Point!

12.② 선생님들이 학생들의 멘탈을 이해하기를 두려워한다는 얘기가 빈칸에 들어가면 되므로 하기 싫어한다는 얘기가 들어가면 된다. 따라서 정답은 ②가 된다.

13.① 이 지문에서는 선생님들이 자신들의 과거의 도덕에 대한 이해를 정확하게 전달하라고 나와 있으므로 과거의 도덕을 희석시켜야 한다는 얘기는 핵심의 반대되는 내용이 된다. 따라서 정답은 ①이 된다.

14.③ 역사의 역할이 이 지문의 핵심 소재이므로 핵심 소재가 그대로 들어간 선지를 정답을 찍어준다면 정답은 ③이 된다.

15~17. 19세기 말에, 프레드릭 윈슬로 테일러(Frederick Winslow Taylor)라는 한 젊은이가 초시계를 필라델피아에 있는 미드베일제강 공장에 갖고 와서, 공장 기술자의 능률을 향상시키는 것을 목표로 하는 일련의 역사적인 실험을 시작했다. 그는 일단의 공장 노동자들에게 다양한 금속가공기계에서 일하도록 했고, 기계의 작동분만 아니라, 근로자들의 모든 동작을 기록하고 시간을 쟀다. 모든 작업을 일련의 작고, 별개의 단계로 나누고, 그런 다음에 각각의 단계를 수행하는 다양한 방식을 시험함으로써, 테일러는 각각의 근로자가 일해야 하는 방식에 대한 일단의 정확한 지침 — 우리들이 오늘날 말하는 '알고리즘' —을 만들었다. 미드베일의 사원들은, 그 새 제도가 자신들을 거의 자동기계나 다름없는 존재로 전락시켰다고 주장하면서, 그 엄격한 새 제도에 대해 불평했지만, 그러나 그 공장의 생산성은 상승했다. 테일러의 엄격한 산업 설계방식은 전국에 있는, 그리고 얼마 안 있어, 전 세계에 있는 제조업자들에 의해 수용되었다. 최대의 속도, 최대의 능률, 그리고 최대의 생산을 추구하는 공장 소유자들은 시간 동작 연구를 사용해서 일을 구성하고 그리고 근로자들의 업무를 설정했다. 그 목적은 모든 작업에 최선의 근로 방식을 알아내고 채택하고, 그렇게 함으로써 제작기술 전반에서 과학이 경험의 법칙을 점진적으로 대신하게 하려는 것이었다. 일단 그의

시스템이 육체노동의 모든 행위에 적용되자, 테일러는 자신의 시스템은 산업의 구조개혁뿐만 아니라 사회의 구조개혁을 일으켜, 완벽한 능률의 유토피아를 만들 것이라고 지지자들을 확신시켰다. 테일러 시스템은 아직도 많이 남아있으며, 여전히 산업제조가 지켜야 할 윤리로 되어있다.

이종현T의 독해 Point!

15.① 빈칸에 들어갈 표현은 엄격한 지침을 내려서 일을 하게 한다는 얘기가 빈칸에 들어가야 하므로 정답은 ①이 된다.

16.④ 밑줄 얘기의 핵심은 과거의 방식을 Taylor의 방식으로 바꿨다는 얘기이므로 정답은 ④가 된다.

17.② 제조업자들은 Taylor의 방식을 좋아했지만 직원들은 좋아하지 않았으므로 2번은 핵심의 반대 내용이 된다. 따라서 정답은 ②가 된다.

18~20. 우리가 이야기를 만들 대, 이야기는 대개 전통적인 이야기들인데, 거기에는 주인공들이 있고, 적대자들이 있고, 그리고 화자들과 등장인물들과 청자들 사이의 규정된 관계가 있다. 이야기들은 고정된 과거, 시종일관되게 과거에 근거한 현재, 그리고 시종일관되게 미래로 향하는 가능성의 지평을 갖고 있는 선형적인 줄거리를 갖고 있다. 다른 한편으로, 디지털 기술은 이러한 고전적인 줄거리를 탈피하는 이야기를 만들어내고 있다. 새로운 의사교환의 접촉(인터페이스)은 새로운 이야기의 상호작용과 구성을 허용하고 있다. 다중의 도메인, 주로 다중의 온라인 역할게임들, 하이퍼텍스트, 사이버텍스트, 이 모두는 전통적인 이야기 구조를 엉성하게 만들고 있다. 디지털 이야기들은 극단적인 경우 저자들, 사용자들, 그리고 미디어의 공동창작이다. 끊임없는 전개되는 이야기 속으로 들어갈 수 있는 많은 입력 지점들이 흔히 많은 공동의 제작자들에게 제공된다. 이러한 최근의 기술발달은 전통적인 구조의 결정적인 특징들을 더 이상 갖고 있지 않는 무제한의 이야기를 가능하게 하는 것 같다.

이종현T의 독해 Point!

18.④ 빈칸 다음을 보면 과거의 작품은 과거에 대한 얘기 → 현재 → 미래 이야기로 이어진다고 되어 있으므로 이에 대한 표현이 빈칸에 들어간다면 정답은 ④가 된다.

19.③ 비교 대조의 글은 뒤에 나오는 소재가 핵심이다. 즉 디지털 시대의 이야기에 대한 얘기가 핵심이므로 이에 대한 선지를 찾으면 정답은 ③이 된다.

20.② 등장 인문들 사이의 관계가 아니라 화자와 등장인물 그리고 청자 사이의 관계에 대한 이야기이므로 ②는 잘못되었다.

21~24. 에너지 음료는 엄청난 양의 설탕과, 카페인, 그리고 여타 자극제가 함유되어 있다. 비록 흔히 운동선수들에게 그리고 운동선수들에 의해서 팔리고 있음에도, 에너지 음료는 스포츠 음료가 아니다. 스포츠 음료는 에너지 음료보다 설탕이나 혹은 다른 감미료가 훨씬 덜 함유되어 있고 그리고 카페인은, 설령 함유되어 있다 하더라도, 거의 함유되어 있지 않다. 이러한 사실도 대학에 재학하고 있는 선수들과 그리고 보다 어린 선수들 사이에서 점증하는 에너지 음료의 인기를 떨어뜨리지는 못했다. 그러나 에너지 음료가 당신을 더 나은 선수로 만들 수 있다는 증거는 아주 피상적인 것이다. 올바른 경우에, 그것은 선수의 기록을 향상시킬 수 있다. 그러나 기록을 향상시키기 위한 카페인의 양은 사람에 따라 크게 다르며, 일단 선수가 카페인에 익숙해지면 그 효과는 대개 감소한다. 그리고 에너지 음료에 함유되어 있는 다량의 설탕은 설사와 위장병을 일으키는 것으로 알려져 있다.

에너지 음료가 젊은 선수들에게 끼치는 영향은 특히 분명치 않다. 최근에 발표된 두 가지 연구가 눈에 띄지만, 에너지 음료에 관한 연구는 거의 이루어지지 않았다. 한 연구에서, 대학생들은 카페인이 전혀 들어있지 않은 것을 포함하여 다양한 정도의 카페인이 함유된 에너지 음료를 받고 시험을 완성하도록 요구받았다. 카페인이 함유된 에너지 음료를 마신 학생들은 마시지 않은 학생들보다 몇 배나 빠른 반응을 보였지만, 더 나은 소요시간과 보다 정확한 반응은 가장 적게 카페인이 함유된 거을 마셨던 그룹에서 나왔다. 두 번째 연구에서, 12세에서 17세 사이의 건강한 아이들이 다양한 양의 카페인이 첨가된 달고, 맛없는 청량음료를 마셨다. 그런 다음 아이들을 다양한 간식이 들어있는 실험실에 풀어놨다. 가장 많은 카페인을 마셨던 아이들은 틀림없이 가장 많은 설탕이 함유된 간식으로 향했다. 그 결과는 아이들에게서 카페인 사용과 고에너지 식품의 섭취 사이에 상관관계가 있을지도 모른다는 것을 암시하고 있다.

이종현T의 독해 Point!

21.② 정확성이 높은 사람들은 카페인을 가장 적게 먹은 사람이라고 나와 있으므로 정답은 ②번이 된다.

22.① telling이 형용사로 효과적인, 강력한 의 뜻이 있으므로 이와 동의어로 받을만한 표현을 찾아주면 정답은 ①번이 된다.

23.④ 이 지문의 핵심은 에너지 드링크가 별 도움이 안될 수도 있다는 얘기가 핵심이므로 이게 들어간 선지를 답을 찍어주면 정답은 ④번이 된다.

24.③ 필자는 에너지 드링크의 효능이라고 말하는 것에 대해서 반박하고 있으므로 믿지 않는다고 할 수 있다. 따라서 정답은 ③번이 된다.

25~26. 합리주의와 경험주의 사이의 갈등은 지식의 본질, 원천, 그리고 한계에 대한 연구에 몰두하는 철학의 갈래인 인식론 내에서 일어난다. 우리는 몇 가지 운 좋은 추측을 해서 참된 믿음을 형성할 수 있다. 우리가 확실히 보증된 믿음을 얻을 수 있는 방법은 분명하지 않다. 더구나, 세상을 알기 위하여, 우리는 세상에 대해 생각을 해야 한다. 그리고 우리가 사고(思考)할 때 사용하는 개념을 얻는 방법이나, 혹은 우리가 우리의 개념을 사용하여 세상을 분류하는 방식이 실제 존재하는 분류와 일치한다는 확신이 혹 있다면, 어느 정도의 확신을 우리가 갖고 있는지는 명확하지 않고 합리부의자들은 감각경험과 상관없이 우리의 개념과 지식을 얻는 중요한 ㅈ방식이 존재한다고 주장한다. 경험론자들은 감각경험이 우리의 개념과 자식의 궁극적인 원천이라고 주장한다. 합리주의자들은 우리 자식의 내용은 감각경험이 제공할 수 있는 정보를 능가하는 경우가 있다고 주장한다. 경험론자들은 보완적 사고방식을 제시한다. 그들은 우리가 우선 경험을 소유하고 있는 한, 합리주의자들이 언급하는 정보를 경험이 어떻게 제공하는지를 설명해 간다.

이종현T의 독해 Point!

25.④ 인식론에 해당하지 않는 것을 찾으면 된다. 원천에 대해 찾는다고 했으므로 1번은 해당하고, 보증된 믿음을 찾는 방법과 세상을 분류하는 방법이 나와 있으므로 2번 3번도 해당한다. 무엇이 가치있고 아니고를 나누는 것은 아니므로 정답은 ④번이 된다.

26.② 밑줄은 앞 문장에 있는 Empirists의 반대인 Rationalists에 대한 얘기이다. Empirists는 경험이 가장 중요하다고 했으므로 Rationalists의 얘기는 경험보다 중요한 것이 있다는 얘기가 들어가야 한다. 따라서 정답은 ②번이 된다.

27~29. 다른 많은 일처럼 관리의 일도 주로 행함으로 배운다. 그러므로 보다 높은 직위로 나아가는 사람들은 제때에 필요한 경험을 쌓을 기회를 꼭 얻는 것이 중요하다. 이러한 경험을 운에 맡기기보다, 기회들을 조직의 인력계획시스템 안에 마련해둘 수 있다. 이것들 중 맨 처음에 해야 할 일은 사람들이 도전적인 일을 하고 사업체의 일부 운영에 대한 전반적인 책임을 질 수 있게 해주는 직책을 만들어 내는 것이다. 이것은 조직이 지나치게 중앙집권적으로 구성되어서는 안 된다는 것을 의미한다. 만일 조직이 업무를 손익단위로 나눌 수 있다면, 임원들은 조직의 나머지 부서들과 상호의존 관계를 유지하면서도, 적절한 영업센터로 자립해 있는 사업체를 운영하는 경험을 쌓을 수 있다.

일부 기업들은 다른 기업보다 이런 형태의 조직에 보다 많은 정성을 쏟는다. 예를 들어, 소매업에서, 관리자들은 비교적 젊은 시절에, 소매점의 관리를 책임질 기회를 자주 갖는다는 것을 고려해보라. 다른 좀 더 기술적으로 정교한 산업에서는 이와 유사한 수익중심단위(profit center units)를 찾는 것이 훨씬 더 어려울 수 있다. 그러나 가능한 곳은 어디든지, 수익중심지들을 설립해서 젊은 관리자들이 5명이든, 백 명이든, 혹은 5백 명이든지 간에 팀을 이끄는 경험을 쌓을 수 있도록 해야 한다. 그들은 전반적인 업무수행에 대한 책임이 자신들에게 있다는 것을 배운다.

이종현T의 독해 Point!

27.① 빈칸 앞 내용은 직원들에게 운영할 수 있는 권한을 주라는 얘기이다. 따라서 빈칸에도 같은 얘기가 들어가야 하는데 빈칸 문장에는 not이 있으므로 직원들에게 권한을 안준다는 얘기가 빈칸에 들어가면 된다. 따라서 위에서 모든 것을 처리한다는 것이므로 정답은 ①번이 된다.

28.① 핵심은 직원들이 부분적으로 경영할 수 있는 권한을 주는 것이 핵심이므로 정답은 직원들이 경영하게 하라는 ①번이 정답이 된다.

29.② 두 번째 단락부터 실제로 부분적으로 경영하게 한다는 사업의 예시들이 몇몇으로 나와 있으므로 사업들마다 다르다는

얘기인 ②번이 정답이 된다.

30~33. 코스모스는 열대 식물의 하나로 대략 20여 종에 이른다. 코스모스는 키가 크고, 우아하고, 늦게 꽃이 피며, 다양하고 깃털 모양의 잎을 갖고 있는 일년생 혹은 다년생의 식물이다. '코스모스'라는 말은 그리스 용어 Kosmos라는 말에서 비롯된 것으로, '장식 혹은 아름다운 것'을 의미한다. 그리고 만발한 그 사랑스럽고 우아한 코스모스를 보고나면, 사람은 이 꽃은 정말로 이름이 잘 지어졌다고 느낀다. 코스모스는 열대와 아열대 지역 아메리카가 원산지이다. 코스모스의 아메리카 원종(原種)더 따뜻한 고지대인 멕시코에서 온 것으로 알려져 있다. 미국에서 자란 초기의 종들은 추위에서 견딜 수 없었다. 왜냐하면 코스모스들은 햇빛을 좋아하기 때문이다. 코스모스가 씨앗이 여물기도 전에 서리를 맞아 죽는 일이 종종 있었다. 그러나 새로운 종의 코스모스가 개발되어 이제는 여름철 꽃뿐만 아니라 가을철 꽃도 되었다.

코스모스가 늦게, 다른 많은 식물들이 제 할 일을 다 했을 때, 꽃이 핀다는 사실은 정원사와 꽃 애호가들에게 코스모스를 더 가치있게 만든다. 왜냐하면 코스모스는 첫 서리가 내릴 때 참으로 진가를 발휘하기(만개하기) 때문이다. 잎이 얇은, 이 늦게 피는 별 모양의 꽃은 화단이나 담장에 아주 매력적일 뿐만 아니라 꺾은 꽃은 실내 장식을 위해 아름다운 꽃다발이 된다.

미국에서 가장 일반적으로 재배되는 종은 7내지 10피트의 높이로 자라지만, 일부 종은 그렇게 키가 크지 않다. 코스모스는 부드러운 줄기를 갖고 있으며, 밝게 빛나는 화려한 꽃들은 노랑 화반(花盤)을 갖고 있다. 방사형으로 갈라진 꽃잎들은 흰색, 연분홍색, 빨간색, 자주색, 조개껍질 색, 노란색, 오렌지색을 포함한 다양한 색이 있다. 사실상 청색을 뺀 거의 모든 색이다. 초기의 원시종들은 직경이 대략 1인치인 꽃들을 갖고 있었다. 그러나 다양한 육종업자들은 이 바람직한 식물을 연구해서 일부 경우에는 줄기를 짧게 하고, 꽃의 크기를 증가시켰으며, 일부 꽃은 하나씩, 다른 꽃들은 다발로 자란다.

이종현T의 독해 Point!

30.③ 밑줄의 의미는 코스모스가 추위에서도 핀다는 얘기가 핵심이다. 따라서 정답이 ③번이다. 1번이 정답이 되기엔 지문 내용이 이젠 여름에 잘 못피고 추위에서 핀다 라고 되어야 하는데 여름에 코스모스가 못핀다는 얘기는 아니므로 1번은 안된다.

31.① 1번의 순서가 잘못되었다. 처음에 여름 꽃이었다가 이제 추위에서도 피는 것이다. 따라서 정답은 ①번이다.

32.④ 지문의 중간 부분에 정워에 두기 좋다고 했으므로 정답은 ④번이 된다.

33.③ 3번 선지가 7~10까지는 맞는 얘기지만 with 뒷 부분부터 더 커지는게 아니라 몇몇은 그만큼 크지는 않는다고 되어있어야 한다. 따라서 정답은 ③번이 된다.

34~36. 무신론과 무정부주의는 복잡한 이념적 유기체가 아니라는 점에서 실제로는 이념이 아니다. 이 단어들 각각은 특정한 유형의 복잡한 집단적인 이념유기체에 대한 반대를 나타낸다. 둘은 모두 그것들이 대적해 싸우고 있는 그 이념유기체가 사람들이 좋은 삶을 영위하기 위해서 반드시 필요하지는 않다고 주장하고 있다. 이 둘 모두를 위한 한 단어가 있어야 하지만 사실은 없는데, 그 대체적인 이유는 교회와 국가가 같은 종류의 "다세포적인" 이념적 유기체라고는 일반적으로 인식되고 있지 않기 때문이다.

"개인주의자"가 아마도 우리가 갖고 있는 단어들 중에 그 어떤 집단적 사고방식과도 거리가 먼 자율적인 인간을 설명하는 것에 가장 가까운 단어일 것이다. 강한 개인주의적 의식은 우리로 하여금 그 어떤 상위의 권력도 우리의 생각을 통제할 권리는 갖고 있지 않다는 결론을 내리게 한다.

무신론과 무정부주의 둘 모두가 크고 대중적이고 복잡한 많은 이념에 똑같이 반대하기 때문에 이 두 (훨씬 더 단순한) 사상을 똑같은 주형 속에 부어넣으려는, 그리고 이 사상들을 실제보다 더 큰 이념적 구조체로 만들어내려는, 그리고 이 사상들에 다른 사상들을 덧붙이려는 경향이 있으며, 간단히 말해 이 두 사상을 단순한 사상에서 복잡한 이념유기체로 변화시키려는 경향이 있다. 이러한 이유 때문에, 무신론과/이나 무정부주의를 믿는 사람들은 그들의 무신론에 대해 강한 신앙을 갖는다거나 존재하는 권력들에 맞서 싸우기 위해 무정부주의 단체들을 결성하는 것과 같은 이상하리만치 모순된 일들을 실제로 종종 확신에 차서 하게 된다.

이종현T의 독해 Point!

34.D 무신론과 무정부주의에 대한 설명문이다. 따라서 이게 들어간 선지를 찾으면 정답은 D가 된다.

35.C 무정부주의와 무신론은 집단적 사고방식이 되지 않아야

한다. 그런데 빈칸 앞 문장을 보면 사람들이 집단을 형성한다고 되어 있다. 즉 집단을 형성하지 않는 이론을 가지고 있으면서 집단을 형성하고 있으므로 자신들의 신념과는 반대되는 행동을 하는 것이다. 따라서 정답은 C가 된다.

36.D 무신론과 무정부주의는 교회와 국가와 반대가 되므로 정답은 D가 된다.

37~39. 일몰 광경을 바라보는 것이 큰 아름다움과 반성의 순간이 될 수 있지만, 그 현상을 연구하는 전문가들은 지평선 아래로 태양이 진 후 몇 초 지나지 않아 나타나는 생생한 녹색 빛의 반원형 또는 원형인 매우 드문 '녹색 섬광'만큼 애호가들에게 좋은 볼거리는 거의 없다고 주장하고 있다. 이 포착하기 힘든 저녁 사건은 오랫동안 허구라고 여겨졌지만, 최근에는 대기과학자들에 의해 긴 행복한 시간(일몰구경시간)의 부작용 이상의 것으로 확인되었다.

햇빛이 지구의 대기권에 부딪칠 때, 그 빛 안의 색들이 파장에 따라 다른 정도로 분산된다. 푸른색이나 초록색과 같은 파장이 짧은 색이 파장이 긴 따뜻한 색보다 더 쉽게 흩어진다. 태양이 머리 위에 있을 때는 푸른색의 빛이 널리 흩어져 있어서 하늘이 푸르게 보인다. 태양이 지평선에 있을 때, 우리는 너무나 더 많은 대기를 통해 태양을 보게 되어서 차가운 색은 통과하지 못하고 차단된다. 붉은색, 오렌지색, 노란색의 빛이 우리 눈에 들어와서 하늘이 전형적인 저녁노을 색을 띠게 된다.

그러나 완벽한 조건에서는, 태양이 지평선을 지나 아래로 내려갈 때 태양으로부터의 빛은 다양한 색의 띠들로 갈라진다. 이 색 띠들은 밑에는 붉은색 위에는 푸른색으로 하여 모든 무지개 색들이 수평으로 펼쳐진다. 태양으로부터의 빛은 대기권 안에서 곡선을 그리며 나오는 것이므로, 실제로는 태양이 졌는데도 그 빛은 지평선을 넘어 곡선을 그리며 온다. 모든 것이 정상이면, 따뜻한 색은 지구의 가장자리에 의해 차단되고, 푸른색은 대기의 의해 퍼지지만, 그러나 초록색 띠는 잠깐 '녹색 섬광'의 형태로 볼 수 있게 된다.

이종현T의 독해 Point!

37.B Green flashes는 태양이 지고난 직후에 나오는 것이므로 이전이라고 한 B가 잘못되었다.

38.A Green Flash가 핵심이고 이게 어떻게 나오는지를 설명하는 설명문이다. 따라서 정답은 A가 된다.

39.B green은 cool color이므로 잘 퍼진다는 것을 알 수 있다. 따라서 정답은 B가 된다.

40~41. 1966년 에디 아놀드(Eddie Arnold)는 컨트리 뮤직 명예의 전당에 들어가게 되었다. 미국 역사상 가장 인기 있는 컨트리 뮤직 가수들 가운데 하나인 아놀드는 가난에서 벗어나기 위해 자신의 부드러운 목소리를 사용했다. 그의 아버지가 돌아가셨을 때, 가족의 농장은 채권자들에게 넘어갔고 아놀드 가족은 소작인으로 전락했다. 평생의 꿈이었던 최고의 아티스트가 되었을 때도, 이 시골 소년은 자신의 뿌리와의 접촉을 결코 끊지 않았다. 연달아 히트곡을 내면서 상당히 세련된 팬층이 형성되었음에도, 그는 항상 자신을 "테네시의 시골 총각"이라 불렀다. 그는 마음속으로 근면한 농장 일꾼으로서의 자신의 배경이 성공한 가수라는 부담스러운 역할을 잘 감당할 수 있게 준비시켜주었다고 생각했다. 처음부터, 그는 컨트리 가수 세계에서 그의 동시대인들 대부분과 분명히 다른 인물이었다. 청바지에 체크무늬 셔츠를 입거나 반짝거리는 금속장식이 달린 옷을 입었던 대부분의 가수들과는 달리 아놀드는 언제나 멋지고 당당한 옷차림이었다. 2008년 5월 그가 사망했을 때 음악계는 로맨틱 발라드의 최고 인기가수 한 명을 잃었다.

이종현T의 독해 Point!

40.② 빈칸 문장에서 그와 동시대 인물의 관계를 찾겠다는 생각으로 다음 문장을 보면 동시대 인물들과 그가 반대되는 관계라는 것을 Unlike를 통해 알 수 있고, 그에 따라 빈칸에는 둘은 다르다는 얘기가 들어가야 한다. 따라서 정답은 ②번이 된다.

41.④ 다음 문장에서 그는 테네시아의 시골 총각으로 불렸다고 되어 있으므로 자기 자신을 계속 농장 사람이라고 생각했다는 것을 알 수 있고, 정답은 ④번이 된다.

42~43. 형식적 경제모델이 현실세계의 정책에 대해 갖는 타당성은 논란을 일으키는 주제였다. 경제학자 노턴(R, D. Norton)과 리(S, Y, Rhee)는 과거로 거슬러 올라가 14년간에 걸친 한국경제에 그러한 모델을 적용하는 데 어느 정도 성공을 거두었다. 생산량, 물가 및 여타 변수에 대한 그 모델의 수치는 실제 통계와 상당히 일치하였다. 그러나 정책과 관련된 그 모델의 가치는 이보다

덜 분명한 것으로 밝혀졌다. 노턴과 리는 장기적인 변수들은 불변으로 놓고 단기적인 정책 변화의 영향을 정확히 짚어보고자 모의실험을 수행하였다. 그들의 모델에 따르면, 원유수입 가격이 높아지면 물가상승률을 증가시키고, 수출이 5퍼센트 감소하면 국내총생산(GDP)이 낮아지고 물가상승률을 증가시키며, 통화 공급량의 증가를 늦추면 물가상승률이 약간 높아질 것으로 보였다. 이러한 연구 결과는 다소 놀라웠다. 많은 경제학자들은 수출 감소는 물가상승률을 증가시키지 않고 감소시킬 것이라고 주장해왔다. 그리고 대부분의 경제학자들이 원유가격의 상승은 물가상승 요인이라고 보지만, 통화 공급의 속도를 늦추는 것이 그것과 같은 것이라고 보는 이는 거의 없다. 노턴-리의 모델은 참된 정책적 관련성을 희생시키고 통계적인 "적합도"만을 강조하는 형식주의적 접근의 위험성을 보여주는 것으로 간주될 수 있다.

이종현T의 독해 Point!

42.④ 이 지문은 노턴과 리의 이론에 대해 잘못되었다고 반박하는 글이므로 이게 들어간 선지를 찾아주면 정답은 ④번이 된다.

43.① 빈칸 다음 문장에서 많은 경제학자와 노턴은 반대관계이므로 둘을 반대로 만들어줄 수 있는 표현이 빈칸에 들어가면 된다. 따라서 정답은 ①번이 된다.

44~45. 만약 당신이 낮 동안 졸음을 느낀다면 당신은 충분한 잠을 자지 못한 것이라고 전문가들은 말한다. 만약 당신이 자리에 누운 지 5분 이내에 잠이 드는 것이 일상적이라면, 당신은 필시 심각한 수면 부족을 겪고 있는 것이고, 심지어는 수면 장애를 겪고 있을 수도 있다. 다른 면으로는 깨어 있는 사람이 아주 짧게 잠드는 현상인 마이크로 수면 역시 수면 부족의 또 다른 특징이다. 많은 경우에 있어서, 사람들은 자신들이 마이크로 수면을 경험하고 있다는 사실을 자각하지 못한다. 서구 산업사회에 만연한 "밤늦게까지 일하고 새벽같이 일하러 가는" 관행은 상당한 수면 부족을 일으켜 왔으며, 그 결과 실제로 비정상적인 졸음이 지금 거의 보편적인 것이 되었다.

모의 운전 장치를 이용하거나 손과 눈의 동작을 일치시키는 과제를 수행하도록 실험을 해보면, 수면이 부족한 사람들은 술에 취한 사람들보다 수행능력이 떨어진다. 수면 부족은 또한 신체에 미치는 알코올의 영향을 확대시키며, 따라서 심신이 지친 사람이 술을 마시면 휴식을 잘 취한 사람보다 훨씬 더 손상을 입는다. 졸음은 잠들기에 앞서 뇌가 취하는 마지막 조치에 해당하기 때문에, 졸음운전은 재난을 초래할 수 있고 또 종종 실제로 그러하다. 카페인이나 여타 각성제들이 심각한 수면 부족의 영향을 극복해주지 못한다. 미국 국립수면재단에서는 만약 당신이 눈의 초점을 맞추기 어렵거나 하품을 멈출 수 없다면, 또는 지난 몇 마일을 운전해 온 과정이 기억나지 않는다면, 당신은 필시 안전하게 차를 몰기에는 너무 졸린 상태라고 말하고 있다.

이종현T의 독해 Point!

44.③ 밑줄 친 부분은 잠 부족에 대한 얘기이므로 잠 부족을 담고 있는 선지는 ③번이 된다.

45.② 이 지문은 잠 부족의 문제점이 핵심이므로 이것에 대한 얘기가 들어간 선지를 찾으면 정답은 ②번이 된다.

46~48. 지난 몇 년간 인터넷 아마추어리즘의 영향에 대한 논쟁과 논평기사를 읽어본다면 논의가 계속 두 가지 점으로 되풀이하여 돌아간다는 것을 알 수 있다. 그것은 블로거들의 활동이 전통적인 언론에 미치는 영향과 위키피디아(백과사전)가 종래의 학문에 미치는 영향이다. 두 경우 모두에 있어, 체계적인 교육을 받고 제도적으로 공인된 엘리트들이 블로거 글렌 레이놀즈가 말한 '다윗의 군대'의 도전을 받아왔으며, 양 진영은 모두 다분히 교조적이고 상대를 무시하거나 방어적인 태도를 취하고 있다. 이런 논쟁은 아주 합당한 것이다. 왜냐하면 블로거들과 위키피디아를 작성하는 사람들은 어떤 것들은 전문 지식인보다 더 잘하고 다른 것들은 훨씬 더 못하기 때문이다. 또한 우리는 어떤 쪽이 더 잘하는지 알 수 있을지도 모른다. 너무나 많은 시간을 들여 이런 논쟁들을 끝까지 진행함에 있어 문제는 인터넷이 열어 놓은 광대한 시장에서 아마추어 저널리즘과 백과사전 글쓰기의 중요성을 너무 과대평가한다는 것이다. 사실은 인터넷상에서 유저들이 만든 대부분의 콘텐츠(ucc)는 전통적인 전문가의 권위에 도전이 되지는 않는다. 그런 콘텐츠는 전문가들이 부재하거나 유저들 자신이 전문가인 영역에서만 효과적일 뿐이다.

이종현T의 독해 Point!

46.C army of Davids는 elite와 비교되는 표현이므로 elite의 반대라고 생각하면 평범한 사람들이 된다. 따라서 정답은 C가 된다.

47.D army of Davids, 즉 아마추어들의 영향에 대한 것이므로 빈칸도 아마추어에 대한 얘기가 들어간다면 정답은 D가 된다.

48.B 이 글의 핵심은 위키피디아같은 곳이 전문가의 영역을 방해하지 않는다는 것이 핵심이므로 이게 들어간 선지를 찾으면 정답은 B가 된다.

49~51. 멀리서 보면 물고기 떼는 커다란 생명체와 유사하게 보인다. 그 수가 대개 두세 마리에서 수백만 마리에 이르는 물고기들은 촘촘히 대형을 지어 거의 한 몸처럼 수백만 마리에 이르는 물고기들은 촘촘히 대형을 지어 거의 한 몸처럼 일제히 선회하고 역선회하며 헤엄친다. 무리를 이끄는 지배 체계가 없거나 너무 약해서 전체 물고기 떼의 움직임에 거의 혹은 전혀 영향을 주지 못한다. 게다가 일관된 지도력도 없다. 물고기 떼가 오른쪽이나 왼쪽으로 방향을 전환할 때, 그때껏 측면에 있던 물고기들이 선두를 맡는다. 물고기 떼의 평균적인 크기는 종에 따라 다른데, 개체들 간의 공간과 물고기 떼의 평균 속도 및 3차원적 형태가 종에 따라 다르기 때문이다. 물고기 떼가 이동할 때에는 군인처럼 정확하게 정렬을 하지만, 휴식을 하거나 먹이를 먹는 동안에는 보다 일정치 않은 방향성을 갖는다. 물고기 떼가 포식동물에게 공격받게 될 때에도 배열이 특정한 방식으로 변한다. 이동하는 물고기 떼 안에서의 공간 확보는 대체로 수력학적 힘(물 흐름의 힘)에 의해 결정되는 것이 분명하다. 개별 물고기들은 다른 물고기가 일으키는 교란에도 효율성이 크게 떨어지지 않으면서 가능한 한 이웃 물고기들과 가까울 수 있는 자리를 찾는 경향이 있다.

이종현T의 독해 Point!

49.A 지문의 중간 부분에 모여있다. spacing of its members가 B이고, species가 C이고, velocity가 D이므로 정답은 A가 된다.

50.B 빈칸 다음 문장을 보면 위치에 따라 리드가 달라지므로 빈칸에도 리더가 계속 달라진다는 얘기가 들어가면 된다. 따라서 정답은 B가 된다.

51.A fish school의 목적에 대해 나와있지는 않으므로 정답은 A가 된다.

52~55. 상품 생산이 다른 모든 종류의 생산을 명백히 압도하는 데에서 취향은 발달한다. 생산물을 시장에 팔 상품으로 제조하게 된 결과, 사람들은 생산의 조건들, 즉 착취라는 형태의 사회적 조건들 뿐 아니라 기술적 조건들에 대해서도 점점 모르게 된다. 소비자는(공예) 장인에게 주문할 때는 전문지식이 다소 있지만, (상품) 구매자가 될 때는 대개 지식이 없다. 이런 점 이외에도, 사실, 대량 생산은 값싼 상품의 생산을 목표로 하기 때문에 나쁜 품질을 숨기는 데 몰두할 수밖에 없다. 대부분의 경우, 구매자가 지식이 거의 없다는 것이 실제로 나쁜 품질을 위장하는데 도움이 된다. 산업이 발전할수록 산업이 시장에 내놓는 모조품들도 그만큼 더 완벽해진다. 상품은 세속적인 광채에 감싸여있다. 이 광채는 '야단스런 신학적 미화'를 낳는 광채와는 전혀 다른 것이지만, 사회에는 어느 정도 중요하다. 고객의 전문지식이 감소하는 것과 같은 정도로 고객의 취향은 더욱 중요해지는데, 고객과 제조업자 모두에게 중요해진다. 소비자에게는 취향이 그의 전문 지식 결여를 교묘하게 위장해준다는 점에서 가치 있는 것이며, 제조업자에게는 취향이 제조업자로서는 더 많은 비용을 들여야 충족시킬 다른 소비 요건들을 충족시키지 않고도 소비를 촉진시킬 수 있는 새로운 소비 촉진제라는 가치를 지닌다.

이종현T의 독해 Point!

52.C 앞 부분에 대량 생산을 하는 사람은 나쁜 질을 숨기는 것에 집중한다고 되어 있으므로 빈칸에는 숨긴다는 얘기가 들어간다면 정답은 C가 된다.

53.C 생산자들이 취향이라는걸 이용해서 질을 숨긴다는 것이 핵심이므로 이게 들어간 선지를 찾으면 정답은 C가 된다.

54.D 전문성이 떨어지는 만큼 취향이 올라간다는 것이 핵심이므로 정답은 D가 된다.

55.D 생산자 입장에서위 취향과 소비자 입장에서의 취향은 다르므로 정답은 D가 된다.

MEMO

이것이 독해다 Part 1 기본유형 총정리

2025년 5월 10일 1판 1쇄 발행

저 자 이 종 현
발행인 남 승 우

발행처 도서출판 상尙학學당堂
주 소 서울특별시 동작구 사당로9가길 6
전 화 02) 595-1692~4
팩 스 02) 595-1394
이메일 shdbooks@naver.com
신 고 2-155호(1968.11.29.)

편 집 엄해숙
표 지 토틀컴

ISBN 978-89-6587-269-6 03740

정가 30,000원